Texas Secessionists Standoff

THE TEXAS EXPERIENCE
*Books made possible by
Sarah '84 and Mark '77 Philpy*

Militant separatists take 2 hostages

Continued from A1

Davis Mountains Resort, where McLaren lives and where the home in which the hostages were being held is located. And checkpoints were set up along the only state highway through the area.

Jo Ann Canady Turner: Separatist member arrested on contempt charges.

Authorities identified the hostages as Joe Rowe and his wife, Margaret Ann "M.A." Rowe, both 51. Joe Rowe suffered a broken right arm and cuts from broken glass, officials said.

By late Sunday, spokesmen for the Jeff Davis County sheriff's office and the Texas Department of Public Safety said they were unsure how many people were with McLaren at his headquarters, a cluster of trailer homes not far from Rowe's home.

Three ambulances were at the scene, but Jeff Davis County ambulance service director Mike Ward said their presence was precautionary.

According to authorities, the standoff began about 11 a.m. Sunday when a group of armed men stormed Rowe's home — with guns blazing.

Rowe was injured by flying glass but declined to be exchanged for volunteer firefighter Jerry Rhea, who offered to replace him, said a man identifying himself as White Eagle, a chief aide to McLaren.

DPS spokeswoman Lucila Torres said Rowe was being cared for by his wife, a paramedic.

McLaren said the hostages were being held under rules of international law.

"They're in Mr. Rowe's house and being well taken care of," McLaren said from his headquarters, about 15 miles outside Fort Davis. "We're not out to injure anybody because under the Geneva Convention we have to take care of them."

Eye for an eye, he said

Within hours after authorities were alerted about the break-in at the Rowe home by a 911 call, more than three dozen deputies, state troopers, Texas Rangers and federal Border Patrol officers had cordoned off the area.

McLaren said the hostages were taken in retaliation for the arrest early Sunday of a Republic of Texas member, who was jailed after authorities stopped his van and found two assault rifles inside.

It was the third Republic follower jailed in recent days, authorities said.

Jack Brisbin, the county judge in neighboring Presidio County, said Jeff Davis sheriff's deputies brought Republic member Robert Jonathan Scheidt, 43, to the county jail in Marfa. Scheidt had a Republic identification card that says he is "captain of the embassy guard," Brisbin said.

Another man who identified himself as a Republic member, John Wenger, was brought to the Presidio County Jail from Odessa on Friday, Brisbin said. Wenger was held on outstanding traffic warrants.

In his radio interview, McLaren said he also was angered by the arrest Tuesday in Austin of group member Jo Ann Canady Turner on two contempt charges. The charges stem from a lien she filed against a moving company that stored her possessions after she was evicted from her home.

A judge set her bail at $25,000 and scheduled a hearing for May 27. She was still in custody Sunday.

After Turner's arrest Tuesday, McLaren said: "When they arrested her, they enacted a declaration of war."

On Tuesday night, the group released a statement saying it had issued warrants for "foreign agents" responsible for Turner's arrest.

McLaren told WOAI on Sunday that his followers were dispersing around the state to serve "arrest and deportation orders" against those officials.

Those named by the group included Texas Attorney General Dan Morales, "the unlawful state Legislature, all United States federal judges and all IRS agents on Texas soil."

Long-running dispute

In Austin, Karen Hughes, press secretary to Gov. George W. Bush, said Bush had been made aware of the standoff and "obviously he is concerned."

Ron Dusek, a spokesman for Morales, declined comment on whether security for Morales or other state officials had been stepped up in light of McLaren's remarks. He said Morales also was monitoring the ongoing events at Fort Davis.

The Republic of Texas contends that the annexation of Texas as a state in 1845 was illegal, and that the group's leaders constitute the legitimate government of the independent nation of Texas.

McLaren and other Republic followers have had a long-running feud over land with neighbors and the Rowes, who lead an area homeowners' association and whom McLaren has called "federal moles."

The movement was started in 1995 by about 50 people, mostly from Central Texas, who had become acquainted with each other during the statewide controversy over property rights. Since then, it has splintered several times with some groups, notably McLaren, becoming more militant.

Late last year, McLaren asked supporters to come to the compound and guard it because he thought he was going to be arrested. A federal warrant is pending against McLaren for contempt of court, and he also is wanted on a state warrant for burglary.

The residents have pleaded with authorities for months to do something about McLaren and his armed guards.

The Rowes' son, Mikel, who lives in Austin, said Sunday night that he is confused about why the group would kidnap his parents.

"I am real worried about my dad," said Rowe, 26, who installs video equipment. "He had a heart attack two weeks ago."

In light of his father's long-running feud with McLaren, Mikel Rowe said, Joe Rowe "knew something was going to happen eventually and that he was marked for it." In fact, Mikel Rowe said, McLaren's group recently had sent a statewide fax marking his dad as No. 1 retaliation.

'Acting on his own'

As the events unfolded here Sunday, other factions of the Republic movement moved quickly to distance themselves from McLaren.

Ray Wanjura, who called himself the secretary if judicial affairs for the Republic of Texas, said: "McLaren has broken the law. He has kidnapped his neighbors. He is acting on his own."

A faction led by Archie Lowe of Rice posted a message on the Internet urging Republic members to stay out of McLaren's dispute with authorities.

Lowe's faction last month "impeached" McLaren as its ambassador for such practices as making purchases with worthless "warrants" backed only by state assets they claim to have seized.

Mike Ward, Bob Banta, Claire Osborn and The Associated Press contributed to this report.

Ron Heflin/1997 AP

Richard McLaren, right, a Republic of Texas figure involved in a hostage-taking incident Sunday, meets with the press in March at his home near Fort Davis. White Eagle, an 'embassy guard,' hands him a folder.

Fort Davis-area residents say standoff was inevitable

By Bob Banta and Claire Osborn
American-Statesman Staff

Residents of Davis Mountains Resort have been pleading with authorities for months to do something about neighbor Richard McLaren.

And for just as long, the self-styled ambassador of the Republic of Texas has been threatening authorities with a showdown.

It finally happened Sunday, with McLaren taking hostage two of his most vocal critics, homeowners association president Joe Rowe and his wife, M.A., in what McLaren said was retaliation for the arrests of two of his followers.

"I feel like it's been festering all this time and something was going to happen at some point," said Joe Duncan, president of the Fort Davis Chamber of Commerce and owner of Hotel Limpia.

"We've been telling people and telling people and telling people this was going to happen," area resident Michelle Behrendt said. "They sat on their thumbs and did nothing."

McLaren has been a thorn in the side of his neighbors for many years, filing property liens against them and harassing them through what he called a "paper war."

"It's really sad for residents who live out there to have to deal with the Republic of Texas. Their whole lives have been disrupted. They've basically been locked out and can't get to their homes," Duncan said.

Charles Sanders, who lives in the Davis Mountains Resort, said, "About 12 to 15 years ago me and a couple of other people had a conversation with him, and he had an automatic Uzi then."

Malcolm Tweedy, owner of the Stone Village Motel in Fort Davis, said he was not surprised by the standoff.

"I've been waiting for this to happen," said Tweedy, who thinks officers should have acted earlier. "It's the job of law enforcement to take care of people who make life unhappy for their fellow citizens."

He thinks the reason for police hesitancy in moving sooner "is because they have been scared by Waco," referring to the Branch Davidian siege four years ago.

The standoff has cast a "black cloud" over Fort Davis, Duncan said.

"A man from Austin called and canceled his reservation at the hotel saying he wanted no part of the Republic of Texas or Fort Davis," Duncan said.

This story contains material from The Associated Press.

Republic of Texas: How it started

Ron Heflin/AP

Richard McLaren, 'ambassador' of the Republic of Texas, talks on the phone in this March photo at the Republic's mountain 'embassy.'

- **December 1995:** The Republic of Texas is created. Supporters meet in a cotton gin in Bulverde and elect John C. VanKirk president. VanKirk claims Texas was illegally annexed by the United States and should be an independent nation. Organizers refuse to recognize state and federal laws.
- **January 1996:** The Republic of Texas asks Gov. George W. Bush to vacate his Austin office.
- **February 1996:** VanKirk says his followers include members of militias, tax protesters and Texans who are unhappy with state and federal bureaucracies. VanKirk says federal agents are plotting to kill him.
- **March 1996:** Ten of 12 members of the Republic of Texas cabinet vote to oust VanKirk. The move is triggered by a disagreement over whether militias should be welcomed by the Republic. Donald J. Varnell and Richard L. McLaren are two leaders who want stronger ties to militias.
- **April 1996:** A Houston title company wins a federal lawsuit ordering McLaren to stop filing bogus liens, which he had been doing for years, contending that property titles and boundaries were drawn illegally in the Davis Mountains.
- **May 1996:** McLaren is jailed May 4 in Monahans for refusing to stop harassing people in the Davis Mountains with the liens. Federal District Judge Lucius Bunton in Midland orders McLaren to stay in jail until he changes his mind. McLaren tells the judge his continued incarceration may incite his followers, saying "things are fixing to get out of hand."
- **June 1996:** McLaren is released from jail.
- **July 1996:** Texas Attorney General Dan Morales sues 25 current and former Republic of Texas leaders. Only four members show up or are represented in court, but a state district judge grants a temporary injunction to prevent the group from filing bogus liens, conspiring to hurt state commerce and harassing public officials.
- **October 28, 1996:** A state judge holds the Republic of Texas in contempt for allegedly violating a court order prohibiting them from filing documents purporting to be from an official government agency. Members are given a week to stop harassing bank, state and business officials or face a $10,000-a-day fine that could double each day the order is disobeyed.
- **December 1996:** In Fort Davis, the movement's mail is cut off.
- **January 7, 1997:** Some state employees are ordered not to show up for work after Morales receives a threat possibly tied to his dispute with the Republic of Texas. Workers return the next day without incident. Meanwhile in the Davis Mountains, families near the Republic of Texas camp grow jittery as strangers move in from as far away as Idaho, many of them carrying guns, some driving cars without license plates.
- **Feb. 2:** Republic officials say the group is divided along political and philosophical lines.
- **March:** Jeff Davis County Sheriff Steven Bailey writes to McLaren, urging him to "take a small step back toward reality" and turn himself in on a burglary charge. McLaren is "impeached" by other Republic of Texas leaders, according to the movement's Web site.
- **April 5:** Republic of Texas members come to Austin to recruit supporters. About 25 people show up at the Best Western Atrium in North Austin to listen to Republic of Texas president Archie Lowe.
- **April 27:** Republic members take two neighbors hostage. A posting on the Republic of Texas Web site denounces McLaren as having "gone completely off the deep end" and warns other Republic of Texas supporters not to involve themselves in the conflict.

Texas Secessionists Standoff

The 1997 Republic of Texas "War"

Donna Marie Miller

Foreword by Gary Noesner

Texas A&M University Press
College Station

Copyright © 2023 by Donna Marie Miller
All rights reserved
First edition

♾ This paper meets the requirements of ANSI/NISO Z39.48–1992 (Permanence of Paper).
Binding materials have been chosen for durability.

Library of Congress Cataloging-in-Publication Data

Names: Miller, Donna Marie, 1956– author. | Noesner, Gary, writer of foreword.
Title: Texas secessionists standoff : the 1997 Republic of Texas "war" / Donna Marie Miller ; foreword by Gary Noesner.
Other titles: Texas experience (Texas A & M University. Press)
Description: First edition. | College Station : Texas A&M University Press, [2023] | Series: The Texas experience | Includes bibliographical references and index.
Identifiers: LCCN 2022029634 | ISBN 9781648430985 (cloth) | ISBN 9781648430992 (ebook)
Subjects: LCSH: McLaren, Richard Lance, 1953—-Military leadership. | Secession—Texas. | Militia movements—Texas—History—20th century. | Government, Resistance to—Texas—History—20th century. | Texas—History—Autonomy and independence movements. | Fort Davis (Tex.)—History—Siege, 1997. | BISAC: TRUE CRIME / General | HISTORY / United States / 20th Century
Classification: LCC F391.2 .M55 2023 | DDC 976.4/063—dc23/eng/20220624
LC record available at https://lccn.loc.gov/2022029634

Cover photographs:
Background photo by Texas Ranger Jess Malone.
Foreground silhouette photo by Jon Freilich and The Associated Press

For Jo Ann

Contents

Foreword, by Gary Noesner — ix

Introduction — 1

Part I. Before the ROT War

1. Jo Ann Canady Turner's Arrest, April 22, 1997 — 11
2. Jo Ann Canady's Childhood — 17
3. Bill Turner — 27
4. Foreclosure — 43
5. Richard Lance McLaren — 52
6. The Birth of the ROT Militia — 63
7. Jo Ann Canady Turner's Incarceration — 79

Part II. The ROT War

8. The ROT Takes Hostages — 93
9. Day One: Standoff at the ROT Embassy — 105
10. Day Two: The Media Creates "Satellite City" — 115
11. Day Three: Texas Rangers Move Closer — 127
12. Day Four: Supporters Attempt to Join the Rebellion — 133
13. Day Five: The Texas Rangers Show Restraint — 139
14. Day Six: Robert Scheidt Surrenders — 143

15. Day Seven: The McLarens Surrender as
    Two ROT Members Escape 149
16. Day Eight: Deactivating Explosives in the DMR 153
17. Day Nine: Mike Matson Dies 161
18. Day Ten: The Search for Richard Keyes
    Ends in the Mountains 167

Part III. After the ROT War

19. State Trial for the ROT, and the Worst
    of Times for the Turners 175
20. The Turners Leave the Country at the
    End of the ROT's First Federal Trial 185
21. The Turners Return as ROT Members
    Await Another Federal Trial 197
22. The Turners Become Home Stagers and
    ROT Members Imprisoned 201
23. Ninety-Nine Years Imprisonment for
    Richard Lance McLaren 209
24. Kelly Turner's Murder 217
25. The ROT Today 221

Epilogue 227
Acknowledgments 233
Notes 235
Bibliography 251
Index 277

A gallery of photos follows page 130.

Foreword

IN THIS informative work, author Donna Marie Miller provides some unique insights about the 1997 Republic of Texas (ROT) standoff in Fort Davis, Texas. Gleaned from interviewing key individuals involved in all phases of the ordeal, she shares the true story of Jo Ann Turner, a seemingly normal person caught up in turning to the wrong people for help while trying to resolve personal problems.

Turner's portrait does not show a hardened criminal or psychotic individual intent on evil, but rather an all too human character seemingly up against the world, dealing with insurmountable problems—either created by or exacerbated by her own behavior and poor decision making. To address her predicament, Turner was drawn into a web of false ideology espoused by an inept ROT leader who offered to help. This association drew her deeper and deeper in and led to her personal undoing.

Charismatic leaders such the ROT's Richard McLaren claim to have all the answers that others need to solve their problems. Presented with certainty, backed up by fuzzy logic, and delivered with manifested self-assurance, such leaders convince their followers of the righteousness of their cause. This is a familiar pattern common among right-wing, antigovernment zealots and the cult movements of the 1990s.

Turner is hardly alone among the many naive and gullible individuals drawn to these movements. Many people are so desperate for relief that they are blinded by false promises of easy resolution for their complex problems. Typically, they blame the government rather than take individual responsibility. Promoting a false interpretation of the law as we know it, leaders like McLaren encourage their followers to embrace a false sense of victimization, a belief that they have been wronged by others, and offer a pathway through which they can leave their worldly and financial problems behind. Turner's part in this story is highly instructive because it shows how a decent person, through poor judgment, can get caught up in events beyond his or her control. The consequences to her life have been dramatic.

This story also reveals the strange evolution of the ROT movement and its leadership. Operating under the premise that the state of Texas was illegally annexed by the United States in 1845, modern-day ROT followers came to embrace the belief that they are independent and separate from the United States and that they are in no way beholden to the laws of our country. This bogus concept inevitably led them to believe they could disregard and flaunt US law and determine for themselves what was legal and what was not. The behaviors spawned by their unorthodox beliefs encouraged ROT followers to break various laws, to issue false financial liens, and to constantly push the margins of legal behavior.

Local law enforcement with limited resources and a desire to avoid conflict understandably felt reluctant to take on a group of heavily armed individuals in their community. Eventually, Richard McLaren and his unit of the ROT used their perch in the Davis Mountain Resort to exert their perceived sovereignty by eventually forcing legitimate law enforcement officers, with no recourse, to take action. In response to the arrest of an ROT member, McLaren ordered the home invasion and kidnapping of two resort residents and triggered a confrontation that the ROT was destined to lose. Miller also provides insight into the damaged individuals who were attracted to McLaren's nonsensical beliefs.

As we have so often seen, followers of such movements mostly tend to be uneducated individuals, with no family support mechanism, no meaningful work history, some with mental health issues, and often with criminal backgrounds. Such individuals are seemingly attracted to false political or religious prophets like bees are to honey. While Jo Ann Turner did not fit the profile of a member of such antigovernment militia, McLaren successfully conned her into following him. Desperate financial needs blinded her to his manipulative tactics.

A key part of this story focuses on Texas law enforcement and how it responded to this significant life-threatening event. Led by the Texas Rangers, responding officials had little recourse other than to secure the safe release of the two hostages and bring the culprits to face justice in a court of law. Dealing with a bombastic loudmouth like Richard McLaren was no easy task, and the decisive action for which the Texas Rangers are noted showed an appropriate amount of restraint while simultaneously preparing to take tactical action to resolve the conflict. As an FBI negotiation advisor called to the scene to assist the Texas Rangers, I was gratified to find a thoughtful and patient conflict management team whose goal was always the preservation of life despite the frustrating and combative behavior that McLaren demonstrated throughout the weeklong ordeal.

Sharing the key lessons learned by the FBI at Waco, both the positive actions and the mistakes made helped me to inform the Rangers of the challenges they faced and how to achieve the best outcome for all involved. They were always open to those assessments and recommendations. Throughout the ordeal, Captain Barry Caver and negotiator Jess Malone demonstrated patience, flexibility, and great restraint. As we always say in negotiation, "Don't get even, get your way." My book *Stalling for Time: My Life as an FBI Hostage Negotiator*, devotes a chapter to this challenging event and the negotiation process involved in the 1997 ROT siege in Fort Davis.

In summary, Miller tells several important stories. One is about the errors in judgment we can make as humans when we work against our own best interests. The other is a cautionary lesson about the risks of following someone whose actions and behaviors in the end address only their own personal needs and shortcomings, almost always exploiting their followers. And finally, there is a lesson about the importance of leveraging a talented law enforcement leadership team with thoughtful decision makers, using the talents and the skills of a good negotiator, and accepting help from advisors who have dealt with similar incidents in the past to help identify positive actions to be taken and problems to avoid.

—Gary Noesner
Former FBI Consultant and Crisis Negotiator

Texas Secessionists Standoff

Introduction

I BEGAN WORK on this project in September 2017 following a public signing for my first book, *The Broken Spoke: Austin's Legendary Honky-Tonk*, published by Texas A&M University Press. At that event, Molly McKnight approached me to tell me about her friend Jo Ann Canady Turner who, twenty years earlier, had helped to start a war for Texas' independence.

Texas Secessionists Standoff: The Republic of Texas "War" is divided into three sections: Part I—Before the ROT War, Part II—The ROT War, and Part III—After the ROT War. ROT stands for the Republic of Texas militia group that declared Texas an independent nation and fought a seven-day war to secede from the United States that began on April 27, 1997, in the Davis Mountains.

Chapter 1 begins with Jo Ann Canady Turner's arrest because that event triggered the seven-day war fought between ROT militia members and three hundred law enforcement agents in the Davis Mountains. Her phone call to her friend, the self-proclaimed ambassador of the ROT Richard "Rick" Lance McLaren, from Travis County Jail on April 22, 1997, helped to incite the standoff that began five days later.

To provide insight into Jo Ann Canady Turner's motivation for joining up with a Texas antigovernment militia, Chapters 2 through 4 provide a flashback into her background. An impoverished childhood and abusive father, a brief courtship and marriage to an alcoholic husband seventeen years her senior, and the foreclosure of their family home all contributed to her poor choices.

Chapters 5 through 7 deal specifically with Jo Ann's association with McLaren, the ROT, and her subsequent forty days of incarceration. I recorded detailed accounts of these events during interviews with Jo Ann once a week in my kitchen or at several local restaurants. After the interviews, she read and approved my transcripts, before I added them to the book.

Provocative personal stories about her life provide the thread that begins each of the remaining chapters in this book.

Chapters 8 through 18 describe the happenings of each day during the siege, beginning April 27, 1997, and ending May 3, 1997. Seventy-five primary sources, including law enforcement officials, attorneys, residents, and FBI agents, provided me with firsthand knowledge about the siege and a four-month manhunt for an ROT escapee that followed.

These events subsequently ruined Jo Ann's otherwise unremarkable life. Chapters 19 through 24 describe her release from jail, her fearful life on the run for fifteen years, grief, and finally absolution. Like the unnamed narrator of Samuel Taylor Coleridge's lyrical 1798 ballad, "The Rime of the Ancient Mariner," Jo Ann suffered an albatross-sized guilt following this seven-day revolutionary war in Texas, but her tragic story continued up until her death on April 8, 2020. After losing nearly every possession she owned to foreclosure, Jo Ann also lost the lives of both her daughter and a husband. She hoped this story would someday help others to avoid a similar fate.

However convoluted, McLaren also shared his story with me from inside William P. Clements Unit Prison in Amarillo where he has been serving a ninety-nine-year sentence. McLaren to this day remains steadfast in his belief that the United States illegally annexed Texas on December 29, 1845. However, attorneys, prosecutors, and federal judges who convicted ROT members of organized crime, bank and mail fraud, and violating the Federal Firearms Act disagree.

Despite McLaren's failings, the ROT survives, split into three separate factions. One prominent faction calls itself the Texas Nationalist Movement, led by Daniel Miller (no relation to this author) and boasts three hundred thousand members who wish "to take Texas back."[1] His book, *Texit: Why and How Texas Will Leave the Union*, continues to support the idea of making Texas an independent nation.

Another group, led by David Johnson and Jesse Enloe, was discredited in 1997 after its members threatened to kill multiple government leaders, including then-President Bill Clinton.[2] Enloe and two others, Jack Abbot Grebe Jr. and Johnnie Wise, received lengthy prison terms as a result.[3]

One of the original ROT members, Ed Brannum,[4] who joined the group in 1995, still leads another faction that meets once a month in Kerrville. For Chapter 25, I interviewed Brannum by phone. He claimed that many ROT members today still use a variety of legal loopholes to avoid paying federal income taxes, and they do not carry Texas driver's licenses.

Since the 1990s, several other antigovernment, right-wing, and tax-defying extremist groups have proclaimed themselves sovereign and not subject to the laws of the United States. These groups made their revolutionary agendas public as they clashed with law enforcement while the media reported the events in front-page news. Examples include Ruby Ridge, Idaho, in 1992; Waco, Texas, in 1993; and the Oklahoma City bombing in 1995.

Other books written about such events include *A Place Called Waco: A Survivor's Story* by David Thibodeau, *Ruby Ridge: The Truth and Tragedy of the Randy Weaver Family* by Jess Walter, and *American Terrorist: Timothy McVeigh and the Oklahoma City Bombing* by Lou Michael and Dan Herbeck.

Former FBI agent Gary Noesner and author of *Stalling for Time: My Life as an FBI Hostage Negotiator*, wrote my book's forward. He also dedicated one chapter of his book to the 1997 standoff with the ROT militia in the Davis Mountains. Mike Cox also provides an autobiographical account of the ROT event in several chapters of his book, *Stand-Off in Texas: Just Call Me a Spokesman for DPS*.

As a former journalist who spent nine years writing for three major Texas daily newspapers, I have written this nonfiction book in a narrative style similar to that of Norman Mailer in his Pulitzer Prize–winning 1979 true crime tale *The Executioner's Song*. Each of my sources provided me with unique perspectives and their own opinions about what happened during the week-long 1997 standoff in the Davis Mountains. The result is an account of these events devoid of my own personal opinions.

For nearly three decades, I have followed news about Fort Davis, Marfa, Alpine, and Big Bend, as I hold a personal stake in the area. Formerly from El Paso, I often travel by car between that city and Austin. I always look forward to seeing the Davis Mountains come into view at about the midway point of my journey. The majestic range rises forty-nine hundred feet up from the Chihuahuan Desert floor, providing twenty-seven hundred miles of National Park land and a 102,675-acre preserve.

Some of my favorite movies have been filmed in the area, including *Giant* and *The Searchers* in 1956, *Paris Texas* in 1984, *Fandango* in 1985, *No Country for Old Men* in 2004, *There Will be Blood,* in 2007, and *Boyhood* in 2014.

I have long considered this part of West Texas as a place for my husband and me to retire someday. We enjoy regular visits to historic Fort Davis to attend the nighttime "Star Parties" during the spring season at McDonald Observatory. Treks to Keesey Canyon Overlook and Skyline Drive Trail allow stunning views in all directions of the remaining wild terrain. At 8,379 feet in elevation, Mount Livermore, also known locally as Baldy Peak, stands as the fifth tallest in Texas. Despite recent history, the Davis Mountains will remain for me as pristine and as glorious as ever.

We Texans enjoy sharing our state's rich history, however mythologized, so I must indulge. Please forgive this brief synopsis of more than two hundred years, condensed unlike Stephen Harrigan's own detailed 925-page and four-pound book, *Big Wonderful Thing: A History of Texas.*

The quest for Texas' independence as a nation began nearly two centuries before Richard Lance McLaren proclaimed himself ambassador of the ROT. Mexico won its independence from Spain on September 16, 1810, and the government quickly began awarding *empresario* land grants to help colonize the Tejas province in the state of Coahuila. Moses Austin,[5] a native of Connecticut, delivered three hundred Anglo-American settlers to Tejas shortly before he died in August 1821. His son and successor, Stephen F. Austin, gained permission from then–Mexican Governor Antonio Martínez to grant each American colonist, as head of his household, 640 acres and an additional 320 acres to men who brought along wives. Martínez further offered 160 acres per child to each family with offspring and another 80 acres per slave to slaveowners.[6] Consequently, the Mexican territory known as Tejas was founded primarily by Americans.

By 1824, Austin had established San Felipe de Austin as the colony's unofficial capital where he served as both the civil and the military authority.[7] In 1833, he unsuccessfully asked the Mexican government for permission to separate Tejas from the state of Coahuila. However,

Mexican troops arrested Austin in January 1834 under suspicion of inciting an insurrection. After being held for eight months in a Mexico City jail, Austin returned home to find that his fellow American colonists had demanded that the Republic of Texas separate from Mexico to create an independent nation.[8]

According to Donald S. Frazier, PhD,[9] formerly a history professor at McMurray College in Abilene, the forefathers of the Republic of Texas possessed grand ideas but had little experience in seeing them through to fruition. Sam Houston became the nation's first president after he and his men defeated Mexican General Antonio López de Santa Anna at San Jacinto.[10]

Following the Battle of San Jacinto on April 21, 1836,[11] and under terms of the Treaties of Velasco,[12] all Mexican troops retreated to below the Rio Grande River, then considered an armistice line, not necessarily a permanent boundary line, between the two countries. Problems arose when the founders of the Republic of Texas attempted to establish the Rio Grande as its southern physical land boundary. The Adams-Onís Treaty of 1819[13] had previously established the Red River as the boundary between Mexico and the former Spanish Tejas.

The Republic's first Texas Constitution allowed for the creation of a convention of delegates in a building located near La Grange in Fayette County, then called Washington on the Brazos. Wealthy Texas rancher George C. Childress presented the resolution calling for Texas' independence and its recognition as a new republic.

Some speculate that Houston may have served as an agent of US President Andrew Jackson who wanted to see the Republic of Texas annexed. However, Houston's successor, President Mirabeau B. Lamar,[14] did not favor annexation and immediately began making alternative plans.

The Republic of Texas declared its independence from Mexico on March 2, 1836,[15] by attempting to claim territory east of the Rio Grande, north from the Gulf of Mexico all the way to the Sabine River,[16] and encompassing parts of Oklahoma, Colorado, Wyoming and New Mexico.

Almost immediately, the United States began attempts to annex Texas. The US pattern of annexation had begun with the Republic of West Florida earlier in the 1800s and in all Florida parishes all the way to

Pensacola.[17] Florida had declared the Republic of West Florida an independent nation just before the US military sent in its troops, secured its interests, and annexed it.[18]

A provisional government would not decide on a proper location for the new nation's capital but instead began vacillating, and at Washington on the Brazos, a convention of delegates wrote a constitution and elected officers on March 1, 1836. That year, the capital moved four more times, from Brazos to Harrisburg, then to Galveston, to Velasco, and to West Columbia, before operating from Houston on April 19, 1837.[19] President Lamar finally moved the Republic of Texas capital, on October 17, 1839, to Austin,[20] a hamlet at that time. Then Lamar began a series of failed expeditions north to Santa Fe to extend Texan control of land in New Mexico.[21]

Lamar's efforts failed when Mexican forces captured the Texans in 1841. A series of complex political and military struggles between the Mexican and Texian governments followed.[22] From March 2, 1836, until February 19, 1844, Mexican troops regularly attacked outposts within the sovereign nation of the Republic of Texas as civilians fought for independence from Mexico. During that period, settlers also continued to fight their own frontier wars against neighboring Native American tribes, including Comanche.[23]

In 1844, members of the Republic of Texas considered an offer of help from US President John Tyler. The president drafted a treaty of annexation that resulted in Mexico severing all of its diplomatic relations with the United States.[24] At first attempt, Tyler lacked the votes to ratify the treaty. However, shortly after he vacated office, he won support from president-elect James K. Polk. Under Polk, both houses of Congress passed a joint resolution to approve the annexation of Texas on March 1, 1845.[25]

In return for the state's annexation, Polk offered to send a fleet of warships to protect the Texas coast from attack by the Mexican military. He promised that Texas could "keep her public lands and pay her own public debts." Polk later signed documents that officially declared Texas a state of the Union on December 29, 1845. J. Pinckney Henderson served as the state's first governor.[26] In addition, the US Army showed up at the mouth of the Nueces to declare the area between the Nueces River and the Rio Grande as part of the United States upon annexation. The

Mexicans opposed Texas' annexation because the land included what the Mexican government considered its own seceded region.

The controversial Mexican-American War began in 1846 over the disagreement about the boundary lines separating the two countries. The war ended with a compromise in the Treaty of Guadalupe Hidalgo[27] that established the international boundaries as the Rio Grande south and the Gila River to the west in exchange for the United States' payment of $15 million to Mexico. However, neither boundary remained permanent, as rivers tend to move by natural means.

As a result of the treaty, however, the United States gained control of five hundred thousand square acres of formerly Mexican-claimed territory that included parts of land in Arizona, California, Colorado, Nevada, New Mexico, Texas, and Utah.[28] Controversially, the treaty effectively also extended the reign and reach of slavery. For the ten years leading up to the American Civil War, Texans owned slaves despite political extremism between northerners and southerners throughout North America. While at the time only one in four Texans owned slaves, a majority supported slavery as a means of supporting statewide agricultural growth.[29]

Texas became the seventh state to secede from the Union thanks to 76 percent of its voters who favored joining the Confederacy just one month before President Abraham Lincoln took office on March 6, 1861.[30] Though only a few battles were fought in Texas before the Civil War ended on April 8, 1865, and a variety of federal forces occupied the state until 1870, the military command changed eight times. A new Texas Constitution, approved in 1876, to this day remains the basic authority of Texas law.[31]

Any separation of the state of Texas from the Union became a moot point with the 1869 Supreme Court decision in *Texas v. White*, which held that the United States is "an indestructible union."[32]

In 1854, the US Army established Fort Davis to protect the migration routes of American pioneers from east to west during a time when Mescalero Apache tribes occupied the region.[33] The 2,265-square-mile area once existed in Presidio County until 1887 when it became Jeff Davis County. Fort Davis became the county seat, named for Jefferson Davis, who from 1861 until 1865 served as president of the Confederate States of America during the Civil War.[34]

Following the Civil War, a large population of Texans living in rural areas of the state began to become increasingly frustrated with a federal government that offered little protection to homesteads against raids by Native Americans and Mexican bandits.[35] While those violent attacks on American citizens have disappeared from West Texas over time, political unrest has stretched well into the twenty-first century throughout the United States.

Throughout the 1990s, informal paramilitary groups began to appear throughout the United States as part of an antigovernment movement. Members of these groups shared common conspiracy theories that had begun with the Silver Shirt Legion and the Christian Front shortly before World War II and continued with the California Rangers and the Minutemen at the close of the war.[36]

At the peak of the modern militia movement, formal groups enveloped sovereign citizen and tax protest movements. These groups included the Arizona Viper Militia, Georgia Republic Militia, Kentucky State Militia, Ohio Unorganized Militia Assistance and Advisory Committee, Southeastern Ohio Defense Force, Oklahoma Constitutional Militia, Michigan Militia, North American Militia, San Joaquin County Militia, Southern Indiana Regional Militia, Southern California High Desert Militia, Twin Cities Free Militia, Washington State Militia, and West Virginia Mountaineer Militia, to name just some.

With the cataclysmic standoffs at Ruby Ridge, Idaho, in 1992; Waco, Texas, in 1993; and in Jordan, Montana, in 1996, nearly every state claimed at least one antigovernment militia group in residence throughout the 1990s.

During the national peak of the antigovernment movement, in remote West Texas, a handful of separatists led by McLaren began their public act of rebellion on April 27, 1997. McLaren declared war against the United States following the arrests of Jo Ann Canady Turner in Austin and Robert Jonathan Scheidt in the Davis Mountain Resort. The militia members referred to themselves as the Republic of Texas (the ROT). McLaren had created a media firestorm years earlier by claiming that Texas had been illegally annexed by the United States prior to the Civil War. His plan had been to retake Texas and to restore it to its former glory as an independent nation. McLaren's plans may have failed, but he successfully besmirched the name of the Republic of Texas forever.

Part I

Before the ROT War

1

Jo Ann Canady Turner's Arrest, April 22, 1997

ON THE MORNING of April 22, 1997, fifty-four-year-old Jo Ann Turner dressed in a pair of Ralph Lauren blue jean shorts, a well-pressed white cotton short-sleeved Burberry blouse, and a pair of Gucci gold-painted leather sandals. Appraising herself in front of her bedroom's full-length mirror, the reflection she saw revealed a beautiful woman aging gracefully.

Jo Ann had defied the aging process by at least a decade. Her dewy, ivory skin had been nipped and tucked by a skilled plastic surgeon. Salon experts had dyed and threaded her eyebrows to give them an eternally youthful appearance. A regular six-week regimen of color treatments veiled her age by producing a lavish head of heather blond, shoulder-length hair perpetually styled into a flip. Her nails had been professionally manicured regularly to produce a perfect ten. She had toned her body through years of exercise, maintenance, and excellent nutrition. Bankruptcy had taken much from Jo Ann, but it would not also steal her looks.

Jo Ann's husband, Bill, had left their apartment before dawn that morning for his job driving for Leal Trucking Company. Jo Ann had planned to spend the better part of her own day searching for employment in the classified ads section of the *Austin American Statesman*.

Though it had been several months since their eviction, she still found it difficult to accept the Shepherd Mountain apartments as home. The two-bedroom unit seemed Lilliputian compared to the Turners' former custom-built house along the banks of Town Lake. Jo Ann herself had designed the five-thousand-square-foot residence on Rivercrest Drive in a Mediterranean style. She and Bill had filled their showplace with one-of-a-kind furnishings, draperies, antiques, and china before losing it all in foreclosure.

Jo Ann saw that the kitchen's aluminum trashcan needed emptying; resignedly, she tied the liner bag securely and carried it outside. She felt the sun warm her skin, smelled the verdant air, and welcomed the sight of the property's solicitously tended fruit trees in a tableau of flamingo pink and white. It seemed that nothing could spoil her day.

Within seconds, however, nine men, dressed from head-to-toe in black, surrounded Jo Ann, pointing fully loaded automatic weapons at her head. The men represented the Austin Police Department's SWAT team, the Travis County Sheriff's Department, the Bureau of Alcohol, Tobacco, Firearms and Explosives (ATF), and the FBI.

"I'm sure that they thought I was going to faint in the parking lot. Most people would have. I wasn't screaming; I was calm," she said.[1]

Jo Ann immediately addressed one of the law enforcement officers as he pointed a gun at her. She noticed he had an alien look, like a character out of an episode from the 1960s *Twilight Zone* television series. Half-moons of pink puffy flesh surrounded his eyes, which peeked out from beneath holes in the black nylon stretch fabric of his facemask.

"He said, 'We're here to take you in.' I asked, 'Take me in where?' He said, 'The judge has ordered your arrest.' I asked, 'For what?' And he said, 'I don't know,'" Jo Ann recounted. "'His first question was 'Do you have any guns in the house?'"

Jo Ann said that she didn't own any weapons and asked if she could quickly change from her shorts into jeans. Without producing a warrant, four officers followed Jo Ann into her apartment. They stood just outside her closed bedroom door as she changed.

It took Jo Ann only five minutes to change into jeans and to write a quick note to Bill to let him know that she had been arrested. When she left the apartment, she remembered to take her keys and purse and to lock the front door behind her.

The thirty-minute ride to Travis County Jail seemed the longest half hour of Jo Ann's life. She watched as her Westlake neighborhood, Town Lake, and Austin's downtown skyline slipped from her view, framed by the glass windows of the patrol car. The sustained hum of the car's wheels and the rhythmic interruptions made by the breaks between asphalt and concrete seemed to hypnotize her. Her thoughts drifted as she replayed her actions over the last year.

"I'm thinking, *Why are they taking me in? It has to be one or both of the two liens that I filed with Stewart Title and the IRS. What else could it be?*" she said.

Neither she nor the driver spoke during the ride to Travis County Jail. The officer pulled the car into the garage, then escorted her to booking. Other officers fingerprinted Jo Ann and photographed her to create a mug shot.

In the Central Booking Facility at Travis County Jail, Jo Ann stood nude while a muscular female jailer dressed in a dark blue and white uniform searched her mouth, her nose, her anus, and her vagina for the presence of concealed contraband or weapons. As part of police standard operating procedures, the jailer poked and prodded her. Tears came to Jo Ann's eyes. Although she felt overwhelmed with shame, she did not put up a fight.

"I felt violated and humiliated," Jo Ann said. "They made most of the men leave the room during the search, but one man remained standing along a south wall staring. The female jailer just giggled and laughed at my shame."

Afterward, the jailer took Jo Ann's clothing along with her purse and locked them in the evidence room. A female guard outfitted her with the traditional orange prisoner garb and flip-flops.

Jo Ann was then escorted to a room with walls of beige-painted cinder blocks. There, seated in a metal folding chair at a small metal-frame desk, sat a pudgy man wearing wire spectacles who appeared to have been squeezed into a dark linen suit at least one size too small for him. He identified himself as a legal representative from the criminal division of the Texas Attorney General's office. His name escaped Jo Ann's attention; she would recall later only that the man held a tape recorder.

That moment would mark the first that Jo Ann would hear the term "paper terrorist" applied to herself and to members of the Republic of

Texas (ROT), although in the days to come, the term would become almost a cliché. The man told Jo Ann that on January 17, 1997, Governor George W. Bush had asked Texas legislators to write a bill that would make the filing of bogus liens punishable by a four-thousand-dollar fine and imprisonment.[2]

He said that Jo Ann would be charged with working with the ROT by filing false liens within the state court system over the last several months in an attempt to financially stall operations for businesses and property owners. He also said members of the ROT had further harassed and intimidated government leaders using the US Postal Service as part of a "paper war" aimed at reclaiming Texas.

Jo Ann recalled often hearing the self-professed "ambassador" for the ROT, Richard Lance McLaren, proclaim Texas an independent nation that had been illegally annexed by the United States in 1845. Through a series of interviews with radio broadcasters and reporters from newspapers and magazines throughout Texas, McLaren had claimed a following of ten thousand supporters, including Jo Ann. Because she had typed several of McLaren's liens, he had promised to help her reclaim her foreclosed home and subsequent auctioned possessions once he became the leader of the newly reformed independent nation of Texas.

■ ■ ■

Jo Ann returned her attention to the man from the Texas Attorney General's office seated directly in front of her.

"He said, 'Mrs. Turner, we would like a statement from you. Do you agree to waive your rights and to give us a statement?' I told him 'Not without my attorney present,'" she said. "Then I asked if I could call my attorney."

After the interview ended, Jo Ann telephoned McLaren from a pay phone inside the jail. She dialed his cell number from memory. When McLaren answered and she heard his familiar voice, Jo Ann could hardly keep herself from crying.

"He asked me what had happened, and I told him. Then Rick said he would file some documents. When I hung up the phone, I felt sure that I wouldn't be incarcerated long—but I was wrong," Jo Ann said.

For the next twenty-four hours, Jo Ann waited for McLaren to rescue her. The following afternoon, feeling desperate, she finally phoned her husband, Bill, to ask him to post her bail. "My husband told me that he tried to get a bond for me. He said he went to several bail bondsmen, but they all told him the same thing—that they could not secure a bond for me because we had no money and no valuable assets," Jo Ann said.

When she hung up the phone, Jo Ann heard an unfamiliar whirring sound just outside the window to her holding cell. "I saw this helicopter outside. I pushed a button beside my cell door and asked, 'What's a helicopter doing out here?' A male jailer's voice said, 'Someone's trying to come and get you released from the jail; it must be somebody from the Republic of Texas militia.'"

Jo Ann did not for a moment consider that the jailer had told her the truth. Rather, she feared that no one would come to her rescue—not the Republic of Texas militia nor even her own husband. Instead, she believed she might die alone and forgotten inside Travis County Jail.

2

Jo Ann Canady's Childhood

SINCE BIRTH, Jo Ann Canady Turner had relied on the charity of strangers. Born May 29, 1943, in Brackenridge Hospital, the oldest public hospital in Texas,[1] she became the first of five children delivered free of charge to her indigent parents, Margaret and Sydney Canady.

The historic hospital's three-story limestone Queen Anne–style building had been constructed with two triangular-shaped gables and two steeples at 1405 Sabine Street. Over the years, its staff had earned a reputation for helping anyone in need regardless of their ability to pay. The City of Austin and Travis County had jointly built the hospital at a cost of ten thousand dollars, and it opened on July 3, 1884, boasting forty patient beds. Originally called the City-County Hospital, it became known as City Hospital in 1907. In 1915, a new forty-five-bed facility opened. The hospital further increased its capacity to 208 patients with the construction of new wings on the south, west, and north sides of the main building between 1929 and 1941. Austin City Council members renamed the hospital in 1929 in honor of Dr. Robert J. Brackenridge, who had helped to finance both its 1915 construction and the three additions while working tirelessly to improve public health care for the city's poor.[2]

Catholic nuns, members of the nonprofit group the Daughters of Charity of St. Vincent de Paul,[3] likely cared for Jo Ann as an infant in the hospital's neonatal unit. While remembering nothing of her time spent there or the knifelike pleats of the nuns' habits, Jo Ann would someday embrace black as her favorite color.

The Canady family initially lived on East 1st Street, later to be renamed Cesar Chavez Street, in a modest three-bedroom redbrick house. Throughout her childhood, Jo Ann received little to no nurturing from either of her parents. Instead, they led busy lives while earning barely enough money to survive.

Sydney Carroll Canady, a native of Austin born in 1903, had worked a series of odd jobs since adolescence. He worked as a grocery store clerk, as a night watchman, and as a dishwasher, and he had once operated his own baggage company before finding long-term employment in the maintenance department at the Texas School for the Deaf.

At home, Jo Ann's father often sat and rolled his own Bull Durham tobacco cigarettes and chain smoked. She recalled his cloudy vapors often hung low surrounding his head and face, giving him a sinister, ghostlike appearance. Although she never saw him drink alcohol, Sydney sipped enough black coffee late into the evenings that Jo Ann noticed the drink made him jittery and restless.

She would later learn from her father's sister, Lillian, that her paternal grandparents had never approved of their son's marriage, although her aunt would remain close to her nieces and nephews throughout their lives.

Jo Ann's mother, Margaret, went by the name Maggie and had worked as a maid at a number of Austin hotels before and after she married. Maggie was born in 1920 and raised in Paige, Texas, a small community just west of Giddings where Jo Ann's maternal grandparents farmed. Maggie grew up plain, the oldest of three children—with two sisters, Helen and Nellie, and a brother, John Jr.

Once she married Sydney, Maggie never wore makeup other than just a little bit of lipstick. She never used nail polish or adorned herself with jewelry when she dressed for church every week. Jo Ann recalls that on Sundays, before church, her mother often prepared fried chicken or a roast beef that she placed in the oven, where it promptly burned.

On July 10, 1944, thirteen months after Jo Ann was born, Maggie gave birth to fraternal twins, Lillian and Jimmie. The Canadys named little Jimmie after the famous country singer and songwriter Jimmie Rodgers. Lillian was named after Sydney's sister. Their Aunt Lillian was married to Frank Nelson, a general contractor in Austin, and the two lived an elite lifestyle far removed from the seedy part of town where the Canadys lived. Meanwhile, Jo Ann's immediate family members would suffer in poverty for years to come.

The families shared little contact except when Aunt Lillian stopped by the Canady home to drop off clothes once owned by her daughter, Patricia Nelson, two years older than Jo Ann. Her cousin's well-made hand-me-downs had been purchased in expensive department stores. The clothes allowed Jo Ann to imagine a future for herself when she could purchase such luxuries brand new.

The 1946 birth of Sydney Jr., the youngest of the Canady sons and his father's namesake, further stretched the family's household finances thin. The Canadys soon downsized into a smaller one-story, two-room shotgun-style stucco house that had been built in 1942 at 2507 East 4th Street.

For ten years, the family slept all together in the front room of the house in three separate beds. Jo Ann and Lillian shared one bed, and Jimmie and Sydney Jr. shared another, while their parents slept nearby (the youngest Canady sibling, Becky, would not arrive until 1960). Everyone took turns sharing one bathroom. Jo Ann recalls that she often stayed awake for hours listening to the sounds that her siblings and mother made in their sleep. She began noticing that her father seldom slept, and in the darkness, he often kept watchful eyes upon her. In the pit of her stomach, his attention began to make her feel uneasy, but she did not yet know the reasons why.

For a short time during her elementary school years, Jo Ann made friends with Lupe Lozano, who lived next door. Lupe frequently invited Jo Ann to her house for a visit. Once a week in the afternoons after school, Jerry and Mary Lozano would allow Jo Ann to accompany their daughter to her weekly piano lessons.

Seated on a sofa across from the piano teacher and Lupe, Jo Ann would listen to her friend practice. As she listened, she tried to absorb Lupe's playing by focusing on her friend's finger placement. Jo Ann also tried writing down what she could understand from the music lessons. Eventually, however, she grew bored with the instruction and with Lupe, who was two years her senior. Meanwhile, Jo Ann longed for more, something as-yet undefined in her thoughts.

The Canady family never celebrated birthdays or traditional holidays. However, unexpectedly, around the time of Jo Ann's eighth birthday,

Maggie bought her eldest daughter a brand-new blue Schwinn bicycle paid for using the layaway plan at Sears department store. Jo Ann taught herself to ride the bicycle by holding onto one of the handlebars with her left hand and using the other to slide along the inclining wall of a neighbor's house located directly across the street. No one held the bicycle seat for Jo Ann as she learned to ride. Not once did she ask for anyone's help, and she never fell. Once she learned to balance, she rode for hours around town. The freedom that the bike afforded her felt exhilarating.

Jo Ann attended the bilingual Metz Elementary School until the sixth grade when her parents enrolled her in Florence Ralston Brooke Elementary School. Though no one ever provided a reason for her transfer, Jo Ann always suspected that it might have stemmed from her father's prejudice against the neighborhood where her family lived.

Jo Ann began seventh grade at John T. Allan Junior High School, in a building that since 1900 had served as Stephen F. Austin High School at the corner of 9th and Trinity Streets. However, Allan Junior High burned down shortly after the academic year began in 1956.[4]

For the remainder of that year and all through eighth grade, Jo Ann attended University Junior High, affiliated with the University of Texas. The yellow-brick school, built in a Spanish Renaissance style, stood on a sloping hill between Red River Street and San Jacinto Boulevard. Before desegregation, the administration allowed for a split school day. Anglo students attended classes early in the mornings and left campus at lunch, and Mexican American students finished the school day in the building.[5]

Jo Ann excelled academically at Allan Junior High. She won the Citywide Spelling Bee in the eighth grade and received a certificate signed by the mayor, Robert Thomas Miller, and Gordon Bailey, then the principal at Allan Junior High. Her spelling bee award bore a large yellow A for Allan. She proudly held on to that first-place spelling bee certificate for decades until one day in 1996 when all of her personal belongings would be boxed up and auctioned during a home foreclosure.

At just thirteen years old, Jo Ann began working two jobs after school; on weekdays, she waited tables for tips at the East Seventh Street Bakery, and on weekend nights, she worked at the Tip-Inn Restaurant. Gonzalo and Maria Gonzales, the grandparents of Jo Ann's new best friend, Bernice Ruiz, owned the Mexican food restaurant then located on Webberville Road.

Bernice's parents, Benny and Alice Ruiz, owned the bakery that also served as an informal community center. It provided a jukebox and small tables and chairs for local patrons to sit while they drank coffee and ate pastries. For Jo Ann, the jukebox was an introduction to the music of the times, and it expanded her universe. When the bakery emptied and closed each night, Bernice would place a quarter in the jukebox, and the two girls would dance to rock and roll music, with Bernice leading.

In the evenings, sometimes as late as midnight, Jo Ann walked alone more than two miles from the restaurant to her family's home. One night after arriving home late, she snuck into the house, being very careful not to awaken her sleeping family members. In the bathroom, Jo Ann changed quickly into her one thin cotton nightgown. Abruptly, the bathroom door opened and her father stepped inside, shutting the door and locking it behind him.

Without saying a word, her father moved toward her menacingly. She recalls that he did not look into her eyes, but only stared longingly at her nubile body. Slowly, he lifted her nightgown to put his hands on her breasts. Jo Ann attempted to push her father away, but he pinned her against the door. He held her firmly with his body pressed against hers while he groped her. Suddenly, she heard one of her brothers knocking on the other side of the bathroom door. Startled, her father released Jo Ann.

Little Jimmie asked to pee. Feeling rescued, Jo Ann unlocked and opened the door before she dashed to the bed that she shared with Lillian to pull the covers up around her. Her father walked slowly to the bed he shared with her mother, all the while keeping his sights on Jo Ann. Torn curtains hanging on the windows allowed moonlight to spill into the room and to reveal the whites of his eyes staring at her from her parents' bed. She barely slept that night, consumed with thinking of ways she would prevent her father from touching her again.

Jo Ann began staying overnight often at Bernice's grandparents' home located just a few blocks from the Gonzales's restaurant. The couple doted on her and fed her most meals before and after she worked waiting tables. Her best friend also began sharing some of her clothes with Jo Ann to wear to school. Bernice and her family provided Jo Ann with a safe and loving adopted family, however temporary.

She attended the ninth through twelfth grades at McCallum High School, and during Jo Ann's freshman year of high school, her mother returned to working as a maid at a local hotel. The boost in the family's income allowed the Canadys to move north into a three-bedroom house on Taulbee Lane. After the Canadys moved, the Ruiz family soon followed, and Bernice and Jo Ann continued their inseparable friendship.

In high school, both girls shared a fondness for athletics. Jo Ann learned to swim in the natural spring-fed Barton Springs that had been purchased by Billy Barton in 1837 before Austin was established as the capital of the Republic of Texas.[6] Jo Ann and Bernice also swam often at Deep Eddy, the oldest swimming pool in Texas.[7]

Occasionally, the Canady children and their mother would all pile into a two-door Ford sedan owned by Maggie's sister, Helen Symes, to drive to Giddings where their grandparents Lillie and John Smathers lived. In Giddings, all of the children chased chickens or sat on the fences to watch the pigs root in their pens while the adults visited inside the house.

At the start of Jo Ann's sophomore year at McCallum, Bernice began driving Jo Ann to school in her turquoise and white 1955 Chevrolet Bel Air. On the weekends, Tony Castillo, Bernice's boyfriend and future husband, visited and drove both girls to the movies in her car. At the drive-in, Jo Ann often sat in the front while Bernice and Tony kissed in the back seat.

Once Jo Ann began dating, she and her dates often went to the Chief Drive-In theater at 5600 North Lamar Boulevard. The drive-in accommodated as many as 814 cars parked with mobile sound speakers attached to the car windows, and the giant three-story screen nightly provided the most current movie releases at the time.[8] Jo Ann and a half dozen of her friends also liked piling into a single vehicle to attend the South Austin Drive-In at 3900 South Congress, which allowed for one thousand parked cars.[9]

Jo Ann's favorite films were scary movies: *The Innocents. The Pit and the Pendulum. The Curse of The Werewolf. Mr. Sardonicus. Homicidal. The Beast of Yucca Flats.* and *Bloodlust.* all released in 1961. She also became fond of Elizabeth Taylor and Richard Burton movies such as *Cleopatra* and *The V.I.P.s.*

During her junior year of high school, Jo Ann entered Texas' newly founded Vocational Office Educational (VOE) program. In 1963, the Vocational Education Act established similar occupational programs nationwide to prepare students for careers in both the business and industrial trades. As part of the VOE program, Jo Ann attended traditional classes for half a day until noon weekdays. In the afternoons, she worked at Woolworth's department store at Sixth and Congress streets.[10]

Before long, a Woolworth's manager put Jo Ann in charge of the cosmetics department, which stretched three long aisles. Jo Ann loved meeting new people and quickly learned how to sell makeup products. Quickly, she developed a loyal following of customers and began earning a commission. She spent almost all the money she earned from her paychecks on clothes purchased at the E.M. Scarborough & Sons department store, then located across the street at 6th and Congress.[11]

When Jo Ann turned seventeen years old, her youngest sister, Becky, was born, and once again the family's finances began to suffer. Not long afterward, Jo Ann realized she had to leave home. Immediately upon graduating high school, Jo Ann applied for a college loan to enroll in Hardin-Simmons University in Abilene. Her roommate was Judith Hedrick, whom she had met while attending Sunday school classes at the Walnut Creek Baptist Church at 12062 N. Lamar. Judith's family had charitably offered to supplement Jo Ann's college tuition for a semester if Jo Ann agreed to be Judith's roommate.

Jo Ann loved attending Hardin-Simmons and especially enjoyed visiting the campus gym. She participated in intramural games for volleyball and basketball, playing positions both as a guard and as a forward. She recalled that the university's rules then prohibited female students from wearing shorts in public while attending classes on campus at Hardin-Simmons. The administration did not allow girls to wear shorts walking to and from the gym. Instead, teachers instructed them to wear a long trench coat over their clothes. Only once they arrived inside the gym could the girls remove their coats.

Dressing in the latest fashions, Jo Ann wore long dark skirts with layered lace and horsehair petticoats. She topped these skirts with starched white blouses and white fold-down ankle-length bobby socks. She wore hard-soled leather penny loafers with coin-sized slots located over the insteps. She also wore classic flat saddle shoes, either black-on-white or brown-on-white. Jo Ann wore her medium shoulder-length hair flipped up or in a bouffant style made popular by then First Lady Jacqueline Kennedy.

Chapter 2

On the weekends, Jo Ann socialized at a popular dance hall then located just 25 miles southeast of Abilene, the Grande Ole Oplin.[12] A live band seldom performed on Oplin's large, elevated stage. More often, a deejay spun records broadcast through a large sound system, advanced for its day, as patrons crowded a massive wooden dance floor. At the Oplin, students congregated from three local universities with religious affiliations: Hardin-Simmons University, Abilene Christian University, and McMurry University.

"I liked to dance to all the pop stuff—including Elvis Presley's music and early rock and roll," Jo Ann said.

Some of *Billboard* magazine's top hits of 1962 also popular with Jo Ann were "The Lion Sleeps Tonight" by the Tokens, "The Twist" by Chubby Checkers, and the "Peppermint Twist" by Joey Dee and the Starliters.[13]

As a conservative Baptist, Jo Ann's roommate did not approve of outings to the Oplin for dancing or dating. Because she and Judith lived such different social lives during the fall semester of 1963, Jo Ann switched roommates. Jo Ann learned that her new roommate, Cathy Harper, from Odessa, was the daughter of a school principal. When Cathy told her that teachers earned limited salaries, Jo Ann switched her major from physical education to business.

Meanwhile, a tall and lean member of the Cowboys' football team attracted Jo Ann's attention. Ken McMinn, the sophomore wide receiver wore the number 188 on his jersey and averaged 87 yards per game the year before, according to the *Abilene Reporter-News*.[14] Jo Ann enjoyed going to all of McMinn's home games, and she learned all she could about the team's statistics. Soon she became a football fan and an expert at narrating the play-by-play, a skill she would maintain throughout her lifetime.

However, by the end of her freshman year at Hardin-Simmons, Jo Ann had run out of money. With her charitable source of income from the Hedrick family cut off, she had no choice but to return home to Austin. Sadly, she lost track of McMinn.

Back in her hometown, Jo Ann found that Austin no longer looked the same as she remembered. Protests of the Vietnam War had begun. In addition, the Civil Rights Act had not yet been signed into law, but Austin's residents had begun protesting the WHITES ONLY signs displayed in public places.[15] Austin Independent School District board members had desegregated all the elementary school campuses through the fifth grade by September 5, 1962, but civil unrest had become a sign of the times.[16]

Jo Ann faced tremendous difficulty finding a job that paid enough for her to live independently. Consequently, while living at home again, she enrolled in several typing, shorthand, and English classes at Durham's Business College.

In the summer of 1964, she took a job working in a clerical pool at the Steck Company, which later became Hart Graphic, one of Austin's oldest printing companies. Jo Ann began looking forward to the day when she would not have to live at home with her four siblings and parents. Her father especially made her feel anxious. She recalled once stepping out of the shower to find him standing in the bathroom's open doorway staring at her womanly nakedness. As her father took a step toward her, Jo Ann rushed forward toward the bathroom door and slammed it closed in his face. Temporarily, she had thwarted his advances, but she knew she might not be safe for long.

3

Bill Turner

ONE NIGHT, Nellie Holder, an attractive middle-aged brunette, asked her niece Jo Ann Canady to cover her shift waiting tables at the Playboy Lounge, a gentlemen's club once located at 51st Street and Airport Boulevard. Austin had followed the nationwide trend in opening a string of gentlemen's clubs after well-known American billionaire and playboy Hugh Hefner had opened his infamous Chicago establishment.[1]

Not knowing what she should wear to work, Jo Ann dressed in a dark skirt, starched white blouse, and simple shoes. Nellie's husband, Howard, agreed to give Jo Ann a ride to the club and dropped her off in front of the lounge. Inside, Jo Ann saw girls waiting tables dressed in a variety of strapless, tight-fitting, and brightly colored body suits, high heels, and heavy makeup. The cocktail waitresses pulled their hair up on top of their heads in the popular celebrity-inspired hairdo of the times called the beehive.

Immediately, Jo Ann noticed the house band performing jazz music on top of a riser positioned in front of a large dance floor. A sign in front of the bandstand read "Bill Turner Combo" and included the musicians' names: Bill Turner on bass, George Harrison on drums, Harold Horner on piano, and Jay Clark on clarinet and saxophone. At nineteen years old, Jo Ann could serve alcoholic drinks, but she could not drink them legally. While she worked, she found herself glancing over often at Bill Turner, who appeared very fit, with a sleek physique. He possessed tan-looking skin and black wavy hair cut close around the ears, and he wore heavily framed glasses similar to those worn by the late famous singer and songwriter Buddy Holly. During a break with his combo, Bill also noticed Jo Ann and made a beeline toward her to introduce himself. They spoke only briefly, but as he introduced himself, Bill moved in close to her and gently touched Jo Ann's arm in a light caress.

"It was not love at first sight. I didn't have a ride home that night, so Bill offered me a ride," Jo Ann said. "Otherwise, I would have had to take a taxi."[2]

During the car ride home, Bill proved himself to be every bit of a gentleman. As they said goodnight, he asked Jo Ann out on a date for the following day to go boating on Town Lake.

The next day, when Maggie Canady left the house to go to the grocery store, Jo Ann paced anxiously alone in the house with her father. She stood as close to the front door as possible; as soon as the doorbell rang, she rushed to answer it with her father standing at her side. Bill arrived at the Canady home dressed in shorts cut to the mid-thigh, allowing his swim trunks to peak out a bit from underneath, and he wore a conservative button down short-sleeved white shirt. Sydney Canady likely never guessed that Bill Turner was seventeen years older than Jo Ann, or if he had, he did not share his suspicions during their brief introductions.

Once outside, Bill opened his car door for Jo Ann and told her that although he moonlighted as a musician, he also held a steady day job investigating car titles for the Texas Department of Motor Vehicles. Playing in a band had provided expendable cash that he freely spent on his beloved "Betsy," a 1957 two-toned white-on-blue Ford Fairlane convertible with matching tuck and roll upholstery.

From the dashboard, Bill retracted the car's roof automatically with one hand while, with the other, he tuned the car radio's dial to a local rock and roll station. He pushed the speaker's volume up loud, then louder. In an instant, vibrations coursed through every inch of Jo Ann's body, as she felt all eight cylinders of the car's engine combust and roar to life. Bill gunned the gas pedal, causing his car to jerk away from the curb. The sudden acceleration and startling velocity caused Jo Ann to inhale deeply the distinct scent of fuel exhaust, which later lingered on her tongue intoxicatingly.

She recalls feeling an overwhelming sense of freedom as the wind whipped her loose blond hair about her face. Closing her eyes, she envisioned her father still standing in the doorway of their family home growing smaller and smaller until he appeared no bigger than a cockroach. The image of him, buglike and dressed in a familiar V-neck white T-shirt and baggy trousers, made her giggle aloud.

When she opened her eyes again, she saw the surrounding city landscape awash in a tapestry of colors: shades of kelly green, chartreuse, and citrine seemingly made in brush like strokes along the hillsides. The trees seemed to wave and to sway at the sound of Roy Orbison singing "Dream Baby (How Long Must I Dream)." Inspired, Jo Ann raised her hands up and over her head joyously. She felt delirious as she allowed the music together with the dreamlike images to transport her far above and beyond the cumulus clouds that dotted the sky that day.

At the marina, they climbed aboard Bill's impressive boat, a natural blonde-wood-planked and chrome metal nineteen-foot 1960 Chris-Craft Capri with red-upholstered seats. He had planned for the afternoon, packing peanuts and chips, as well as drinks for them both in a picnic basket. When he offered Jo Ann a beer, despite her being underage, she gladly accepted.

She had dressed in shorts and a midriff blouse worn over a bright yellow polyester swimsuit. She quickly stripped to reveal her modest two-piece—not quite a bikini because it did not reveal her belly button, but it accentuated her full bosom.

The sun deliciously warmed her bare skin and she blushed in spite of herself when she noticed Bill's eyes wandering the length of her pale lithe body. She lay back against the boat cushions, proudly pushing her elbows up behind her and jutting out her chin as she closed her eyes. As she did this, Jo Ann felt the rolling tremors delivered by the boat's inboard engine as it turned a long driveshaft from the craft's midsection along its bottom to a propeller located at its stern. The sheer force of the metal blades spinning against the lake water doused her in a delightful mist that glistened on her skin.

The couple spent the entire afternoon boating on the lake before visiting a hangout where Bill promised to introduce her to all his friends. It seemed to Jo Ann that everyone knew Bill Turner at The Pier,[3] a historic place that had served as a fishing lodge when it opened in 1928 and became a speakeasy during Prohibition. Throughout the 1960s, the establishment had remained a popular teen hangout that offered a café, a pool hall, and an outdoor dock. Bill possessed a gentleman-like charm and confidence, and he drew a lot of admirers at The Pier who seemed to Jo Ann about her own age.

Bill told Jo Ann that he had grown up water skiing and boating on Town Lake and that he frequently demonstrated his skills from the legendary water ski ramps. Hollywood actress and author Sissy Spacek would one day mention the same ski ramps in her 2012 autobiography, *My Extraordinary Ordinary Life*.

The two cruised in Bill's boat through a small channel that cut into the shoreline, and he docked in front of a small, dark, wood-shingled cabin. Once inside, they lay down on a small twin bed where they necked and petted one another for hours until the sun began to set. As Bill touched her, Jo Ann felt unfamiliar sexual stirrings. Secretly she wished that the day would never end and that she would never have to return to her family home again.

Along the horizon, the sky evolved into a beautiful rainbow sherbet sunset with layers of crimson, purple, orange, and yellow. Bill returned his boat to the marina and kissed Jo Ann tenderly. He told her that he had to prepare for his jazz combo's gig later that night at the Continental Club. However, from that first meeting, the two became a couple.

While driving Jo Ann back to her family home, Bill provided a brief history. He had worked for the JR Reed Music Company selling instruments to musicians at local high schools until he went to work for the Texas Department of Motor Vehicles (DMV) in the early 1960s. Until shortly before they met, Bill had also managed the Continental Club on South Congress Avenue[4] that was owned by Bill Morin; the swank supper club featured mostly topless dancers. His Bill Turner Combo continued to play jazz there occasionally until Martin Schuler took over the club's lease and turned it into a tavern.[5] During the 1970s, Schuler began leasing out the venue to private entertainment brokers who booked fairly famous rock and roll bands.

Within a month after their first date, Bill took Jo Ann out to dinner at a local Mexican restaurant, Matt's El Rancho. Beforehand, he had purchased a small diamond solitaire and a bouquet of red roses. After they ate their meal, Bill proposed to Jo Ann by candlelight, with a wine toast while a mariachi band played nearby.

"He did not get down on his knee. I think he was too embarrassed for anyone else to see him, so he just leaned over towards me. He said, 'I really do love you; I don't know if you love me, but maybe I can change that. I would like for you to marry me,'" Jo Ann said.

"My mind was already made up. I was so much in love. I told him 'I think a lot about you, and I think I love you.' Everything happened so fast; I had never loved anyone."

The magic of the moment combined with the wine created a dizzying effect that went straight to Jo Ann's head. It seemed to her that the night had popped right out of a wonderful fairytale. They married on November 5, 1963, months after Jo Ann turned twenty and Bill was thirty-six years old, before a justice of the peace in the Travis County Courthouse.

The Turners spent their honeymoon in Nuevo Laredo, a small town along the Texas-Mexico border. They attended a bullfight and afterward dined at the Tack Room at 1000 Zaragoza Street. Jo Ann remembers that the restaurant, with white tablecloths, crystal glasses, and fancy china, served a somewhat exclusive local clientele.

When they returned to Austin, the two moved into a house on Cloverdale Lane, close to the former Robert Mueller Municipal Airport.[6] In his free time, Bill sometimes flew single-engine planes that he leased. He told Jo Ann that he had obtained his pilot's license several years earlier after being denied military service because he was flat-footed and wore glasses.

After they married, Jo Ann eventually met Bill's family. Bill's father, Cleofas Turner, worked as a stonecutter in the local quarries both in Austin and Lampasas. Bill's mother, Anna Ross Turner, seldom worked outside of the home but contributed to the family's income by washing laundry at boarding houses around town.

While both the Turners and the Canadys accepted the couple's marriage, Bill's mother and Jo Ann's father frequently provided reasons not to visit the newlyweds. Whenever Jo Ann invited them over, the other extended family members never stayed very long after dinner.

Everything Jo Ann learned about her mother-in-law's personality quickly began to make her wary, especially one story in particular Bill told her that revealed Anna's controlling nature. Bill told Jo Ann that his sister, Peggy, and her husband, Gene Messick, were devout Jehovah's

Witnesses. Gene had been drafted into the US Army, but he had refused to serve on religious grounds, and the government sent him to prison for two years. Before Gene left for prison, Peggy became pregnant. After she gave birth, she and the baby lived with Bill's mother, Anna. For years, Anna sought full legal custody of her granddaughter. However, the court case remained unresolved up until the little girl died at just four years old due to a congenital heart condition.

Jo Ann found that Cleofas's personality could not have been more opposite from that of his wife. Jo Ann knew her father-in-law to be a congenial, happy-go-lucky guy who had once suffered a stonecutting accident that had left him crippled for life. Following his surgery, one leg forever remained shorter than the other, and consequently, he walked with a limp. Cleofas possessed brown skin and black hair that he liked to attribute to his Native American ancestors in Indiana. He admitted that he knew little of his kin, except the names of the Native American tribes that had lived in the northwest portion of the Indiana Territory during the 1700s, including the Wea, the Piankeshaw, and the Shawnee.[7]

Jo Ann also began to suspect that Anna suffered from an undiagnosed bipolar disorder.[8] Her mother-in-law often exhibited severe changes in mood and energy that soon played a role in helping to sour Jo Ann's feelings toward her.

The newlyweds also began arguing often. During one of their squabbles, Jo Ann learned that Bill had been married not just once but twice before. With his first wife, Wilma Rayne, Bill had fathered two children—a boy and a girl—Terry and Barbara. The couple had married young and had lived in Portland, Oregon, for about twelve years before returning to Texas. Bill told Jo Ann that he had been married to a second wife, Janelle Nygard, for only five years before their childless union dissolved. Soon Jo Ann began questioning her own reasons for marrying so young.

Bill began coming home from his music gigs smelling of alcohol and cigarettes. He would stagger in the front door, wobble-legged like a toddler across the living room floor, and throw down his car keys. Afterward, he would fall, fully dressed, upon the king-size bed in their master bedroom. Jo Ann developed a routine in undressing him by taking off his shoes and socks first, then his belt, and pulling down his suit pants while he lay sprawled out slack on his back, white-bellied and bony as a fish.

Always talkative, Bill's personality had initially seemed to Jo Ann as the polar opposite of her father's. However, she slowly discovered Bill could be controlling and selfish with his money. He seldom shared what he earned playing with his band even when bills piled up and money became tight. Over the next several years, Jo Ann would turn often to her older sister, Lillian Lehman, for financial help after both of their brothers, Jimmie and Sydney, died.

Jo Ann's world brightened a little when she gave birth to their son Jeff on June 23, 1964. Throughout Jeff's elementary school years, he loved sports: he played tennis, soccer, and Little League football, and he enjoyed swimming. Jo Ann remembered Jeff as an affectionate and friendly boy who always had a lot of friends around the house.

However, the Turner family dynamics began to change in August of that same year, when the Texas DMV transferred Bill to McAllen, Texas. Relocated to the small town, the family enjoyed few distractions in the evenings. Bill increasingly drank too much, grew jealous of Jo Ann's affections for Jeff, and often accused her of loving their son more than him. Jo Ann would attempt to soothe Bill's jealousy by bestowing him with little bursts of affection. Occasionally, she would make a special dinner for just the two of them, light candles, and dress in a sexy negligee afterward, but nothing seemed to soothe Bill's jealousy.

One night, without provocation, Bill began hitting their son with a belt. Jo Ann immediately threw herself between them and threatened to call the police to make him stop. Afterward, Bill seemed contrite and apologized, but that night marked only the first of many that would follow.

Jo Ann found a job translating documents from English into Spanish at the Edinburg, Texas, offices of Mayor Alfonso "Al" Ramírez, the town's first Hispanic mayor. Weekday mornings, she drove twenty-one miles north from McAllen to Hidalgo County's seat. The county was named after Miguel Hidalgo y Costilla, the former leader of the Mexican Revolution.[9]

She worked as Ramirez's administrative assistant in his two-person office and quickly became interested in translating US immigration application forms. While she loved her new professional responsibilities, her marriage and family life continued to suffer.

During the weekdays, Jo Ann's son spent long hours in daycare because no family members lived nearby to offer support. Bill's work with the DMV required him to travel all over the county, though he usually ended up close to home by the end of the day. Jeff stayed in daycare until six o'clock most weekday evenings when either Bill or Jo Ann managed to pick him up.

Often on the weekends, the Turner family's tensions escalated into arguments and more beatings in which Jo Ann protectively pitched herself between Bill and Jeff. Jo Ann soon came up with a plan to hire a live-in housekeeper to thwart her husband's anger and to babysit Jeff.

Jeff learned to speak Spanish from a number of different women who lived off and on with the Turners and cleaned their home on weekdays. On Saturdays, the family's maid would catch a bus for home to the interior of Mexico, near San Luis Port of Entry.

In 1965, Jo Ann found another job sixteen miles southeast in Weslaco translating the daily news for broadcast at the KRGV television station or Channel 5 News, in Rio Grande Valley, Texas.[10] The station also provided several opportunities for Jo Ann to record television spots in Spanish. At the time, Molton "Ty" Cobb,[11] the famous former baseball star, hosted a live weekly television show on KRGV TV and asked Jo Ann to record a few commercials in Spanish. Soon the producers at the station began asking her to translate other broadcasts from English into Spanish.

Then in 1967, the Texas DMV again transferred Bill, this time to Houston. Jo Ann did not seek another broadcasting job but instead worked temporarily as a secretary at a private law firm in a downtown building owned by Humble Oil and Refining Company. The law offices occupied several floors in the prestigious Humble Building. However, Jo Ann found secretarial work boring, so eventually she resigned.

After Jo Ann left the law firm, she went to work for architects Jenkins, Hoff, Oberg, and Saxe. Her new job entailed working as a receptionist, but she also organized architectural plans and put together design packages for clients. The work both challenged Jo Ann and provided her with a steady and healthy income that contributed to the Turner family's nest egg.

One weekend, Bill and Jo Ann traveled three hours to Austin to meet with a real estate developer who had been Bill's friend for years. Buddy Wendlant lived in a condominium in the Tarrytown neighborhood off

Exposition Road. He offered to drive the Turners around town to look at some vacant lots offered for sale along Town Lake.

The landowners, Walter Bohn and his wife, Frieda, lived in a large rock house—the first home to be built on Rivercrest Drive. For ten thousand dollars, the Turners purchased a one half-acre lot in the cul-de-sac on which to build their own dream house.

One lake channel cut through the center of the property where the Turners would begin building a boathouse and a dock. After they returned to their home in Houston, the two realized they should have asked the Bohns if they could purchase the adjacent lot. They called Wendlant again to inquire about the second lot and delightedly learned it was still available. The following weekend, the Turners returned to Austin to buy the adjacent lot along the lake for eleven thousand dollars. The Turners would make payments to the Bohns faithfully every month on time for more than twenty years—that fact would someday prove to be ironic for Jo Ann during a 1996 foreclosure.

The Turners built their boathouse first to store Bill's boat so that whenever they drove from Houston on weekends, they could enjoy outings on Town Lake. Bill would eventually sell his Chris-Craft and purchase a 1981 Bill Gammon Glastron Carlson high-performance speedboat. Gray and white in color, with white interior tuck and roll upholstery, the boat sat eight people comfortably. Made of fiberglass and sleek in design, with an inboard engine, it allowed four passengers to sit up front on a rounded and luxurious single upholstered seat cushion.

Jo Ann took a new job working as a secretary for Gulf Oil Company for the next five years. Meanwhile, Bill's job with the Texas DMV allowed him a steady and solid salary with nice retirement benefits but offered little in the way of excitement. Although Bill performed in a dance band occasionally while they lived in Houston, he often complained to Jo Ann that he missed playing with his Austin musician friends.

The Turners moved into a suburb west of the Memorial area of Houston in a brand-new house they purchased. The neighborhood stood close to Lakeside Estates, a development of middle-class homes and manicured lawns doted on by contracted landscapers. Houston had become a busy metropolis with lots of traffic, and the city boasted a lively entertainment district.

Chapter 3

After living in Houston for five years, they finally took Jeff with them back to Austin to visit his fraternal grandparents. However, the family reunion turned sour from the moment the Turner family arrived at Bill's childhood home. Anna grabbed Jo Ann by the shoulder and almost tore off her daughter-in-law's blouse. That violent act startled Jo Ann, and she decided never to visit her mother-in-law again from that day forward.

"I told Bill, 'We're not coming back here anymore. I am not coming back with you. If you want to come see your mother, you'll come by yourself,'" Jo Ann said.

Also, while they lived in Houston, Bill's temper again began to flare regularly. During his angry outbursts, Bill often beat Jeff mercilessly with a belt in Jo Ann's presence. With each swing of the strap, Jo Ann screamed at Bill and attempted to grab his arms to stop him from hitting their son. In the process, Jo Ann often became the unintended target of Bill's attacks.

Only one person in the Turner household would soon possess enough charm to brighten Bill's dark moods. The Turners' daughter, Kelly, was born May 22, 1971, at Memorial Hermann Southwest Hospital in the Bel Air subdivision of Houston. Her father immediately began to dote on her.

Throughout the early 1970s, Kelly remained in daycare until six thirty daily when either Jo Ann or Bill could pick her up. In the evenings, they ate dinner together as a family and afterward watched television or watched Jeff play with his baby sister.

A few times in the years that followed, the entire Turner family took short three-day vacations to beaches in either Galveston or Corpus Christi. For those trips, Jo Ann would pack chips, dips, and veggies to bring along for the day. Jeff and Kelly played together in the shallow waters along the beach while Bill and Jo Ann often stayed up on the shore, watching their children from folding chairs beneath the shade of an umbrella and drinking beer.

Slathered in sunscreen, the children played among the ocean waves within their parents' sight; Jo Ann noticed that Jeff had become a risk-taker. A strong swimmer, Jeff always swam out far into the waves, beyond the sandbar, unafraid of the rip currents. He never wore a life jacket, unlike his sister, who did so obediently because Bill insisted.

In 1972, the Turner family returned to Austin to live, and they rented a duplex off Spicewood Springs Road, between North MoPac/Loop 1 and

Mesa. The house, built upon a rock bed, seemed to Jo Ann to be filled with scorpions, making her fearful that the strange creatures might sting one of her children. As a preventative, she often sprayed strong Deet insect repellent throughout every square inch of their home, inside and out. It would be years before she would learn that the product's chemicals also had been linked to terrible human illnesses and deaths.[12]

At Dobie Middle School, Jeff joined the school band to please his father. The school's band teacher, Vic Williams, had often performed as a guest musician in Bill Turner's Combo at the Continental Club. Jeff asked his father if he could play drums, but Bill said he wanted his son to play something musical. Eventually, the two agreed on woodwinds, so Jeff took up the clarinet in the school's concert band.

On the weekends, Jo Ann began answering phones and setting up appointments for Smith & Jones Real Estate Company. After she gained some experience and studied, she passed her real estate test. Within weeks, she rented an office in Wind River Office Park. Jo Ann, together with Joyanna Harrison, the former wife of George Harrison who had been a drummer in Bill's combo, also leased a second office, located at North Lamar Boulevard and 39th Street. Jo Ann enjoyed working forty to fifty hours a week and on weekends as an independent real estate agent selling primarily FHA and VA homes.

Bill and his son's relationship continued to deteriorate when Jeff entered Lanier High School. Their fights escalated so badly one night that Jo Ann called the police and pressed charges against her husband. Bill spent that night in Travis County Jail.

Afterward, because Bill showed less and less interest in Jeff, Jo Ann alone began attending her son's band performances, football practices, and other extracurricular activities. However, Jeff eventually began to skip school and to be charged with truancy on a regular basis.

By December 1979, Jo Ann had taken another job, working forty hours a week in the administration offices at Shoal Creek Hospital, a position she would hold for the next thirteen years as an administrative assistant to William Dyer.

The Turners moved into a new house in Austin's Quail Creek neighborhood. Kelly's fraternal grandparents bought her a swing set for the backyard, and they built a treehouse in the front yard for Jeff. Jo Ann felt encouraged when Bill helped with both projects.

Jo Ann continued to work two jobs, and sometimes three, to help make ends meet. She seldom stayed home for any length of time. Weeknights she worked as an independent Realtor, and on weekends, she moonlighted as a network marketer selling for National Safety Associates, known as NSA Water Filters. The company would, in 1993, be ordered to refund some of its customers owing to a multilevel sales scandal.[13] She also sold HerbalLife products, which, in 2019, would be linked to liver failure.[14]

Jo Ann encouraged Kelly to become involved in extracurricular activities at Eanes Elementary School and later at Hill Country Middle School. However, Kelly showed no interest, although she did briefly join the Girl Scouts of America and later became active in the youth groups at Hyde Park Baptist Church. On her own, Kelly also liked to jog and to stay physically fit.

Everything seemed to change again for the Turners when Bill announced he quit his job at the Texas DMV. He told Jo Ann that he planned to combine his retirement pension with a loan given to him by his mother, Anna Ross, to buy a fleet of trucks and to start his own trucking business, Turner Trucking.

At the same time, in 1983, the Turners began building their dream house on Rivercrest Drive in Austin. They had little trouble qualifying for an adjustable-rate mortgage to build their house while using the land as collateral. The lakeside property had appreciated tremendously over the previous two decades, as its value grew into the tens of thousands of dollars. Jo Ann obtained a bank loan to hire general contractor Bill Turpin, who drew up the plans for the home's construction. Turpin tweaked the architectural plans over several visits before they met with Jo Ann's approval. She hired additional subcontractors, including drywall installers, electricians, plumbers, as well as flooring and window installation experts. The Turners often met with the contractors at Turpin's condominium in Westlake.

Turpin constructed the Turners' split-level house with three bedrooms upstairs and the master bedroom down. Inside the grand entrance to the home, on the lower level, hung a huge chandelier from a cathedral ceiling with spiral staircases leading up to the bedrooms. Huge floor to ceiling windows stretched along the back side of the house, allowing for spectacular views across the lake.

The Turners moved into their newly built house early in August 1984. Jo Ann cherishes a photograph taken that Christmas of the four family members sitting in front of the fireplace in the upper living room.

"We had a beautiful tree. I went to The Christmas Store and bought this beautiful German-made Christmas tree with all of the lights. I had some custom bows made to put on it—they were blue, kind of bluish white," Jo Ann said.

Jo Ann told Jeff and Kelly that they could each invite one friend for Christmas Eve dinner and to spend the night. Christmas morning, Jo Ann arose very early to put a turkey in the oven and prepared cornbread dressing, sweet potatoes, and fresh green beans—all the traditional items for dinner later in the day. Christmas morning, she fried some bacon and sausage and made pancakes. The children who had spent the night with Jeff and Kelly left after breakfast, and the Turners sat around the Christmas tree opening their presents.

However, after the holidays ended, arguments between Bill and Jeff again escalated. Bill, always the disciplinarian, would not tolerate what he referred to as Jeff's "back talk," while his son refused to cower to his father's demands.

"Dad and I were clashing so bad. He was quite the drill sergeant but wasn't. So, like he ran a military household; and me being a fourteen- to fifteen-year-old young man, I thought 'I can do it better than him,'" Jeff Turner said.[15]

Jeff lived in the Turner family's luxurious home for only a short time after dropping out of high school. During his junior year, he hitchhiked out of town and across the country with a girl the Turners hardly knew. After spending a year living as a dropout, Jeff returned to town to enroll in Austin High School, and graduated in 1985. Following graduation, he moved to Dallas to train to become a ballet dancer.

In Jeff's absence, however, his bedroom remained vacant as the remainder of the Turner house regularly filled to capacity, with guests sometimes spilling out onto the outdoor decks and the boathouse overlooking the lake. Bill held jam sessions at home at least once a month with local musicians. News about the sessions spread by word of mouth or telephone (the Internet did not then exist). The musicians all knew each other and had played together at different venues over the years. Regulars included local legendary guitarists Jody Meredith, Bert Rivera,

Jay Clark, and the late Jerry Lightsey. Occasional visitors included local celebrities, such as Willie Nelson, who, already a renowned musician, had become a well-known local star of the 1980 movie *Honeysuckle Rose*.

Musicians played late into the night; sometimes Jo Ann hired both a caterer for the sessions and a maid service to clean up afterward. She often hired a bartender to serve drinks. Anyone invited also brought food. Camilo Joe "C.J." Villegas, a Tejano drummer and the original co-owner of Austin's El Mercado restaurant located on South First Street, together with his wife, Gudelia, attended the parties. Villegas always brought his own set of drums and a large platter of enchiladas that he had prepared.

Jo Ann would sit with the "band widows," as the women married to the musicians referred to themselves. She quickly became close friends with Shirley Rivera, Louise Lightsey, Maida Meredith, and Dorothy Harrison, who was then married to drummer George Harrison.

The jam sessions at the Turners' house also drew local judges and political figures. Harriet Mitchell Murphy, the first African American woman appointed to a judgeship in Texas and a civil rights advocate, attended.[16] Political consultant William "Peck" Young seldom missed a jam session. His clients ranged from the feisty former Texas Governor Ann Richards to 1988 presidential candidate Michael Dukakis.[17]

One day in 1984, on her way from Shoal Creek Hospital in her 1980 Cadillac Eldorado to eat lunch at home, Jo Ann T-boned another car at the busy intersection of Mt. Bonnell and Ranch Road 2222. Before a traffic light was eventually installed in 2017, that intersection had earned a reputation as treacherous due to a blind left turn drivers often had to make into westbound traffic on Mt. Bonnell.[18] As a result of her injuries, Jo Ann underwent surgery to fuse several disks together in her spine; afterward, the injury limited her movements and gave her pain for the next nearly four decades. Months of rehabilitation kept her from working while the Turner family suffered insurmountable debt from Jo Ann's medical bills.

The Turners had possessed a beautiful house, nice friends, great jobs, and expensive jewelry. To outsiders, their lives may have appeared idyllic up until 1989 when Bill's trucking business began to fail. A statewide savings and loan crisis had affected most of Austin's small businesses, but local major companies also suffered. Texas served as the epicenter of the S&L crash nationally; in Austin the financial effects would linger for nearly a decade.[19]

The Federal Savings & Loan Insurance Corporation closed or resolved 296 institutions between 1986 and 1989 as inflation and interest rates rose. As interest rates set by the federal government rose, mortgages lost value. In 1989, Congress passed the Financial Institutions Reform/Recovery and Enforcement Act. The Resolution Trust Corporation closed 747 S&Ls with assets of more than $407 billion.[20]

Furthermore, following the Carter administration's Motor Carrier Act of 1980, the deregulation of the trucking industry created unprecedented competition nationwide, and the nation's recession further magnified its effects.[21] By 1994, the bank had foreclosed on Bill's small trucking business and repossessed all of his trucks. As a result, Bill began driving for Leal Trucking Company. The Turners discussed a plan to save their home and their belongings. Jo Ann carried the burden of the family finances alone by working two jobs. However, things quickly worsened.

Jo Ann continued to work part time as a real estate agent, but potential clients became increasingly hard to find. Bill seldom performed in clubs in town because the local establishments had stopped hiring bands. The Turners could no longer count on Bill's moonlighting to supplement their lavish lifestyle. Music venues in Austin had suffered since Congress passed the National Minimum Drinking Age Act of 1984, which reversed the legal drinking age from eighteen years to twenty-one years old. The law required the states, including Texas, to increase the minimum age required for the public consumption of alcohol or risk losing 10 percent of their federal highway funds. Bars in Austin that had once drawn college students ages eighteen years and older now found it more difficult to keep their doors open, to pay their liquor licenses, and to pay their rents.[22]

As a result, life for the Turners changed drastically; Jo Ann and Bill stopped buying fancy clothes, they no longer ate their meals in fancy restaurants, and they hosted fewer parties. Then they stopped paying their federal income taxes to the IRS.

Out of desperation, Jo Ann considered listing their house on the market with another Realtor. Times being what they were, the Turners knew that they would not be able to sell their home for more than one hundred thousand dollars, although it had once been appraised by the Travis County Appraisal District for twice that amount. In addition, when the interest rate on their adjustable home mortgage[23] finally maxed out at 17 percent, the Turners stopped paying their thirty-four-hundred-dollar monthly mortgage payments.

4

Foreclosure

As the Turners' finances worsened, Jo Ann began looking for creative ways to earn extra money. She expanded the line of products that she sold through network marketing. In addition to selling NSA Water Filters, she sold nutritional products for two companies: Vox, based in California, and Jeunesse Global, located in Florida.

She also took on a networking partner, Troy Wright, from Virginia. He and his wife, Denisha, had recently married and relocated to Austin. Together Jo Ann and Troy began building their list of investors. They offered multiple levels of investing. As top-level investors, Jo Ann and Troy earned the highest percentage of commissions from sales by people who invested at the lowest or most recent levels that earned less. They also sponsored huge marketing events inside luxury hotels located in Austin, Dallas, and Houston attended by hundreds of people.

Jo Ann concentrated on attracting people with whom she most wanted to associate, people with money to spend and those she believed possessed similar work ethics and goals for capitalizing on their investments. In time, she perfected a scripted sales pitch.

She became relentless at seeking out new investors—she earned commissions from the sales of each of her recruits. She worked tirelessly, late into the evenings, with her investors, talking to them by phone or in person, if necessary, to train them in networking sales.

"I was concerned about the people that were in my 'downline'—that's what we called it—the people at a lower level in our organization. I evaluated them all of the time," she said. "I looked at their numbers, asked what was going on. If someone was falling down, then I needed to call them—I never waited for them to call me because if you do that, by then it's probably too late—they're probably giving up. My motto was 'never give up.'"[1]

Meanwhile, Jo Ann also attended a networking meeting in Dallas to learn about the prospects of selling solid gold bars. There she met a woman who would become a life-long friend, Molly McKnight.

"I just remember how gorgeous she was," McKnight said.[2]

McKnight said she had been invited to the Dallas networking meeting organized by her close friend Margaret Lewis, formerly married to Dwight Douglas "D. D." Lewis, from Knoxville, Tennessee. Dwight Lewis, a linebacker, played for Mississippi State and then for the NFL's Dallas Cowboys for thirteen seasons, from 1968 until 1981.[3]

Not long after their initial meeting, Molly moved back to Austin, and she called Jo Ann. When the two met for lunch, Molly told Jo Ann that she had previously also sold products for World Class Travel Network. Within weeks after meeting, she and Jo Ann began selling solid gold bars for Gold Unlimited Network based in Delaware. By 1999, executives for that company would be indicted and charged with operating an illegal pyramid scheme;[3] however, until then, the Texas network would continue its branch operations. Jo Ann and Molly sought out their friends, neighbors, and relatives as investors to sell gold and encouraged each one to, in turn, sponsor their friends within the network. Each investor earned a descending percentage of a commission based on the team's total sales.[4]

By 1992, the Federal Trade Commission would crack down on NSA's sales tactics. Several high-level distributors in the company would be investigated for earning large commissions on a monthly basis from lower-level sales personnel.[5] Regardless, if anyone had asked them at the time, both Jo Ann and Molly would have defended themselves as legitimate business professionals. They insisted that only amateur entrepreneurs who could not properly move their products within the network deserved to be labeled operators of a pyramid scheme.

"Someone would buy twenty-five thousand dollars' worth of the product, and then the person who sold it would not help to get rid of it either through reselling the product or recruiting more people," Jo Ann said. "You can't just go out there and recruit one hundred people and not help them sell the product. Their investment wouldn't move the product. That's what these guys were doing—not helping to move the product."

Two years earlier, the United States had fallen into a deep recession marked by inflation, high unemployment rates, and a glut in oil prices.[6] Since then, Jo Ann had increasingly noticed a drop in the number of people who wanted to invest. Her successful career in network marketing ended along with her last hope of improving her family's dire financial situation. Just as she began to feel desperate for the first time in her adult life, what seemed like the answer to all of her financial problems arrived by US mail in the form of a postcard sent from the Republic of Texas (ROT).

Inside her lakefront home in Westlake, one of the wealthiest neighborhoods in Austin, Jo Ann opened her mailbox one day to find a business postcard from J. C. Van Kirk, then the president of the ROT. On the postcard, Van Kirk had typed his phone number and written a note that read, "If you're about to lose your house, you need to call us." Immediately, Jo Ann went to her landline telephone and dialed the number.

"I had never heard of him, nor ever knew of him—until he contacted me with that postcard," Jo Ann said. "I told him that I feared that we would lose our house because we had not paid our mortgage in a couple of years because my husband's business went sour, and subsequently I was not successful with my networking and real estate business."

The next day, Van Kirk visited Jo Ann at her house to discuss her financial situation. Jo Ann told him that the mortgage costs on the Turner house had escalated because she and Bill had acquired an adjustable-rate mortgage (ARM).[7] She explained that, in 1983, she and Bill had agreed on an ARM at their bank because the rate had been slightly lower than for a conventional loan. The terms for the ARM favored the bank that carried the note. The ARM could change several times over the life of a loan, and the Turners' rate would increase from 3 percent to 17 percent. The starting rate had lasted less than a year as their payment of one thousand dollars per month more than tripled by 1996.

Over the next three months, Jo Ann met three times with Van Kirk's assistant, whom she knew only as June, and she paid the woman fifteen hundred dollars per visit.

Chapter 4

"I went to her house. She was always sitting on the bed in the middle of her bed because she was so overly overweight; she was a big, big woman, and I guess that she just couldn't get up and sit in a chair. I thought to myself, *Oh, this is disgusting*, but I was so desperate at that time that I ignored all that," Jo Ann said.

"I was just so distraught, I did not pay enough attention; I just kept giving her money, giving her more money. I am sure she was giving J.C. part of it. It was a con situation. When I look back, I can't believe I did all that, but I was so desperate. I was so distressed."

Finally, Jo Ann realized that Van Kirk and his assistant could not successfully help her to resolve her mortgage crisis. Soon afterward, Van Kirk promised to put Jo Ann in touch with his associate, Richard "Rick" Lance McLaren.

When McLaren and his common-law wife, Evelyn Ann Horak McLaren, arrived at the Turners' home, he immediately set up his laptop computer and printer on Jo Ann's dining room table. She found Richard engaging, although a bit scruffy. She recalls that he stood about five feet ten inches tall, with very thin, scraggly, curly hair, "looking very much like Albert Einstein," with an unkempt manner. He dressed in jeans, a flannel shirt, a sports coat, and tennis shoes.

Evelyn seemed easygoing, and Jo Ann found her very likeable. The woman had short bleached-blond hair and dressed neatly in a simple blouse and pantsuit and wore sensible shoes. She told Jo Ann that she worked full time for the US Postal Service.

After typing up all of the information that Jo Ann had provided, Richard and Evelyn spent the night in the Turners' guest room. The couple left the next day after breakfast, but not before they promised to help Jo Ann to keep everything she owned.

Meanwhile, a representative from the Alamo Title insurance agency of Austin attempted to hand deliver a delinquency statement on December 28, 1995, to the Turner home at 3510 Rivercrest Drive, but Jo Ann would not answer the door. Then a FedEx carrier attempted to deliver a statement the next day, December 29, 1995. However, Sheryl Clark at Alamo Title agency received the statement "address unknown/return to sender" in early January 1996. Three months would pass as Jo Ann waited anxiously for further action that would bring about foreclosure.

Then, early on the morning of March 11, 1996, Jo Ann sat at the breakfast bar in the kitchen of her spacious home on Rivercrest Drive drinking a Bloody Mary cocktail. She stared out her home's windows at a gorgeous view of the water across Town Lake, the ducks, and the pecan trees. She noticed that the leaves on the trees had already begun sprouting tiny green leaves, when suddenly she heard knocking at her front door.

Travis County constable Karen Marie Sonleitner from Precinct Two began banging on the Turners' door and shouting.

"She was hollering out there: 'Mrs. Turner, Mrs. Turner, we're here to move you out,'" Jo Ann said. "The constable yelled, 'Come unlock this door.'"

Yet Jo Ann did not rush to unlock the door right away. Instead, she yelled through the closed door.

"I said 'I'm calling the judge. I wasn't informed that this was going to happen. You don't have a search warrant to come in here and take all my stuff,'" Jo Ann recounted.

"She said, 'Oh yes we do have a search warrant, and it is signed by the judge, but the judge is not in town, so you can't reach him.' So, I said, 'Just wait a minute.' I still didn't unlock the door. I went back to the phone on the breakfast bar, and I made a phone call."

Jo Ann immediately called Michelle Faucett, who at the time served as Van Kirk's secretarial assistant. Faucett apologized and said that she could not do anything because the Travis County Sheriff Department had become involved. Jo Ann hung up the phone and reluctantly went to her front door to open it.

A mob of people rushed past Jo Ann as she opened the door. The constable handed Jo Ann a copy of the foreclosure from Alamo Title Insurance of Texas, as others pushed past Jo Ann, nearly knocking her down. Immediately, the intruders began asking questions.

"'Do you have any guns? Mrs. Turner, do you have any guns in the house?' they asked," Jo Ann said.

Peeking outside her home's front door, Jo Ann saw several semitrucks lined up in a row along the cul-de-sac in the front of her house.

"Things kept going through my mind, like, *What can I salvage?* I had suitcases open, and I threw things into them," Jo Ann said.

She picked up her mother-in-law's silverware in the dining room and set it aside with the intention of returning to it later. Then she went back to the master bedroom where the movers had begun packing up her other personal possessions. In the master bathroom, she remembered her jewelry and put it in her purse right away.

Jo Ann returned to the living room to find movers packing up two beautiful antique clocks. She immediately protested.

"The constable said, 'Sit down and shut up, or I will handcuff you and arrest you. In fact, I would like for you to leave right now.' I told her, 'I'm not leaving,'" Jo Ann said.

Employees with Alar Moving Company together with representatives from McGuire's Clocks packed up two antique German clocks and moved them out of the Turners' house. Jo Ann fondly remembers one very special clock that had been mounted on the living room wall. She had paid three hundred dollars for the clock to the late Gisela Sterling, who had served as an Austin High School German teacher for 30 years. Another unique freestanding clock, Jo Ann recalled, bore an engraving inside that read "Berlin 1939."

Another woman whom Jo Ann did not recognize, Jody L. Hagemann, approached her, and as an attorney for the FDIC, she ordered Jo Ann's things to be removed from her home as part of foreclosure.

About that time, Bill came home from work after Jo Ann called him. He parked his pickup truck as close to their house as he could and positioned it between the semitrucks. He immediately began helping his wife to collect their personal possessions. The movers took everything the Turners could not load into their cars.

Then Jo Ann ran across the street to ask a neighbor, Steve Eckhart, if they could pack their clothes in wardrobe boxes and store them in his garage until the following day.

"I kept all my clothes, for whatever good that did us; I had no place to go to wear them," Jo Ann said.

Altogether, twenty-five people worked all day long to pack up the contents of the Turners' home. They packed up furniture, crystal, and china once owned by Bill's mother. From the walls, they took expensive artwork, some painted by local artists, such as French Smith, Jack White, and watercolor artist Mary Doerr.

The movers took Bill's upright bass. They took all the Turner children's personal belongings; they even boxed up the Turners' baby pictures. Jo

Ann would learn later that Shapiro & Dunn PLLC had contracted Gaston & Sheehan Auctioneers to sell all the Turners' belongings.

Bill and Jo Ann left their home for the last time a little after six o'clock that night. At that moment, the Turners realized they had no idea where they would spend the night. Then Jo Ann remembered seeing a newspaper ad for Homestead Village that offered a weekly rental rate. So that's where they went, unloading everything that they owned in the world into that hotel room.

In the days that followed, Jo Ann tried to hide her emotions whenever she spoke to Bill about their eviction because she worried that he might become volatile. One day during their week as a homeless couple, she found an ad in the *Austin American-Statesman* that offered a ninety-nine-dollar move-in rate at Shepherd Mountain apartments. The "no questions asked" offer also advertised "no credit check." That day, Jo Ann paid the move-in fee at the leasing office, took possession of a set of keys, and the Turners moved into their two-bedroom and nearly vacant apartment. The Turners acquired a year lease at the Shepherd Mountain apartments for unit 933, with a view of the pool and the clubhouse.

Bill went to work the next day as usual, driving trucks for the Leal Brothers. Alone inside their apartment, Jo Ann felt depression overwhelm her as she attempted to absorb the reality of all that had happened. The more she replayed the events of the previous day in her mind, the angrier she became. Not for a moment would she allow all of her family's belongings to be sold at auction. She felt determined; Travis County had not seen the last of Jo Ann Canady Turner.

5

Richard Lance McLaren

EVERY DAY, Jo Ann managed to rouse herself out of bed, avoiding the temptation to wallow in self-pity. She wanted to do whatever she could to change her life for the better as quickly as possible. Every day, she drove to a local grocery store to buy food to cook for dinner that night. At the store, she also often bought a newspaper to thumb through the classified sections to look for jobs. Soon she began calling friends and contacts that she had made through network marketing. However, too many of her contacts had either heard her story or asked what had happened to her after she seemingly disappeared.

Using a cell phone that she had purchased prior to her eviction, she again called Rick McLaren.

"Rick just kept saying, 'Well, hang in there, Jo.' He called me Jo. 'We're working on some paperwork,' he would say, or 'this is all going to change.' It never did. It just got worse," Jo Ann said.[1]

What little remained of Jo Ann and Bill Turner's relationship slowly began to unravel.

"When we lost the house, Bill blamed me because I had been in charge of the finances. He felt it was all my fault," Jo Ann said.

"The fact that he wasn't playing in a band anymore was my fault also. He said that I kept him from playing his music. It was all my fault; everything was my fault that happened. Anything bad that happened was my fault."

Bill told Jo Ann that he no longer trusted her, and the two stopped speaking to one another. They ate their meals in silence whenever he came home from work. In the evenings, because they no longer owned a television, they read the newspaper. Bill, who rose at five o'clock every morning to go to work, went to bed early in the evenings, by eight, leaving Jo Ann alone with her thoughts. She would sit on the sofa and read the newspaper cover to cover.

During the days after Bill left for work, Jo Ann walked over to the main lobby of the Shepherd Mountain apartments to watch the news broadcasts on a large television monitor mounted on one wall. She soon learned the names of all the staff members who worked in the office. Jo Ann had always been a social person in both her personal and her professional life, and she fed on her interactions with people. However, she feared divulging too much to anyone about her personal situation. From all appearances, she maintained a friendly composure when hanging out in the community room at the apartment complex, while being careful to avoid drawing any attention to herself.

Weeks passed slowly for Jo Ann. She heard nothing that made her suspect that she might be arrested, but she feared the worst was yet to come. Nearly every morning, Jo Ann drank a Bloody Mary to help her cope with the stress she felt while reading the daily newspaper and looking through job listings. In the evenings, Bill would return home from work, and again they would eat their dinner in silence.

"I couldn't believe this happened to us; we lost everything: a house on the lake, money, cars, our furniture, and personal items," she said. "I prayed to God to forgive me and my family for this awful experience and to give me the strength to move forward and to learn from this."

One day, Jo Ann telephoned Joyce Isaacs, a radio anchor with KVET-AM radio station in Austin to tell her story live on the air. Isaacs suggested that Jo Ann take her case to court before wishing her well and signing off.

The next day, Jo Ann filed a temporary restraining order (TRO)[2] against Alar Moving Company in the courtroom of 200th District Court Judge Paul Davis. She told Davis that she wanted to keep Alar from selling her personal property at auction. She watched as the judge's assistant walked past her to hand a written note to Davis. Jo Ann saw the note clearly: "This is the Republic of Texas lady."

Davis told Jo Ann that he had to deny her request because the parties named in the restraining order had not appeared in court. He asked Jo Ann to reschedule another hearing for a future date.

The very next day, Jo Ann entered the courtroom of Travis County's 261st District Court Judge Pete Lowry. She notified his bailiff that she wanted to present a TRO against Gaston & Sheehan Auctioneers. Within minutes and without hesitation, Judge Lowry approved the TRO. Jo Ann drove as fast as she could to the offices of Gaston & Sheehan Auctioneers. When she arrived at three o'clock, she notified a receptionist that the TRO she possessed would prohibit the company from auctioning any personal items removed from the Turners' home. A man Jo Ann did not know soon appeared to tell her that the auction of her belongings would proceed as scheduled. Then he asked her to leave and threatened to take drastic action. Suddenly she felt hysterical; she barely recognized her own voice when it came out of her mouth in a series of shrieks.

"I told him 'I want to see my things. Where do you have them? If you intend to sell my things, I have a right to see them. This is a public auction, isn't it? I want to see what you are auctioning,'" Jo Ann said. "But he only threatened to phone the police if I didn't leave. I had no choice."

Jo Ann left frustrated. Once she arrived home, she finally allowed herself for the first time to cry uncontrollably. She remembers crying on and off all through the night. The next morning, she called Judge Lowry's office again. A receptionist answered. Jo Ann told her what the man at the auction company had said and that he just ignored her TRO.

"She told me 'The TRO was dropped yesterday afternoon by the judge,'" Jo Ann said. "Then I asked, 'Who informed you that it had been dropped?' The receptionist said, 'Mr. Kimball called to say that Ms. Jody L. Hagemann, his lawyer, took care of it.'"

As Jo Ann hung up her cell phone, it rang almost instantly in her hand, making her jump. She did not recognize the number or the male voice on the other end of her phone when she answered.

"He said, 'Mrs. Turner, you have already been warned to drop this lawsuit. Do you want to live?' and he hung up," Jo Ann said.

Slowly, Jo Ann began to realize that neither she nor Rick McLaren nor any other members of the Republic of Texas (ROT) could prevent the auctioneers from selling all of her possessions. She suddenly feared all her options had evaporated.

Chapter 5

Within days, a woman whom Jo Ann did not know called to say that she had purchased an unmarked box at a local auction. An official at Alar Moving Company had given the woman Jo Ann's telephone number. She and Jo Ann met in the parking lot of what used to be the Simon David store in the Arboretum shopping center. Inside a box that the woman offered, Jo Ann recovered some, but not all, of her children's baby pictures.

As Jo Ann closed her eyes for a moment, she mentally walked herself through her former home, picturing everything she had lost and fearing that she would never see any of her possessions again. She knew of only one person to ask for help, and that person was Rick McLaren.

■ ■ ■

For most people who met him, McLaren remained a mystery, an enigma. If anyone learned anything about him, the information likely came from a third party. He never talked about his personal life nor his work background. The one person who seemed to know the most about him had seen McLaren perhaps only a dozen times over a span of more than forty years.

Charles "Chuck" Samson III remembers his cousin "Rick" only as a tall, lanky boy who often talked fast and enjoyed sharing his strong opinions on a multitude of subjects.[3]

Samson recalls that as a young man McLaren never drank, never smoked, and never cussed, but to a fault he could talk up a storm. When he became the leader of the ROT antigovernment militia, McLaren also frequently pushed his agenda.

"You didn't have to worry about making conversation because he could pretty much fill in all the gaps, you know? He was very energetic. He was always thin and always seemed to have a lot of energy. He was always a nice, polite person," Samson said.

Samson and McLaren first met when they both attended the funeral for their mutual grandfather, Charles H. Samson Sr., on December 1, 1969, in Jackson, Ohio. McLaren's mother, Mary June Samson McLaren, and Chuck's dad, Charles H. Samson Jr., were siblings. Several years later, on March 6, 1977, the two cousin reunited again to attend another funeral, this time for their mutual grandmother, Marie Gertrude Morris Samson, in Wilmington, Ohio.

According to Samson, his family also had often traveled by car from their home in College Station, Texas, to visit their grandmother in Ohio during the holidays. During those family reunions, he and McLaren shared a room together and enjoyed staying up late at night telling jokes.

McLaren was born on August 18, 1953, in St. Louis, Missouri.[4] Samson recalls that his father told him that Richard's father, Robert "Mac" McLaren, left his wife soon after their son's birth. Mary June and Richard then moved into her parents' family home in Kirkwood, a suburb of St. Louis, Missouri. The large plantation-style two-story home, constructed of red bricks and limestone mortar, featured four wooden, whitewashed pillars that provided a wide front porch. Both upstairs and downstairs, five tall windows framed in white storm shutters faced the lush front yard trimmed in evergreen bushes. A long, narrow sidewalk led to the street in the quiet, upper-middle-class suburb. He and his mother moved to Wilmington, Ohio once McLaren entered elementary school.

Though McLaren spent much of his adolescence living in Ohio, he schooled himself in Texas culture. He researched and wrote a report about the Alamo as a fourth grader,[5] as the state's history began to pique his interest. At some point during his adolescence, he read an article in *Texas Highways* magazine that boasted beautiful and expansive landscapes, and he began planning a move to West Texas. In high school, he joined Future Farmers of America, the tennis team, and the school newspaper but lost the latter position after criticizing the administration.[6]

He graduated from Wilmington High School in Ohio on May 31, 1972,[7] and worked a series of odd jobs in sales, carpentry, and food service before moving to Fort Worth in 1973.[8] He married his high school sweetheart, Sandra Kay Denkenberger, on April 24, 1975, in the Assembly of God Church in Wilmington.[9] However, from all appearances, the marriage did not last long.

In the fall of 1975, after enrolling in Texas A&M University, Samson and a girlfriend took a trip to attend the state fair and to visit Six Flags over Texas amusement park. On the way, they took a detour to visit McLaren at his apartment in Fort Worth. The McLaren newlyweds had likely separated, because Samson recalls that McLaren at the time lived alone and had accumulated a passionate collection of vintage cars, including several Buicks.

"He had two or three cars, and he kept them up real nice, and he was a pretty good mechanic," Samson said.

McLaren's mom, Mary June, served as a librarian at Sterling C. Evans Library at Texas A&M University and would continue to do so for twenty-six years until she retired.[10] She died at age eighty-three on February 26, 2004, and her body was laid to rest at College Station Cemetery.

Charles H. Samson Jr., who held a PhD in engineering, had helped his sister Mary June obtain her job on the Texas A&M campus. He served as head of the civil engineering department for fifteen years and later as acting president of Texas A&M University from July 1980 until August 1981.[11]

Nearly two decades passed before McLaren contacted his cousin again, in 1994, to ask if he could stay over for a few days with Samson and his new wife, Sherese. The visit was the first of several trips McLaren would take over the next two years to visit the Samsons in Austin.

When McLaren arrived, Samson soon discovered that his cousin had transformed into a prematurely balding middle-aged man who favored wearing jeans with a dress shirt, a sports coat, and tennis shoes. From all appearances, McLaren seemed to enjoy the simpler things in life.

"He would come and visit, and he was real impressed with Austin's Metro bus system," Samson said. "We took him to a couple of places, but most of the time he took the transit system around."

McLaren enjoyed attending wine tastings throughout the hill country. Samson learned that McLaren also had taken an interest in researching the state's political history from inside the city's local libraries and on the University of Texas campus.

"We had some discussions at that time about the research he was doing. You could tell by talking to him, he was very adamant about the principles behind the Republic of Texas, but I had never heard the words 'Republic of Texas' from him or anything—if he mentioned it, it went right by me," Samson said. "He was talking about a Fort Davis group—a lot of the ranchers and the wine owners out in West Texas, saying that they did not like the government putting restrictions on their property."

Soon, McLaren mentioned to his cousin that he had "homesteaded" on land located in the Davis Mountains near a natural spring that provided fresh running water. He told Samson that in 1983 he had settled into a tiny trailer and lean-to parked among the mountain's ponderosa pine trees and that he eked out a living by working in a local restaurant as a dishwasher.

Carl Covington, an Alpine master electrician and owner of Covington Enterprises, recalls meeting the ROT leader in 1995 while McLaren worked in the dining room at the Blue Mountain Bar and Grill, next door to the 1912 historic Victorian-style Hotel Limpia.[12] Previously, McLaren had been employed at several other local restaurants.

As part of Covington's business, he serviced refrigerators and stoves in local restaurants including those at Hotel Limpia. While Covington worked on appliances, he often visited with McLaren in the hotel kitchen.

"We didn't talk about politics or world issues or state issues or anything like that," Covington said. "He just seemed like a regular guy. He didn't strike me as flaky or 'out there in left field.' He just seemed like a guy who worked in a kitchen."[13]

McLaren later secured work at a local winery and would eventually teach winemaking classes in Fort Davis. However, he also spent eleven years fighting with residents in the Davis Mountain Resort (DMR) over land rights. The DMR amounted to little more than about fifty miles of dirt roads tracking through about ten thousand acres of scrub brush and rough mountain terrain, said Jerry Rhea,[14] a retired local dirt contractor and volunteer fire chief.

Not long after moving into the DMR, McLaren began refusing to pay road maintenance fees and property taxes, said Joe Rowe, who at the time served as president of the resort's Concerned Property Owners Association (CPOA). As early as 1985, McLaren had filed his first lawsuit against the CPOA, contesting its homeowner fees.[15] He received twenty lots, eighty-seven thousand dollars in cash, and two buildings: an old firehouse that he named his "embassy" and a dilapidated trailer outside the town of Fort Davis on land in the DMR.[16] McLaren's property previously had been owned in 1972 by Global Land Corporation and was repossessed by Rio Grande Savings and Loan.

At Jeff Davis County Courthouse, McLaren also began serving lawsuits, affidavits, land surveys, and deeds of trust against his neighbors. Rowe said McLaren formed the Davis Mountains Land Commission and set up a book of records with Sue Blakely, then the county clerk at the Jeff Davis County Courthouse.

"Sue hated Rick McLaren; she hated him with a passion. She didn't want to be his clerk. Nobody wanted to be his damn clerk," Rowe said.

With his newly acquired authority in the Davis Mountain Land Commission, McLaren also began filing court documents for both residents and nonresidents alike at the Jeff Davis County Courthouse.

"If people wanted to, they could file a document just like you could with the county. You know, you file a marriage certificate, you could file your last will and testament, and people did," Rowe said. "They would file all their records of buying and selling property, and they would file them with this Davis Mountain Land Commission (DMLC) set of books and records. What McLaren was trying to do was to get established as a legal entity."

Soon after he established the DMLC, McLaren appeared before Jeff Davis County Commissioners to request that the court recognize his commission as a legal entity. McLaren also attempted to establish his land in the Davis Concerned Property Owners Association (CPOA). Then he went back to ruminating and mulling over what his next opportunity in life was going to be. Soon he decided he was going to reestablish the Republic of Texas.

Mary Lynn "Rusty" Wofford, who with her husband Johnny Wofford owned the Paradise Ranch Bed and Breakfast, spent twelve years and more than one hundred thousand dollars fighting McLaren's seventeen separate claims against their eleven-thousand-acre ranch. Originally known as the Friend Ranch, the property was purchased in 1939 by J. W. "Skinny" Friend. When he died in 1973, Mary Lynn Wofford inherited it. The land had been owned by four generations of her family. She would finally win her battle in court September 17, 1996.[17]

Johnny Wofford[18] said that McLaren attempted to claim four hundred and sixty-two acres of the Woffords' ranchland that abutted his own along the far northwest corner of the DMR.

"He just swamped our legal system here, our state district, the county and even federal court with fraudulent filings for years," Wofford said. "It got to the point that when we finally got a clear title of that piece of land and sold it, fifty percent of the proceeds from the property went to pay our legal fees."

The trouble had begun fifteen years earlier when Johnny Wofford retired as supervisor of the Marfa sector of the US Border Patrol that once stretched from the Rio Grande all the way through North Texas into the Oklahoma Panhandle. Wofford remembers seeing two Border Patrol agents, including his supervisor, standing outside his office when he reported to work at six o'clock one morning. In his office, he discovered a fax sent from McLaren threatening Wofford, Wofford's wife, their children, their bank accounts, and their land holdings.

In his fax, McLaren stated that he intended to file a lawsuit against the Woffords' homestead where it stood at the entrance to the DMR, Wofford said.

"I thought he was an idiot; I thought he was a guy who was working the system trying to get something for nothing—that's what it amounted to," Johnny Wofford said.

Following McLaren's attempted multiple lawsuits against the Woffords, he began filing liens against land owned by Larry Stewart—no relation to Stewart Title Company—who had helped to develop the DMR.

In 1992, McLaren had sued developers LJB Enterprises and Larry Stewart, claiming that they did not possess a clear title for the DMR because the land surveys by the Texas General Land Office[19] had been cancelled. In 1994, Stewart voluntarily surrendered one hundred acres of his own land in the DMR in exchange for McLaren's promise to drop all lawsuits against him.

Joe Rowe said Stewart signed over property within the DMR to the CPOA on the condition that McLaren would also release the *lis pendens*[20] that he had filed on Stewart's land in Port Aransas. Stewart badly needed to sell the ocean front property to pay his family's medical bills.

According to Rowe, Stewart's daughter Janel had a son, D.K., who had been involved in a terrible car wreck, leaving him paralyzed. Janel Stewart later had been diagnosed with a brain aneurism and died. With mounting medical bills, Stewart could not generate any cash because everything he owned had been tied up in a *lis pendens* that McLaren had filed against him.

"Stewart was broke; I mean he was broken physically, financially, and spiritually," Rowe said.

McLaren also filed a lawsuit against Donald Davenport McIvor (since deceased) to obtain an easement just a few feet inside the boundary of the U Up U Down Ranch.[21] The family had raised cattle on forty thousand acres of the McIvors' ranchland since 1882 when G. S. Locke purchased it. Still, according to McIvor's son Scott, McLaren disputed one patch of wetland that he claimed did not fall within the legal boundary that had been established by McIvor's great-grandfather.[22] McLaren had referred to the wetland as a spring, but it amounted to little more than a wet piece of land after a rain. The wetland existed about a half mile inside the McIvors' ranch boundary.

"My dad got lawyers and he fought him. I mean, I can't remember how long it went, but I think my dad said it cost him about sixty thousand bucks for lawyers," Scott McIvor said.

McIvor successfully brought McLaren to court. During a recess in court proceedings, he addressed McLaren directly, face to face in a hallway. He asked McLaren what might satisfy him. McLaren told him that he wanted the spring, so McIvor deeded McLaren the land. "My dad said, 'If I had known that, before this started, I would have done that and we wouldn't had to have spent all the money that I've spent trying to fight him,'" Scott McIvor said.

Long-time residents of Fort Davis strongly disliked McLaren for his land-grabbing ways. "They all just absolutely detested him. They wanted him to go away. No one that I knew liked him. My understanding was, he never bought anything out there—land-wise or anything," said Mike Ward,[23] a former fire marshal and emergency management coordinator for Jeff Davis County.

About two hundred fifty full-time residents, many of whom retired as oilfield workers, had built about four hundred fifty structures within the DMR by the late 1990s. "There are some nice houses back in there, and there's also a lot of old run-down mobile homes that looked nice in the seventies when they were rolled out there, but by now they're pretty well falling apart," Ward said.

Ward worked forty hours a week at the McDonald Observatory's Visitor's Center as a computer programmer when he wasn't volunteering his time as an emergency medical services driver for Jeff Davis County.

"Davis Mountain Resort folks have a reputation for being stubborn, almost like survivalists—like: 'We'll take care of ourselves out here.' So anytime I've tried to evacuate Davis Mountain Resort because of a fire or whatever, you can get maybe like a quarter of them to leave, but the rest of them are like, 'Nope, I'm going to stay here and protect my house,'" Ward said. "It's a little bit of the wild west out there."

During frequent visits to the Jeff Davis County Courthouse library, McLaren became fascinated researching the adverse possession law.[24] The Texas law allows a person other than the legal property owner to acquire ownership by moving onto land and physically making changes to the land or adding improvements, such as building fences or structures. If the recorded landowner—who in most cases does not live in the state or area—does not impede the development or provide a clear title, then the developer may file a claim of adverse possession to gain possession and ownership of the property.

"McLaren became an expert at Adverse Possession Law in the 1990s," said Bob Dillard,[25] publisher of the *Jeff Davis County Dispatch* newspaper since 1993. The ROT leader befriended Dillard soon after the publisher also became a Jeff Davis County Judge.

"I could see him as the kind of guy who you could sit down with and wouldn't be ashamed of sitting down with and drinkin' a beer with or having a cup of coffee with and just visiting about things—about life, but he had these really outrageous ideas about the law and about land law," Dillard said. "Of course, his head was always going in fourteen different places, or you know—directions."

Dillard at the time remembered thinking that McLaren resembled most other DMR residents, people who had worked hard all of their lives and who wanted to be left alone. "They were building cabins and lean-tos with just what money they could scrape together," Dillard said. "Joe and M.A. (Rowe) had a hell of a nice house."

McLaren lived in a small mobile trailer with a ramshackle wooden lean-to attached to one side. After McLaren moved in, Dillard hired the Ohio transplant to perform some manual labor on his own property.

Dillard also recalled meeting McLaren's mother, Mary June, when she visited her son in Fort Davis a few times throughout the early 1990s.

The inside of McLaren's trailer and lean-to could not have afforded Mary June and her son much privacy in its less than five hundred square feet of living space. A swamp cooler attached to the outside of one window may have provided some comfort in the hot summer months when temperatures easily reached one hundred degrees. However, McLaren's propane-fueled space heater could not have kept out much of the chill when temperatures outside dipped into the low twenties. The sounds made by a scarce rain falling on the structure's metal roof must have been deafening. Anyone—especially a librarian transplanted from Ohio—who was unaccustomed to the wild whistling winds of West Texas that rattle and shake even the most solid of foundations, might have felt terrified in the darkness.

6

The Birth of the ROT Militia

DURING THE fall of 1994, Jo Ann Turner attended a Patriot Rally in San Antonio at the invitation of her new friends Richard and Evelyn McLaren. They told her that they planned to help to reestablish Texas as an independent nation.

John Hamilton, a congressional candidate who had served as the commander of the De Witt County Volunteer Unit of the Texas Constitutional Militia (TCM) declared the rally's goal: "to return both Texas and the United States governments to constitutional republics."[1] On November 12, 1994, members of the TCM group gathered for a Statewide Militia Muster and Patriot Rally just outside the Alamo Mission.

The separatists chose the Alamo to hold their rally because the eighteenth-century Franciscan mission located in the heart of San Antonio had served as the site of Texas' thirteen-day war for independence from Mexico from February 23 through March 6, 1836. The distinctive scalloped white limestone façade of the two-story monument with its four vacant niches still stands as a symbol of freedom to most Texans. However, Alamo Plaza appears to be squeezed into a historical space of just three acres and surrounded by trendy commercial real estate that serves as the epicenter for tourism in San Antonio outside the River Walk.

Speakers that day included Larry Pratt of Gun Owners of America; Larry Dodge of the Fully Informed Jury Association; Gary Graham and J.C. Van Kirk of the Take Texas Back group; Tinker Spain of the

Committee to Repeal War and Emergency Rule; and Alex de Pena, a San Antonio activist. Bill Utterback served as the coordinator of the Southern Region of the TCM and project coordinator at the rally.[2]

Jo Ann had helped to organize volunteers for the rally attended by at least one hundred other people. She stood in the shadows and silently witnessed McLaren speaking with intensity and conviction at the event. She noticed a disparity in the number of women versus men in attendance; about 80 percent were men.

"I got the feeling that the ROT didn't focus on women that much. They focused on men—weapon-toting men," she said.[3] "I felt there was some hidden message that they wouldn't share with everybody, that they were going to declare some type of action—not war, but some type of action—to reclaim the state."

Like everyone in attendance, Jo Ann provided her name, phone number, and email address. Those who wanted to speak came forward; however, Jo Ann simply observed and listened.

"They said things like 'You don't have to lose your home—we can help you with that.' They stated that they were going to file all these documents in the county courthouses, but they didn't say what they were. They did say that they had 'a remedy' for people like us," Jo Ann said. "I kept on believing that something good would come of it."

At the San Antonio rally, she met Dessie Andrews,[4] who identified herself as Dr. Andrews. Jo Ann thought Andrews possessed a kind face, devoid of makeup, with a pixie haircut and dressed very casually in jeans and a T-shirt. She told Jo Ann that she held a doctorate degree from Timothy Bible College located in Bastrop. Andrews asked if a group of ROT members could begin meeting in Jo Ann's office on Angus Road. The office provided a nice-sized conference room that could accommodate up to twenty people. Jo Ann had used her conference room only occasionally to conduct training meetings for newcomers to her network marketing business.

The following week, members of the ROT met in Jo Ann's office conference room as she sat nearby at a desk working silently at a computer. She listened yet kept her eyes focused on her work while the ROT members conducted their meeting. She noticed a hierarchy led by Van Kirk, as the president, who established directors for various purposes.

At the meeting, Jo Ann recalled, a few of the ROT members squabbled, and as verbal arguments escalated, members threatened to fistfight. "It would start out verbal, but it would escalate into a fist-fighting thing. One of the officers would go back and separate them, I suspect because of their differences of opinion," she said.

At that first meeting, the group met for about an hour and a half. Afterward, no one offered to pay Jo Ann for the use of her conference room. McLaren asked Jo Ann if she would be willing to accommodate future meetings for the ROT, and she agreed. He told Jo Ann that the ROT meetings would be held once a month in different locations, including in San Antonio where Van Kirk lived.

Though not a native Texan, McLaren, in the early 1990s, began to identify himself with the state's political and historical revolutionaries. He began to assume a "Texian" identity derived from researching nonnative heroes such as Sam Houston, Jim Bowie, William Barret Travis, and Davy Crockett. As McLaren claimed the title of ambassador of the ROT, he also hoped to brand himself as the authority on its unique heritage.[5]

McLaren began by mailing threatening letters to political heads of state and national leaders. Together with ROT president Archie Huel Lowe,[6] he drafted a letter on September 18, 1995, sent to then–Texas Governor George W. Bush asking him to vacate his office.[7] The request went unheeded and McLaren's letters unanswered.

In the letter McLaren wrote to Bush, he stated that the United States had not properly annexed Texas in 1845.[8] He reasoned that under international law, a treaty must be signed between the two sovereign nations and in this case, between the United States and Texas, before annexation may occur. McLaren claimed that less than a two-thirds vote of the US Senate had approved Texas' annexation.

Despite some state officials' indifference to his threats, McLaren planned to move forward with plans to reestablish the ROT as a free country under the terms of a treaty with the Law of Nations.[9] Meanwhile, he and other members of the ROT group began to write what they often referred to as the "Great Lien" against the state of Texas.

Members of the ROT soon began referring to themselves as the heads of the newly established government "reconstituted in 1995 to accept the

1836 Republic of Texas Constitution as the official contract between the Texian people and their government." On December 13, 1995, at an old cotton gin in Bulverde, Texas, McLaren penned a letter to all the nations of the United Nations to proclaim the "rebirth of the sovereign nation of the Republic of Texas."[10]

A little more than a year later, on January 16, 1996, about two hundred ROT members met on the steps of the Texas capitol in Austin to declare the second-largest state in the union free from the control of the United States. That day, ROT members also notified the United Nations and the World Court in the Netherlands of their intentions.[11]

However, McLaren's "paper war"[12] did not officially begin until April 1996 when he filed a ten-million-dollar lien against Stewart Title Company in Jeff Davis County.[13] US District Court Judge Lucius Desha Bunton III first summoned McLaren to his Pecos federal courtroom on May 2, 1996, after Houston-based Stewart Title brought a civil suit against McLaren for filing the bogus liens. When McLaren did not appear in court, Bunton issued a warrant for his arrest on contempt charges. On behalf of Stewart Title, Houston attorney Michael T. Morgan secured a $1.8 million judgment for fraud and slander against McLaren.

"Liens and documents in various courthouses that were viewed by me as being bogus were cluttering public records and creating title problems for people who didn't deserve it," Morgan said.[14]

As a result of Bunton's order of contempt against McLaren, the Ohio native spent one month in Ward County Jail in the City of Monahans. Following McLaren's release on a ten-thousand-dollar bond, he failed to uphold Bunton's conditions to cease and desist his filing of false liens. Bunton then issued a second warrant for McLaren's arrest, and in response, McLaren faxed a statement to the local media stating that Bunton's court held no jurisdiction.[15]

About that time, then–Texas Attorney General Dan Morales directed all county clerks to stop accepting McLaren's filings of false liens statewide. Morgan said that because McLaren had ignored Bunton's summons to the US Western District of Texas[16] as early as April 4, 1996, the ROT leader had to be brought to court under force by US Marshals.[17]

A letter Morgan later presented as evidence at McLaren's trial had been addressed by then–US Secretary of State Warren Christopher and signed by Douglas Ralph,[18] who was then the ROT's vice president, and Donald J. Varnell, who at the time served as the group's secretary. The letter stated, in part,

1. We demand the immediate release of our ambassador, Richard Lance McLaren.
2. While he is in your custody and care, we demand that he be treated in a manner befitting a diplomatic agent, and that he be granted full rights as a prisoner of war under the third Geneva Convention....[19]

McLaren refused a court-appointed attorney and represented himself at the trial. Because McLaren had also refused to recognize the jurisdiction of his court, Bunton ordered the ROT leader held in civil contempt. However, McLaren remained unflappable.

"Judge Bunton was an imposing figure for any who knew him. He wasn't physically a big man, but he was a *big* man. McLaren said something to the general effect, 'Judge, I think I should let you know that the Republic of Texas' grand jury has indicted you.' I took a couple of steps back when he said it because I didn't know what was going to happen," Morgan said.

"Judge Bunton just smiled and said something like 'Well, let me know how that comes out.' He just kind of rolled with it."

Dessie Andrews recalls that McLaren telephoned her from the Ward County Jail at the start of his month-long jail stay on May 6, 1996, to ask if she would temporarily assume his duties on behalf of the ROT group remotely. At the time, Andrews lived in Canyon Lake just outside Austin.

"I became the focal point for all the ROT faxes and everything. That's when I first saw the Great Lien, and it wasn't made out to the people of Texas; it was made out to a constitutional militia," Andrews said. "Because that's what these guys were going to do—they were going to get all the money—and put it in a trust and abscond with it. It was shocking to me."

After Ward County released McLaren from jail, Andrews called him at home to ask about the Great Lien. "He sidestepped and would not answer my questions, so I knew it was wrong," she said.

By November 1996, the Republic of Texas groups had accumulated more than $41 billion in civil contempt of court fines in Texas,[20] according to Ward Tisdale, a former deputy press secretary for the office of Attorney General Morales.

"When this group first started to appear, it was kind of comical. The whole idea of Texas separatism is still part of the folklore in Texas—that we were once an independent nation and that could happen again—but it's often taken with a huge grain of salt. So, my recollection is that at first it was like, 'Oh, these guys are just kind of buffoons,'" Tisdale said. "But over time as the liens became more and more prevalent and the clogging of the courts began, the attorney general was going to hear from folks at the local level that 'this is a problem, and we need your help.'"[21]

Tisdale said that the ROT group "crossed the line" when they used the local courts to abuse the legal system by filing fraudulent liens against government agencies, businesses, and both private and public individuals.

McLaren soon began to align himself with members of the Washita de Dugdahmoundyah tribe of Native Americans.[22] The tribe had attempted months earlier to claim sixty-five thousand acres of land from the United States based on an 1848 treaty. *Texas Observer* reporter Debbie Nathan identified the leader of the mostly African American tribe from Monroe, Louisiana, as Empress Verdiacee "Tiari" Washitaw Turner Goston El-Bey.[23]

Meanwhile, Lowe became the ROT's new president, and Andrews became his business aide. State District Judge Joseph Hart ordered the group to rescind any notes previously sent to 175 Texas banks demanding the transfer of funds from the state's financial accounts to the ROT.

"The Great Lien stated all of the assets were owned by the Republic of Texas. Rick called in the assets for the state of Texas. He called them in, and he started issuing checks against the assets of the Republic of Texas. He said that it was his right. That's when I thought they had gone stark-raving mad. All of them had gone stark-raving mad because they actually believed that they could take the Texas coffers," Andrews said.

In hindsight, Andrews felt betrayed when she learned that McLaren and the other ROT members had been motivated by money, not politics. "The Great Lien was really created out of greed in the beginning. They pulled the wool over the rest of [our eyes] by having us think it was a political thing they were doing in order to free the country," Andrews said. "This was the group that we thought would bring freedom from the United States."

On January 3, 1997, Morales issued a statement to the media announcing that he would prohibit the newly reformed ROT from meeting in the rotunda of the Texas State Capitol. He said that the group had not followed the required protocol to set up their meeting legally.[24] At about that same time, the ROT filed a multitude of liens against international figures including Pope John Paul II.[25] In addition, the group asked for $92 trillion in "war reparations" from the US government.

Seven days later, Representative Will Hartnett of Dallas introduced a bill to the Texas Legislature that made the filing of false liens a state criminal offense. On January 17, 1997, Governor Bush referred to the filing of false liens by the ROT as "paper terrorism" and proclaimed a state of emergency by asking legislators to speed up the law-making process.[26]

By February 2, 1997, the ROT group had split into three factions for what they referred to as "political reasons." President Archie Lowe and Daniel Miller led one group; David Johnson and Jesse Enloe[27] represented a second; and ROT's former president Van Kirk led a third with Richard Lance McLaren.

The three groups continued to share one solid and unified philosophy: members did not intend to pay taxes to city, county, state, or federal governments. McLaren also planned to file a multimillion claim against the federal government.[28]

On March 4, 1997, Jeff Davis Sheriff Steve Bailey wrote a letter to Rick McLaren asking him to surrender himself on alleged burglary charges that had been filed by his neighbors. McLaren refused to comply.

Meanwhile, the Texas Senate jurisprudence committee, on March 10, 1997, approved changes to the Texas Property Code intended to prohibit persons and organizations from filing bogus liens. However, the code would not officially become law until later that summer. Two days later, Morales won a restraining order against the ROT for filing false liens.

By March 13, 1997, the Texas House of Representatives passed the "bogus lien bill," and six days later the bill passed in the Texas Senate to become part of Chapter 12 of *The Texas Civil Practice and Remedies Code*. Section 12.002. It authorized the collection of money based on damages from anyone who filed a false lien.[29] However, the new law would not take effect until May 21, 1997, according to Houston attorney Michael F. Hord Jr.[30] The legislature later would amend the bill on September 1, 2007.

Beginning as early as January 1996, McLaren had used the Internet to spread his message of sedition and to research methods of filing liens against property owners and businesses. One of McLaren's ROT lieutenants, Robert "White Eagle" Otto, had contacted Todd Jaggar, who at the time operated the only Internet service in the tri-county Big Bend region, the Overland Network, located in Fort Davis. At Otto's request, Jaggar installed Internet service at the ROT embassy in Fort Davis.

"Then I found out it was for McLaren and the ROT group that they had out there in the Davis Mountains Resort, and you know they were kind of notorious around here for like trying to pay for auto repairs and stuff with Republic of Texas 'script,' not money. So, I told him that 'Yeah, sure you can have Internet service—my only requirement is that you pay me in United States currency, not—you know, funny money,'" Jaggar said.[31]

"The fee was twenty bucks, and they would hand me either a twenty-dollar bill or two tens and some change, or whatever it was—never a check. I don't think I ever received any kind of check."

Jaggar never met Rick McLaren, but Evelyn McLaren came into his office "a couple of times" to pay the ROT's monthly provider fee. The McLarens paid Jaggar's fees for Internet service on time every month for more than a year. "They were just another customer as far as I was concerned," Jaggar said.

Then on April 7, 1997, Jaggar received a subpoena bearing the official Texas seal from the office of the Attorney General Morales. The subpoena requested everything—email addresses, physical addresses, all email correspondence between McLaren and anybody within the ROT, as well as the IP addresses of any websites ROT members had visited. The subpoena also requested every known web address or the IP addresses of anyone who had ever visited the ROT website. Eight Internet providers cooperated with Morales's request, but Jaggar's Overland Network did not.[32]

"I noticed it was signed by a court reporter. I'm not a lawyer, but that didn't seem right to me. I knew that a subpoena needed to be signed by a judge," he said.

Jaggar immediately sought the advice of attorney W. Scott McCollough, a former staff member for the Texas Attorney General's office who had become a representative with Wireless Internet Service Providers Association (WISPA), an organization that supports fixed wireless broadband and equipment in mostly rural areas.

According to Jaggar, McCollough told him that nine other Internet providers across the state had received the same subpoena from Morales demanding ROT emails, log-ins, user identifications, subscriber applications, and billing information including credit cards and checking account numbers.[33] About that time, *Washington Post* reporter Sue Pressley interviewed McLaren who claimed he had ten thousand followers across the Internet.[34]

However, Jaggar's company and only one other had questioned the legality of Morales's subpoena. McCollough advised both Jaggar and the owners of Internet Texoma not to abide by the subpoena because it violated the Electronic Communications Privacy Act passed in 1986.[35]

Within days, McCollough also sent a letter addressed to Morales requesting an officially signed subpoena. Morales responded by threatening to hold the Overland Network owner in contempt.

"Basically, that turned into a Mexican standoff where he had a lawsuit against me and I had a lawsuit against him," Jaggar said. "Meanwhile, whatever was going on with the ROT—whatever emails were being sent, I collected that. It was definitely going through my server, but I wasn't deleting any records or anything like that."

Then Jaggar received another letter—this time from McLaren.

"Basically, what it said was—and this is kind of hilarious—they were appointing me, Todd Jaggar, and Overland Network 'a diplomat to the Republic of Texas,'" Jaggar said. "Therefore, anything that they (the Texas Attorney General's office) had with me on record was covered under 'diplomatic immunity.'"

Suddenly the ROT became the subject of a media storm regarding privacy rights.

Morales cancelled his subpoenas and instead announced plans to file an "investigative demand" for the ROT's Internet service provider and communications information.[36]

However, Morales never followed through on those plans, Tisdale said. "I think it was one of those cases where the intention was good, but after really looking at the law and the privacy concerns, it was better to kind of stand down and to not go in that direction."

Meanwhile, members of the ROT continued their military-like maneuvers within the Davis Mountain Resort (DMR). McLaren's neighbors began reporting to Sheriff Bailey that they had witnessed men dressed in camouflage clothing firing live ammunition into the nearby foothills. Bailey, in turn, contacted Texas Ranger Captain Barry Caver for his help.

"Nobody cared about the ROT until they started playing with guns up there in the mountains," Jaggar said.

A Dallas affiliate for NBC contacted Jaggar to ask him to photograph and videotape "any suspicious activity" he observed inside the DMR. To verify the validity of the request, Jaggar telephoned *NBC Nightly News* reporter James D. Cummings, who confirmed and offered to pay Jaggar one hundred fifty dollars per day for his freelance services.

"So then comes the day when the shit hits the fan. I heard that it was going down up there, and I dropped everything; I got the video camera that NBC had left me, and I headed up to the DMR," Jaggar said.

At the Point of Rocks roadside rest area in the Davis Mountains, Jaggar met with Texas Rangers who advised him to keep a low profile at the scene.

Within twelve hours, NBC sent a professional film crew out to the site. Jaggar recalls the camera crew arrived at ten thirty on the night of April 28, 1997. As a neighborly gesture, Jaggar purchased take-out meals for the NBC crewmembers and loaned the station's crew chief his own cell own phone because the network phones experienced limited reception throughout the Davis Mountains. Then representatives from *Time* magazine also contacted Jaggar to ask him to photograph the siege.

Jaggar would eventually take down the ROT's website and discontinue the group's Internet service at the official request of prosecutors for the Eighty-Third Judicial District Court.[37]

"There was a ton of media attention on this whole thing about me taking down their website making the rounds on the Internet," Jaggar said. "My whole system in Fort Davis was all running on a 256K ISDN line."[38]

Overland Network at the time operated a browser with very little memory compared to today's technology standards; Jaggar's Internet service worked on a dial-up system, at 28.8 to 33.6 kilobits per second, or kbps, in terms of the measurable bandwidth of data provided per transmission.

* * *

Fearing what she read in the newspapers about the ROT and Richard McLaren, Jo Ann Turner decided one night in March 1997 to hide out inside the home of her friend Dessie Andrews at Canyon Lake. Because Jo Ann had personally filed several liens on behalf of the ROT against Stewart Title, the Internal Revenue Service, and Travis County, she thought it would be only a matter of time before law enforcement officers tracked her down in Austin.

"I walked through the backwoods to her home so that her landlord couldn't see me. I messed up a brand-new pair of shoes walking through those rocks," Jo Ann Turner said.

Andrews then drove Jo Ann to Fort Worth to stay at the McLarens' apartment to hide out for a month.

"I was running from what might be waiting for me back home in Austin. I just felt like 'they' were looking for me back in Austin. 'They,' meaning all of the court people, the judicial people," Jo Ann said.

Like McLaren, Jo Ann enjoyed being an early riser. Each morning, she started making coffee in the McLarens' kitchen by six o'clock, and McLaren would join her around six thirty. "He was always completely dressed for the day. I never saw him in his pajamas, ever. I only saw him fully dressed, and Evelyn as well," Jo Ann said.

After Evelyn dressed, she also joined her husband and Jo Ann in the kitchen for coffee. Evelyn would leave for work in time to arrive by eight o'clock at the local branch of the US Postal Service in Fort Worth.

The McLarens talked very little to Jo Ann except when the three of them went out to dinner every evening at Applebee's.

"I was trying to be real low-key because I was staying in their apartment at their expense; so, I didn't want to be domineering or anything like that in the conversations. But when you spend a month with somebody, you kind of get to know them. I'm a very good observer of people," Jo Ann said. "I observed that Rick and Evelyn were very, very different—on opposite sides of the spectrum. I think Evelyn was searching for companionship; Rick provided that. She was sort of searching for someone who would sort of take care of her, and eventually she was taking care of him."

During her month-long stay, Jo Ann said, she never saw the McLarens hug or kiss or show any type of affection. They shared no pet names for one another. As far as Jo Ann could see, the McLarens had no friends. Evelyn had two daughters from a previous marriage, but while Jo Ann visited, she never met them. No one ever came to the apartment to visit either Evelyn or Richard in the month that Jo Ann stayed there.

Other than the McLarens, Jo Ann occasionally saw other ROT members when she accompanied McLaren to a temporary branch of the ROT located in Grand Prairie, not far from Fort Worth. Once they arrived, for part of one week McLaren put Jo Ann to work at a typewriter typing his documents. Jo Ann noticed that outside the center, a ROT flag flew alongside of the American flag. Inside, things remained businesslike during just the four days that she worked.

"At the typewriter I'd be typing away—all kinds of documents for the Republic of Texas. I can't tell you what the subjects were or what they said," she said.

"We would stay about six hours each of those four days I was there. I never met anyone who came in because I was only supposed to be working at the typewriter. No one came over to talk to me. I was kind of like the secretary that no one talks to unless they need you. It was really strange. It was like I was in an office where I didn't know anybody, and they didn't care about me—I wasn't important."

She preferred to remain anonymous; Jo Ann understood that none of the ROT members knew that she had been staying with the McLarens.

"Rick had mentioned to me that there had been some visits by government officials. He said they 'came by just to see what they [the ROT members] were up to,' but no one would really divulge any information," she said. The McLarens provided twenty-four-hour accommodations for Jo Ann in exchange for her typing and editing skills.

On March 24, 1997, McLaren sent a press release to the media throughout Texas and to parts of New Mexico, Colorado, Kansas, and Oklahoma claiming that the lands belonged to the reestablished Republic of Texas.

McLaren, then the official author of all legal documents created for the ROT, also stepped up his series of media campaigns by running ads in the local newspapers. He also began broadcasting live-on-the-air announcements as a caller to radio stations and stating that Texas had been illegally annexed by the United States on December 29, 1845.[39]

Meanwhile, as news about the ROT spread, people began sending in donations, Andrews said. She immediately became involved in every aspect of the ROT, including attending a secretive meeting held in Lufkin. Andrews observed that the ROT's own currency was plated with gold and silver used to fashion medallions that bore the official Republic of Texas seal.

"They [ROT members] sent someone to keep me out of an afternoon meeting. That's when Darrell Franks introduced 'the banks,'" Andrews said.

She said that Franks offered to sell dozens of bank charters to ROT members with the promise that the banks would soon restore the Republic of Texas' reserves of silver and gold. Franks was "an ostrich farmer from Shiner," who once held the position as treasurer for the ROT.[40]

In Lufkin, Franks told ROT members in attendance that he had one hundred banker positions to sell at a price of two thousand dollars each. Andrews witnessed people writing checks or pulling out cash to give Franks.

"I saw this feeding frenzy going on in the middle of the hallway at this hotel. There was this big round circle of people and there were other people running up and jumping over the other people to get to the inside of the circle—physically jumping up and over and to get closer. It was Darrell Franks in the center. He was selling those banker positions," Andrews said.

"What he told them was: 'You can pay two thousand dollars to become a banker; there is a gold fund for the Republic of Texas, so every banker is going to get one hundred million dollars in gold.' Those people in the feeding frenzy believed it. They were going to get one hundred million dollars in gold, and they were supposed to give it to people to pay off their debts so that they could begin debt-free in the Republic of Texas. And if they ran out of money, or one hundred million dollars, it would be replenished by another hundred million dollars."

Andrews said that what she saw that day in Lufkin left her feeling appalled at the actions of the ROT members. "Franks walked off with two hundred thousand dollars that day and left behind a lot of disappointed people who felt they couldn't get in," Andrews said.

Andrews then called a meeting of ROT members in Waco on a Sunday about two weeks later.

"I was furious. Darrell Franks had called a bankers' meeting in Dallas—unbeknownst to me—on a Saturday. He talked to these people and said, 'There is going to be a woman who will speak the devil's language and she is the devil. We are God—we, the bankers,'" Andrews said.

"I stood up with that entire council behind me, and I said, 'This is unconstitutional, and it can't stand.' I thought I was going to be lynched on the spot—killed. I barely got out of that meeting with my life, and that's the truth."

From that moment on, Andrews said, she saw ROT members divide into two factions: "the bankers" and "the others."

"It was split about fifty-fifty. We were having meetings, and the bankers influenced them. It was the end of that particular moment. You can't distract people like that. It was the end. Still, it took a lot for it to die. The State of Texas government and the people in the US government became very concerned about this Republic of Texas movement because they knew that they were going to be ousted if it continued," she said.

Using the Texas media, Attorney General Morales began to refer to the actions of the ROT as "paper terrorism."[41] Morales used his attack on the ROT as a political platform by sending a letter to every court and to every official.

"The message said: 'If you suspect that someone in front of you is in the Republic of Texas or has any affiliation with the Republic of Texas, they are to be arrested on the spot and taken to jail immediately,'" Andrews said. "So, anybody who went into court and argued, 'I don't have a license; I don't have to pay the fine,' were deemed members of the Republic of Texas and immediately hauled to jail."

Since 1995, the ROT had notoriously employed a practice of "harassment, intimidation, fraud, and theft using phony liens, affidavits, orders, summonses, and warrants," according to Juan Batista, a reporter for *Indybay*.[42]

One day while staying at the McLarens' apartment in Fort Worth, Jo Ann saw McLaren send a document by fax to a phone number in Puerto Rico.

"Afterwards he said he had acquired one million dollars in cash. That's what he and Evelyn were living on. He got it, and we would go to

Applebee's almost every night to eat dinner—so often that I got so sick of Applebee's. He would pay for dinner with his American Express card that he got from Puerto Rico," Jo Ann said.

That's when Jo Ann learned that McLaren had joined forces with five other men from Louisiana as part of a group that called itself the Washitaw Empire, beginning with a bogus check writing scheme that members cashed in Puerto Rico to buy computers, clothes, and guns.[43]

"A lot of their documents were official-looking, and they were able to bamboozle people," Tisdale said. "All these forms of fraud seem to always come down to one thing—greed—and this was no exception."

Eventually, what Jo Ann observed by living with the McLarens for thirty days convinced her to return to Austin and to begin to distance herself from the ROT. She had a strong sense that whatever business the McLarens had embroiled themselves in might bring them a great deal of legal trouble. She did not want any part of it. Although she feared what her future held, her present association with the ROT began to frighten her more. When McLaren offered to drive her back home to Austin, Jo Ann could not pack fast enough.

By January 1997, Morales would become embroiled in his own politically fatal actions. The attorney general inadvertently incriminated himself while attempting to help his Houston attorney friend Marc D. Murr avoid prosecution in a case involving the State of Texas and several tobacco manufacturers.[44]

Eventually, Morales's threats against the ROT grew faint. By the fall of 1997, Morales would announce that he would not seek reelection. Afterward, the news about Morales's involvement in the state's tobacco litigation would hit Tisdale and other staff members in the office of the attorney general hard.

"We didn't sign up for that," Tisdale said. "We were all really saddened and felt betrayed by that whole thing."

In 1999, John Cornyn would become Texas' new attorney general. The *Texas Tribune* would name Morales "an unreliable narrator" in 2003 after he pleaded guilty to filing a false tax return and altering government records, including a $3.2 billion settlement that had been awarded to the state as part of a $17.3 billion tobacco litigation case.[45]

7

Jo Ann Canady Turner's Incarceration

As Jo Ann tried to sleep, sounds of rats munching things in the dark from the corners of her jail cell kept her awake. She could make out their furry silhouettes from their long and pointed aquiline noses to their scaly tails as they scurried across the tile floor. Tasting bile in the back of her throat, Jo Ann somehow managed to swallow her fear.[1]

The jail cell appeared the size of her former walk-in closet inside the luxurious master bedroom of the home she had lost to foreclosure along Town Lake shoreline. With her back pressed against a damp cinderblock wall, Jo Ann felt chilled to the bone wearing only her prison-issued clothing.

She lay with her feet up on the bare mattress of her lower bunk, shivering with hands pressed together beneath her head in a prayerlike pose. She wished for a pillow or a sheet, as she smelled the musty and pungent scent of mildew mingled with the brine of anonymous sweat, likely left behind by the bed's previous occupants.

Otherwise empty, the cell provided only a stainless-steel sink and toilet. Her full bladder painfully and frequently began testing her prudence at the lack of privacy. In the hours while she waited, a husky female guard twice passed outside Jo Ann's cell. Dressed in a white starched long-sleeve shirt and black tie, black jeans, and boots, the guard did not speak to Jo Ann, who tightly closed her eyes, avoiding the woman's gaze.

Chapter 7

She thought the facility seriously needed an upgrade; the neutral-colored and peeling beige paint inside Travis County Jail had remained relatively unchanged since its construction in 1986. The complex stretched a full block in Austin's downtown between 10th and 11th streets, and Guadalupe and Nueces streets. One of the oldest buildings, the Heaman/Sweat Historic County Courthouse, had been used only for hearing civil cases but also housed the County Clerk's Office and Law Library. However, on the night of April 22, 1997, the jail facility held many pretrial detainees, including Jo Ann.

The next day, Jo Ann learned that she had been arrested on two contempt charges for violating an earlier order by State District Judge Joseph H. Hart[2] to stop filing fraudulent liens. One of the liens cited in the charges was a lien she had filed against Alar Moving and Storage Company after Alar had removed all of her family's belongings following an eviction from their West Austin home in March 1996. She and her husband Bill had lost their home because they had not paid their mortgage and property taxes for two years on the premise that they were citizens of the newly reformed Republic of Texas (ROT).[3]

On the morning of Wednesday, April 23, 1997, Judge Hart asked Jo Ann a few pointed questions and listened to her deposition[4] before setting her bail at twenty-five thousand dollars. He appeared to be a natural Texan of German ancestry with blue eyes, a square jaw, wide dimples, and a toothy grin. Although his blond hair had already begun to recede, Jo Ann thought him to be attractive.

"Judge Hart asked me, 'Mrs. Turner, are you a member of the Republic of Texas militia?'" Jo Ann said. "I answered 'no.'"

"He asked me 'Did you file false liens against Stewart Title Company on behalf of the Republic of Texas militia?' All I said in response was, 'I want to see an attorney.'"

Almost immediately, the local media began to publicize Jo Ann's arrest. On April 23, 1997, Steve Scheibal, a staff writer for the *Austin American-Statesman*, publicly identified her as "the former secretary" for the ROT.[5]

Later that afternoon, Travis County deputies escorted Jo Ann into a long van with mesh metal grating covering the windows that otherwise might have resembled a gray school bus. They transferred her to Travis County Correctional Complex at 3614 Bill Price Road in Del Valle.

Twenty prisoners, both male and female, rode on the bus with Jo Ann that day. The seats faced forward as on any school bus, though she sat alone. Jo Ann noticed right away that only she had been both handcuffed and shackled. The guards had bound both her ankles and waist in iron bands connected by a long slender chain that hobbled her so she could take only small steps at a time. They also had cuffed her wrists at her waist. Her shoulders ached from the strain, and the skin on her wrists burned with the constant irritation. At the correctional facility, guards separated the two groups according to gender. The men went to one building and the women to another, in a series of eight security buildings that housed inmates.

Inside the rural facility, Jo Ann surrendered to a second full-body search. As she undressed, she began to feel increasingly fearful about the possibility of sharing a jail cell with another female inmate. The intake area had been built in a semicircle, at nearly 180 degrees. Several guards monitored the incoming inmates through large windows from inside an attached room and recorded the proceedings electronically with video cameras. Again, the guards asked the female prisoners to strip and to put on new uniforms, a sort of neutral beige-on-beige.

Guards then led Jo Ann and the other inmates to their cellblock. Every bed was occupied. There were two beds in each doorless cell and one commode positioned completely in the open. The communal shower was positioned in the center of the common room and had neither doors nor curtains. Immediately, the guards assigned Jo Ann to a cell with a young, slender Black woman who spoke with a Caribbean accent. The days that followed blurred in Jo Ann's memory.

"I don't recall interacting with my roommate at all. She seemed fairly quiet. She was a drug addict—she did share that with me. She said she had some children," Jo Ann said.

Every day when she awoke, Jo Ann left her cell to sit in a chair at one of the long metal tables positioned in the center of the common room to wait for breakfast to be served. The morning meal usually consisted of a slice of dry toast, some powdered eggs that had been scrambled, and a cup of coffee.

On the fifth day of her incarceration, Sunday, April 27, 1997, Jo Ann watched a television monitor mounted close to the ceiling in the common room display her mug shot taken days earlier. "That's when I saw the CNN news reports about me and what was going on in Fort Davis," she said.

She watched in silent horror as broadcasters reported that members of the ROT militia had attacked Joe and Margaret Ann Rowe, residents of Davis Mountain Resort (DMR) and held them captive in their own home. The ROT members referred to their hostages as "prisoners of war."[6] In exchange for the hostages, the ROT asked for Jo Ann's release and the release of another of its members, Robert Scheidt, who had been arrested in Fort Davis.

"It wasn't until I saw it on the news that I knew what was going on in Fort Davis. The newscaster kept mentioning me and said I was the only Republic of Texas militia member arrested in Austin. They called me 'an operative' at one point. They said I was 'the operative for the Republic of Texas.'"

At the time, Jo Ann didn't understand the definition of an *operative*.[7] Later she would learn that the media considered her a paper terrorist working for the ROT. "It was very frightening because it led me to think that if and when I went to trial, the outcome would be very serious. I didn't know what they would say or what they would do to me," she said.

The guards told her that a representative from CNN had called to request an interview with her on April 27, 1997, but Jo Ann refused. Later, she watched the television as a broadcast anchor for CNN reported that Jo Ann was being held in Travis County Jail on two contempt charges stemming from liens that she had filed. The broadcaster also reported that the ambassador for the ROT militia, Richard "Rick" Lance McLaren, had referred to Jo Ann's arrest as "a declaration of war."[8]

Throughout Jo Ann's incarceration in Del Valle, Bill Turner drove to work regularly and went home to their empty apartment every night. Meanwhile, inside the Travis County holding facility, Jo Ann relied on skills that she had learned during her years leading a network marketing business.

She had acquired the uncanny ability to size up a person after only a few minutes of conversation. Drawing on a combination of clues she interpreted about each person she observed, Jo Ann became an expert salesperson. She noticed a handshake, eye contact, body posture, and what someone said and how he or she spoke. She also knew how to use these intuitive skills to her advantage. Jo Ann knew to find the strongest and most influential person in her cellblock and to befriend her; if she could win over the leader, she knew that the rest of her fellow inmates would follow.

Immediately, Jo Ann befriended a six-foot-tall, hefty Black middle-aged woman in the cellblock who identified herself as Natasha. The woman wore cornrows in her hair, and she had strong cheekbones and large almond-shaped caramel-colored eyes. To Jo Ann, Natasha appeared to possess the ability to read another person's thoughts from facial expressions alone. When she spoke to Jo Ann, she stood very close—nearly nose to nose—and spoke with a whisper-like softness.

All the other inmates seemed to look to Natasha as their leader. Soon Jo Ann began offering Natasha portions of her meals in return for protection inside the facility. Lunch consisted of a bologna and cheese sandwich. For dinner, the guards served strange concoctions they referred to as "casserole," or a mystery loaf made from a variety of meat byproducts along with mashed potatoes and a hard-crust bread roll.

Throughout the day, the scent of eggs and bologna often lingered for hours after being cleared from the common room. Determinedly, Jo Ann vowed never again to eat anything that looked remotely like an egg or an egg substitute. While she had always disliked bologna, the processed mystery meat served inside the prison reeked with both a fecal and metallic smell.

Because Natasha referred to her as Mrs. Turner, everyone else in the cellblock began addressing Jo Ann the same way in a show of respect and because she appeared to be the oldest inmate in the lockup. After skipping so many meals, however, Jo Ann soon began to look emaciated. During her forty days of incarceration she would shrink from the one hundred thirty pounds she weighed at the beginning of her ordeal to just a little over one hundred pounds. Standing five feet eight inches tall, she thought that her weight loss gave her a ghastly appearance.

Bill never visited Jo Ann during her stay at Travis County Correctional Complex; he told her on the telephone that he felt "too distraught" to visit. In the evenings, Jo Ann's thoughts often drifted to Bill, whom she imagined inside their comfy apartment, oblivious and calm, while she lay alone in her bottom bunk cell bed. She tried in vain not to listen to the cacophony of sounds coming from neighboring cells that held her fellow inmates.

Chapter 7

"A lot of those women snored because they had breathing problems and because they were so fat. I would hear some talking, and the deputies would hush them up. The guards would say over the loudspeaker, 'So and so, in so and so room, be quiet. If we have to tell you again, we're going to lock you up in solitary,'" she said.

"It was hard to sleep and to relax because I didn't know if someone might come in at night to attack me. I did have some fear the whole time I was there, even though the majority of those women liked me and seemed to protect me, but I never knew what they were going to do."

Jo Ann attempted to shower daily despite the horrid, unsanitary conditions. The guards also required the inmates to take turns cleaning the toilets, sinks, and floors of the shower stalls. On her hands and knees, Jo Ann mopped up the muck and human hair left behind in the floor drains, using only a sponge and a bucket filled with a strong pine-smelling cleaner. While she worked, fearful thoughts consumed her every moment.

"I just had this fear that I would never get out of there, or if I did, I would be constrained in a prison cell for the rest of my life," she said. "I was convinced that's what they were going to do with Rick McLaren based upon the news reports that I was hearing. I thought, *Well. I'm next.* I just didn't know how I was going to get out of there, especially if I couldn't get a lawyer, so I slept very little. I always kept my back to the wall when I did sleep, and I kept a lookout towards the entry to the cell. I had a lot of time to think."

Often, Jo Ann's thoughts turned to her activities over the prior several months. "I kept asking myself whether I had done the right thing or not. Perhaps if I had not asked for Rick's help, everything would have been over long before now, and maybe I would not have had to go to jail," she said. "I didn't see how I was going to escape some type of punishment. I just didn't know what was going to happen to me."

She began praying aloud at night alone in the darkness of her cell. "I'm not overly religious. I do pray to God. I said prayers; I bargained," Jo Ann said. "Initially it was 'God please help me to survive all of this and help me. Help my husband and my family to understand that it is not because of them that I am here. Please forgive me for what I have done to them and help them to understand what is really going on and to show some mercy for me. If I have done something wrong, please tell me what the outcome is going to be.' I just hated the unknown and not knowing what was going to happen."

Neither of her adult children, Kelly nor Jeff, visited Jo Ann during the time of her incarceration, nor did they call her on the telephone. "I wondered all the while if they were angry with me or ashamed. It bothered me. When I called, all I did was ask Bill if the kids were okay. He said yes and that they were surviving as best as they could, but no one came to visit me, not one person," Jo Ann said.

"The loneliness and isolation were unbearable at times. It seemed like an eternity, as if I had been there ten years instead of nearly forty days and nights. I had no hope of ever getting out. I began to seek some solace and friendship from the women who were incarcerated with me, but nothing brought any comfort. There was no singing, no storytelling, or hobbies—no normalcy from my previous life."

On Sundays, the jail facility provided church services for the inmates. The guards bused both the male and female inmates who had asked to attend chapel to another building on the grounds. Jo Ann went along just to escape her cell for thirty minutes once a week.

None of the inmates who attended the religious services spoke. The men sat on one side of the chapel, and the women sat on the other. The chaplain offered no communion, and no one stepped forward to receive a blessing or a healing touch.

As the chaplain talked, Jo Ann recalled the last time that she had attended church services, nearly forty years earlier. For most of her childhood, Jo Ann had attended both Sunday school classes and services at Walnut Creek Baptist Church. She recalled that her mother, Maggie Canady, faithfully had driven her children to church every Sunday, though Jo Ann could not remember ever seeing her mother pray.

As Jo Ann's thoughts returned to the church services inside the chapel at Travis County Correctional Complex, the guards began to lead the inmates, including Jo Ann, to the waiting bus that carried them back to their respective cellblocks.

After returning to the cellblock, the cellmates often started fights, which Jo Ann observed as racially motivated. "It was primarily between a Black and a White lady and not always the same women each time. It's just that the White ladies didn't like the Blacks, and they let it be known, apparently, from the comments I heard them make. My comment was always, 'Well, so far, they've been my friends. You haven't been my friend.' For whatever reason, the Whites just didn't associate with me," Jo Ann said.

"The Blacks were the majority, and I was going to go with the majority and the ones that were treating me right. As long as I fed Natasha my meals, everything went all right. It was all A-okay. No one made any passes at me. I know it happened in the cellblock. I feared that also, and that's why I had such a hard time sleeping at night, thinking that somebody might come and try to molest me. That didn't happen, thank goodness. I don't know what I would have done if it did."

The fights in the women's cellblock usually began in the common room. They consisted mostly of a lot of tousling and tumbling or hair pulling, or both. The guards attempted to stop the inmates before they hurt one another too badly. The guards always removed those inmates who fought and isolated them elsewhere. It seemed to Jo Ann that the punished women returned to the cellblock less agitated.

The inmates talked very little about themselves, except when Jo Ann asked them questions. "To try and get to know them a little bit, I would try and ask them, 'Do you mind telling me what's going on with you and why you're here?' Most of them were drug addicts and prostitutes. I put people at ease, and they shared their stories with me," she said.

"There was one girl who had been in and out of jail for several years. I think her name was Betty. I asked, 'For how many years?' She said, 'Oh, about twenty years.' She said she could not kick the habit of the drugs, and she kept prostituting because she didn't have a husband and she had three children that she had to support. I just felt so sorry for her, but there was nothing I could do."

In addition to sharing her food, Jo Ann promised Natasha that someday, when and if she were ever allowed to leave the facility, she would send a little money for her to spend in the commissary. Jo Ann eventually would keep that promise.

■ ■ ■

On Monday, April 28, 1997, Travis County State District Judge John Dietz[9] summoned Jo Ann to his courtroom. At first glance, Jo Ann thought Dietz looked as though he had no neck to support his round head atop of his squat body. As he spoke, she noticed the judge's mouth often formed an unnatural O shape, appearing both toothless and dark, like a frog's. Dietz proceeded to shout a series of questions at Jo Ann, seemingly in rapid succession. That day began the first of several when Jo Ann would be called to Dietz's courtroom over the next several weeks.

"Dietz asked the same questions every time I went to court, every single week. I would answer no. I was respectful. I would say, 'No, your honor, I didn't file any bogus liens. I was filing some paperwork to try to prevent my house from being foreclosed.' Second question: 'Did Rick McLaren ask you to file any liens?' I said, 'No, he didn't ask me to file any liens, and I don't consider them bogus liens.' Third question was: 'Are you a member of the Republic of Texas militia?' I would answer, 'No, your honor, I am not.'"

Meanwhile, as San Antonio attorney Nick Milam visited the Travis County Courthouse on unrelated business that day, he saw Judge Dietz stick his head out of his judge's chambers.

"Dietz said, 'Hey Nick. I want your ass over here right now to serve as counsel for this lady who is not represented,'" Milam said.[10]

"I started talking to her, and I couldn't believe it. It was the most ludicrous thing I had ever heard of in my life. So, you know, I'm trying to figure out with Dietz, 'What's your basis for holding this lady?' I went in and I talked to the state's attorney, and he was all up in arms. They had the Texas attorney general down there and all kinds of shit."

The attorney general, Dan Morales (who would later be indicted in an unrelated matter),[11] referred to the ROT members' tactics as "paper terrorism" in a statement released to the local media.

"I was very, very surprised. I was looking at them and saying, 'You guys are really, really overreacting, and why don't you just turn the lady loose and go file your civil actions—get rid of it?'" Milam said. "They were really, really, really charged up—I mean really wound up. I was thinking, *Is there a nuclear war going on or what?* I could not for the life of me figure out what the story was with these guys."

The national media also ran stories about the ROT as Morales began to spin a few of his own locally.

"I couldn't figure it out for the life of me what was going on. The media people were just going on and on about this. I thought, *Wait. wait. There's no crime here; there's no underlying crime. I mean nobody's got hurt here. This is a civil matter."* Milam said. "I'm pretty sure that Dietz agreed with me on that."

Morales and others at the Texas State Capitol perceived Milam's legal representation of Jo Ann Turner as contentious.

"They were like super-serious. I was worried. To tell you the truth, I was worried that they would come after me," Milam said. "Eventually, Dan and his people sat down and had a look at the law—which was something they should have done first and realized that there really wasn't any basis for doing this and realized after looking at this lady that she's somebody's grandma and not, you know, some sort of a whatever—'terrorist.' I didn't get it."

Also, Milam said that Morales and others at the Texas Capitol expressed concerns that the ROT members' claims might hold some truth, that Texas had indeed been illegally annexed in 1845.

"They were really, really, really angry and concerned that these people were challenging the sovereignty of the state of Texas. That really had them going. Why get worried like that and why get all bent out of shape except for the fact that a lot of the stuff that they were saying really is true?" Milam said.

He said that the ROT also disregarded the fact that Texas had officially seceded from the United States as part of the Confederacy on April 12, 1861, during the Civil War. When the war ended on April 9, 1865, the Union reclaimed Texas. Any discussion on the subject of Texas' annexation became null and void.[12]

"You know, it was a long time ago," Milam said. "Texas is part of the United States, but Texans are not really the same as the rest of the Americans, although they are becoming more and more like the rest of Americans."

Jo Ann never confessed to delivering McLaren's documents to the Travis County Courthouse, to Stewart Title Company, and to the IRS office in Austin or to filing them under his name. She realized that McLaren's purpose in filing against Stewart Title Company had been to prevent the company from foreclosing on homeowners across the state of Texas. The Shapiro & Dunn law firm had filed the Turners' foreclosure on behalf of Alamo Title, not Stewart Title, however, Jo Ann believed that filing a lien against the latter somehow would invalidate her own foreclosure once the ROT took control of Texas.

Filled with despair, Jo Ann watched the television interviews with Attorney General Morales who referred to what members of the ROT did by filing liens against businesses as paper terrorism. Meanwhile, Rick McLaren had referred to Jo Ann "as a prisoner of war," according to the press.[13] Still, as she continued to attend routine court hearings with both Hart and Dietz alternately, Jo Ann sensed that the two justices seemed to be easing up on her.

"Just by the way that they were talking," she said. "I remember during the last two court appearances, the judges did not ask me if I knew why I was there. I later found out that they do that—bring prisoners into court—every week so that they can collect their fees from the state, so that the judges and everybody can be paid."

Meanwhile, Jo Ann felt trapped in the series of repetitive court rituals, the likes of which she would later equate to actor Bill Murray's recurring scenes from the 1993 movie, *Groundhog Day*. The difference between that film and her life seemed painfully obvious. She lacked humor and Jo Ann felt sure no happy ending awaited her.

Part II
The ROT War

8

The ROT Takes Hostages

SEVERAL media professionals from all over the world, including a news reporter from Japan, began requesting interviews with Jo Ann Turner while she was at the Travis Country Correctional Center.

"I refused them all. I just didn't want to discuss it with anyone not knowing how that might work against me. Every newsbreak, every news hour—whenever the news came on, it was all about me and Fort Davis where another Republic of Texas member had been arrested," she said.[1]

By day three of her incarceration, Jo Ann again called Bill to ask him if he had had any luck securing the money needed to pay her twenty-five-thousand-dollar bond so she could be released from jail.

"He told me: 'I guess you'll just have to stay there until they decide what they're going to do with you.' He was very distraught," she said. "Bill wasn't angry; he was concerned and sympathetic. He just said he felt like his hands were tied and no one wanted to help him or me."

Looking at the baggy uniform that the jailers had given her to wear reminded Jo Ann that she possessed a whole wardrobe of beautiful clothes in her apartment. Jo Ann's previous work both as a real estate agent and a hospital administrative assistant had required her to dress professionally every day. She had often shopped at Dillard's and had acquired an expensive wardrobe with accessories to match; she favored tailored suits in black.

Bill also dressed well, making quite a visual impression at five feet eleven inches tall, and although he was a little on the thin side, his hair had never faded to gray.

Jo Ann thought that she and Bill must have once looked like a real-life Mattel Barbie and Ken; standing side-by-side, they made a handsome, well-dressed couple, and they took pride in being physically fit. However, for years, they secretly had spent more money than they earned. Anyone who knew the Turners since the late 1980s would not have suspected that a foreclosure lurked in their future.

By aligning herself with Richard McLaren and the ROT, Jo Ann once had hoped to prevent her family from losing everything they owned. She realized now that the collaboration had only served to expedite the inevitable.

■ ■ ■

As the sun began to set over the majestic peaks of the Davis Mountains on Saturday, April 26, 1997, wide ragged ribbons of purple, crimson, and yellow spread across the horizon. Silhouettes of ponderosa, pinyon pine, oak, and juniper trees dotted the ancient volcanic peaks at their mile-high elevations. In the valley below lay grasslands filled with wildlife: scrub jays, white-wing doves, curve-billed thrashers, and rock squirrels.

A lapis-colored twilight sky had descended upon the scene to provide spectacular views of Jupiter and its moons, of Venus, Saturn, and the Milky Way. Temperatures in the Davis Mountain Resort (DMR) fell to a crisp thirty-four degrees that night, promising a late spring snow. Inside the home of Joe and Margaret Ann "M.A." Rowe, the couple celebrated Joe's birthday with their son, Mikel, and Mikel's wife, Jennifer.

The Rowes had mentioned to Mikel their suspicions that earlier in the day while they were out shopping, someone had illegally entered their home on Tomahawk Trail. Upon their return, things had just seemed slightly disarranged.

Years earlier, the Rowes had built their two-story adobe brick and wood-beam home by hand with the help of a few craftsmen who had traveled daily one hundred miles from across the Mexican border. Their home stood on a peak along a twenty-one-mile-long and twisting road near the entrance to the DMR overlooking the Chihuahuan Desert,[2] the largest desert in North America.

At fifty-two years old, Rowe had retired from a twenty-six-year career working for Shell Pipeline Company. He enjoyed spending his days reading, smoking cigarettes, collecting guns, and living off the grid. Standing about five feet eight inches tall, with a shock of shaggy gray hair that fell to his shoulders, Rowe often dressed in Levis and a dark T-shirt layered beneath a flannel shirt worn like a jacket to obscure his slight frame. The Rowes kept to themselves, like most of their neighbors who lived in trailer houses or ramshackle structures scattered along the DMR's dirt roads.

However, for several months, McLaren and his ROT group had bothered the Rowes with frequent military-like maneuvers on adjoining properties. Shortly before sundown on this April day, Rowe spotted some ROT members dressed in camouflage uniforms and armed with rifles pointed at him just along the ridge above his home.

"They had their rifles and their telescopes and binoculars, and they were lookin' down this way, obviously examining the goin' ons," Rowe said.[3]

At that time, Dan Alexander owned the property behind the Rowes' home, but Joe Rowe knew that the house was empty. The Rowes had made a neighborly agreement to watch Alexander's property during his absences. When they saw the ROT members with guns, Joe and Mikel Rowe jumped into Joe's pickup and headed up the hill toward Alexander's house. At the top of the hill, the Rowe men confronted some ROT members standing near their vehicles.

"I hollered at them. I told them, 'Y'all get your Republic of Texas asses off of Dan Alexander's property and get out of here,'" Joe said.

"They hollered something back, and I said, 'Get your asses off this property. I'm gonna call the law.' Then I turned around and drove off."

Joe recognized a white van as the same he had seen frequently driving up and down the road in front of his home toward the ROT's headquarters. He drove home immediately to telephone his friend Steve Bailey, the Jeff Davis County sheriff.

Rowe recounted the phone call: "I said, 'This crap has gone on long enough. You keep comin' out here and saying there's nothing I can do about it. You've got a search warrant, but you ain't got but one deputy and I don't expect you to go up there in that canyon where they've got those booby traps and those trip wires and there's fifteen or twenty people up there with automatic weapons. But they do come out, and when they come out, you ought to damn well arrest them if that ain't too much to ask.'"

Rowe told Bailey that he suspected that Los Angeles transplant Gregg Paulson[4] and his German wife, Karen, had violated the rules and regulations of the National Firearms Act[5] by modifying their semiautomatic weapons with trigger housings that enabled a rapid-fire assault.

Only days before, Rowe recalled, Bailey had said he would search and arrest any member of the ROT if he caught one driving outside the resort. Finally, the opportunity arrived during the early morning hours of April 27. While he was still on the phone with Bailey, Rowe could see from his living-room window that the white van had stopped along the road in front of his home and that a man had exited. The driver stopped to replace his license plate before driving toward town.

Afterward, as Rowe listened to his police scanner, he learned that at the intersection of State Highways 166 and 17, Sheriff Bailey had arrested the van's driver.

"Boy, that started a bunch of the most confusing radio traffic you ever heard in your life," Joe said.

For years Joe had served in the DMR as a member of the volunteer fire department and, along with M.A., the emergency ambulance service. Their home's position at the top of a hill provided excellent reception for interdepartmental emergency communications by way of a police radio they operated. A time or two, the Rowes had provided backup dispatch communications for the local DMR ambulance service.

Members of the ROT likewise operated a police scanner and radio from inside their headquarters. The Rowes reasoned that whatever they heard broadcast over the radio, the ROT members had likely heard the same dispatches.

Over the police radio, they heard Bailey call a dispatcher in Marfa who provided emergency communications for the entire tri-county area of Jeff Davis, Brewster, and Presidio counties. The sheriff announced that he had stopped an ROT member, identified as Robert Scheidt, at the intersection of State Highways 166 and 17.

Simultaneously listening to their ham radio, the Rowes also overheard the familiar voice of Rick McLaren, the ambassador of the ROT, speaking from the group's headquarters. McLaren instructed his ROT members to raid the empty Jeff Davis County Courthouse where he said the sheriff and his deputies would take Scheidt. Unbeknownst to McLaren and his followers that Sunday, the courthouse remained closed. As a result, Bailey's deputies did not take Scheidt to the courthouse but to the Presidio County Jail in Marfa.[6]

"I heard Bailey say, 'I want some backup; I've got a man on the ground'—to him that meant, 'I've got him out of the car,'" Rowe said.

ROT members listening to the radio talk at their own headquarters likely interpreted Bailey's words to mean that he had shot Scheidt. To add to a string of confusing garble, Texas Ranger David Duncan contacted the same dispatcher to request a coroner at the scene of a traffic fatality. Duncan referred to an unrelated single-car crash off US Highway 67 that had occurred a few hours earlier in Presidio County.

"About that time, we heard somebody on the radio say, 'When's the coroner gonna get here?'" Rowe said.

As soon as Rowe heard the word *coroner* over the radio, he also heard McLaren call his men back to the ROT headquarters and cancel orders to attack the local courthouse. What he heard next led him to take the ROT members' communications personally.

"He said, 'Come back. Come back. We're going to change our plans, change our strategy,'" Rowe said. "'Take the place; do what you gotta do, but she's okay.'"

From listening to months of the ROT's amateur radio talk, Rowe understood the talk as a type of code. Rowe interpreted McLaren's reference to "the place" as the Rowes' homestead and the reference to "she" to mean Joe's wife, M.A.

About then, Rowe remembers hearing his blue heeler, Luca, get up from the porch and bark "an odd bark." Next, he heard the sound of car tires on the gravel road directly in front of his house.

"People come and go out here all the time, and Luca loves nearly everybody, except for the few ones that she don't like—she don't like. She's a damn good judge of character," Joe said.

He opened the front door a crack of perhaps eight inches, enough to see through the bronze-tinted glass storm door. A bit of snow lightly covered the ground outside in the yard. Parked in the driveway, he saw an abandoned white Jeep Eagle.

Suddenly, Joe saw Gregg Paulson come right up to the edge of the porch and kneel. Paulson and his wife, Karen, both wore military-style camouflage fatigues and boots. As Karen crept around to the back of the Rowes' house, she began peering into the living-room windows. No sooner had the two Paulsons taken up their positions than a late model Volkswagen bug came speeding down the road toward the Rowes' house.

The driver hit the brakes abruptly in front of a radio antenna tower located just a few yards from the residence. Out jumped a boyish-looking nineteen-year-old, Richard Keyes, who quickly crouched behind the Rowes' pickup truck. Rowe saw that both men pointed modified automatic weapons at him where he stood in his home's doorway.

"Gregg Paulson was down behind that rail out there, and I stood right inside the door, and he hollered at me. He said, 'We come to take the place,'" Rowe said.

"I said, 'Get your ass outta here and go back and tell Rick I don't want nothin' to do with you.' He said, 'We've come to take you.' And I said, 'I don't want to be taken; get your ass outta here.' He said, 'We're armed and there are more of us than there are of you.' And I said, 'I can see that.'"

However, Rowe had enjoyed collecting a wide range of pistols, including a 9 mm, which he held in his hands as he stood just inside the entrance to his home's mudroom.

"The nine millimeter had a white dot on the sight, and I set that white dot right between Paulson's eyes. He said, 'There's more of us than there are you.' I said, 'I know that, but I've got you.' And he said, 'I see that.' He knew that I had that pistol, and I was looking at him right between the damn eyes."

Rowe also noticed that Gregg Paulson held a semiautomatic 7.62 SKS[7] that had been modified to operate as fully automatic. "If you pull the trigger one time, it will give you a three-round burst, *blrrrt*—three shots. No clicking—just three shots, fully automatic. And the SKS was kind of the militia people's weapon of choice," Rowe said.

As he held his gun on Paulson, Rowe called to his dog, which still stood on the front porch between himself and Paulson. "I'd read their ROT manual, see. I know exactly what their procedure is supposed to be. It says very plainly: 'In a hostage situation, if pets are involved, you neutralize the pets,'" Rowe said.

"Luca walked off the porch, and I saw him [Paulson] kind of look. I said, 'I'll lay my pistol down if you won't shoot my dog.' He said, 'Okay.'"

Just inside the home's front door stood a cat's scratching post. Rowe moved away from the storm door briefly to lay his pistol down on the post. As he did so, the light coming from the bathroom window behind him betrayed his position. His silhouette moved ever so slightly as to provide Paulson a target, albeit a moving one. Suddenly, Paulson fired.

"He gave me the three-round burst," Rowe said. "I'm not a very big target and I tried to move as far as I could away from that doorway."

Paulson fired three shots that shattered the Rowes' storm door. The first bullet passed through Rowe's upper arm and lodged in the doorframe behind him, a second bullet exited through the wall above Rowe, and a third crashed through the glass shower door in the bathroom behind him.

"Then the glass—and we're talkin' about the glass out of the storm door, a double-pane window—the glass goddamn was everywhere," Rowe said. "There was glass and little pieces of wood, pieces of aluminum off that door frame, and there was just crap goin' everywhere. I thought I was dead because all that stuff hit me—some of it hit me in the face, then the shoulder. It hit me in the chest, and this damn wound here started bleedin'."

For a second, Joe thought that perhaps a second shooter might have fired from behind him through the bathroom window to cause the shower's glass door to explode. M.A. ran to the phone in the kitchen and dialed nine-one-one. Once the dispatcher answered, she began screaming, "They're shootin' in the house; they've shot my husband. He's hurt."

Keyes then entered the Rowes' house armed with an AR-15,[8] a popular hunting rifle, and quickly snatched the phone out of M.A.'s hands. Next, both Gregg and Karen Paulson entered the residence.

"They had me fairly well subdued, and they came stormin' in," Joe said. "Here comes Karen circlin' back around. They stomped in with mud all over their feet. Here comes Richard Keyes, just jumpin' up and down all hyper—hyper as a bunny rabbit. M.A. started eatin' their asses out for tromping mud in on her clean floor."

Next, M.A. sprang into action to stop her husband's bleeding while the Paulsons held their guns on the Rowes. Joe Rowe was bleeding profusely. He had suffered a heart attack in early February that same year, and a doctor had prescribed Coumadin, a medicine used to prevent blood clots and stroke. The blood thinner contributed to the amount of blood loss Joe experienced that day.

M.A. put a compress on her husband's arm, tied a towel around it, and stopped the bleeding. Then she led Joe upstairs to the loft to help him to sit him down in a recliner.

Karen Paulson and Richard Keyes immediately went to separate bathrooms, downstairs and upstairs, to begin storing water in the bathtubs. Afterward, Gregg Paulson came upstairs to gain a commanding view of the site where the two state highways intersect less than a mile away. Upstairs, he found Rowe's spotters' telescope,[9] and he used it to conduct surveillance on the road leading into the DMR.

Paulson also began gathering up Rowe's gun collection and placing the weapons on top of a chair in the den. However, he did not ask Rowe to unlock the safe that held the rifles. Still inside the house, Keyes took a .32 caliber pistol from the Rowes' pile of weapons and put it in his back pocket. Then he went outside and started the Jeep Eagle. He positioned the car sideways across the cattle guard to block the road, then shot out the Jeep's tires.

"He done shot the tires out of their get-away car," Joe said. "Keyes comes back inside the house wiping his hands, saying, 'I done it, boss.' Gregg asked, 'What's all that shootin'?' Keyes said, 'I shot the tires out.'"

Keyes then proceeded to use the Rowes' landline telephone to make some personal calls.

"After Keyes made his big move on the car, he got on the phone, and he started callin'. He was from Kansas, and he called I guess everybody he knew from grade school on up," Rowe said.

The Rowes would later learn that Keyes had telephoned members of his own family across the country to tell them about the drama unfolding in the Davis Mountains.

Paulson told his wife to come upstairs and to "keep a lookout" for anyone who might attempt to drive toward the house on the road, Rowe said.

Meanwhile, Texas Ranger David Duncan had called Captain Caver in Midland and asked him to come out to the Wofford Ranch, located about five miles from the Rowes' homestead. At the same time, Deputy Pat Reyna, from Valentine, Texas, came charging up the road leading to the Rowes' house in his patrol car but stopped short of the cattle guard when he could go no farther.

"Richard Keyes stepped up to the front door, pulled out his rifle, and said, 'I've got him, I've got him, I've got him,'" Rowe said. "Paulson shouted to Keyes, 'Don't shoot him; don't shoot him.' About that time, Pat had the sense to go back down that hill and turn around and get out of here, and boy, I'm glad he did."

After the Paulsons took control of the Rowe house, Gregg dispatched Keyes to strip the Texas flag off the flagpole in the yard.

"I always said, 'If that Texas flag ain't flyin,' I've got a problem,'" Joe Rowe said.

As the afternoon waned, both the Paulsons and Keyes announced that they wanted something to eat. M.A. had prepared a huge lasagna the night before and now offered it to her captors.

Meanwhile, Rowe began to sense that Keyes didn't like women, especially women who were as assertive as M.A. "My .32 automatic ended up layin' on that bar, and every time M.A. would come and go, she would look at it. That's what Richard Keyes did—I know in my mind he laid it there hoping she would use it, giving him a reason to kill her," Rowe said.

However, M.A. did not attempt to retrieve her husband's pistol. Instead, Rowe began talking to Paulson about Rick McLaren. Paulson talked about how much he really disliked Rick as a person but told Rowe that he agreed with the philosophy of the ROT.

"I could tell he was gettin' worried about me because he wanted me to live. He didn't want me to die because then we're talkin' about murder," Joe said.

The Rowes asked Paulson if their friend, Jerry Rhea, could deliver a medical jump kit to treat Joe's traumatic injuries, and he agreed. M.A. immediately called the dispatcher to ask for the jump kit and some bandages for her husband to be delivered to the house.

Rhea,[10] who served as DMR volunteer chief of the fire department and as the DMR's emergency medical services (EMS) technician, answered the call. Rhea also spoke to Paulson on the two-way radio usually reserved for the fire department.

"The agreement was that I could come up there and that he wouldn't shoot me," Rhea said.

Rhea said he drove the ambulance with his wife, Karen, in the passenger seat along with EMS attendants Larry and Linda Sims. At that time, none of them really knew much about the hostage situation other than that a small group of ROT members held the Rowes against their will and that possibly Joe Rowe had been shot.

Naturally, the Rangers needed to know Rowe's condition as well as how many people were in his house and how heavily armed they were. Rhea became their primary source of that information.

Rhea had met Gregg Paulson earlier that year; the man had introduced himself as "Sergeant Paulson." Other than Rhea, few residents in the resort knew anything about him. Rhea lived about three miles from the Rowes' house where it stood near the cattle guard at the entrance to the resort. As part of his job as volunteer fire chief and an EMT Rhea roamed all over the fifty-plus miles of dirt roads within the ten-thousand-acre resort when he wasn't working as a dirt contractor.

Often when first-time visitors arrived at the DMR, Rhea offered them directions to McLaren's property. Many didn't know how to find the ROT leader's house. Rhea always identified himself to strangers as the volunteer fire chief in a friendly way that earned their trust. Now he hoped that the ROT members would not shoot him. Rhea grabbed the jump kit and left his wife and the Sims couple inside the ambulance, parked down the road from the Rowes' house.

"I had to kiss my wife goodbye, because all I knew for sure when I left the ambulance with the jump kit was, I was going to meet a fella who was holding two people hostage, and I didn't know for sure if I was coming back," Rhea said.

With the jump kit in hand, Rhea slowly walked up the road to the Rowes' house. When he knocked on the Rowes' front door, Paulson came to the door, opened it, and stuck out his rifle. Touching the end of the rifle to Rhea's forehead, Paulson said, "No funny business."

"I repeated 'No funny business.' When I said that, he moved the rifle away from my head. From that point on, he never pointed it at me again. I took that to mean that he and I had an agreement. I was there to check on the Rowes' condition—between me and him, that's what I was there for, and also I wouldn't attempt to overpower him, and he would allow me to come into the house and do what I was there for—to check on the Rowes."

Rhea entered the home in front of Paulson, and they walked through the kitchen into the living room. He saw the pistol lying on the kitchen counter and walked right past it.

Next, he saw Joe and M.A. sitting on the couch in the living room. Rhea went right to Joe and asked how he was feeling. Joe answered that he was "doin' all right." M.A. had bandaged her husband's arm and had set it inside a homemade sling. When Rhea unwound the bandages, he saw that M.A., aided by her certified EMT-basic training, had successfully stopped the bleeding.

Rhea stayed at the Rowes' house for less than one hour. While he expressed concern about Joe's prescribed use of the blood thinner Coumadin, Rhea realized his patient wasn't in any immediate danger.

"I offered to stay in M.A.'s place and let her go out, but she didn't want to. I did give her the opportunity. I told her I could stay," he said. "She didn't want to go. She said she wanted to stay with Joe, and I said okay."

When Rhea asked Paulson if he could leave, Paulson followed right behind him. "He was right there with me the whole time, but never pointing a gun at me, but he was right there behind me—with his long rifle is what I call it. He had it cradled in his arms. He had it right at the ready, but he never again pointed it at me," Rhea said. "Him and I had a gentleman's agreement; it was between him and me, and he kept his part of the bargain and I kept mine."

Rhea left the Rowes' house, returned to the ambulance with Karen and the Sims still waiting inside, and they drove back down the road to the Wofford Ranch, the new command center for the Texas Rangers. For the next nine days, Rhea would sleep in his ambulance nearby, always at the ready.

Close to sundown, Rowe asked Paulson if he could go outside to feed his dog, Luca. Rowe also wanted to put his dog inside a kennel where she usually stayed at night when the temperatures outside dropped. Paulson called Karen downstairs, and she accompanied Rowe outside as he placed Luca in her kennel.

"Karen marched right along beside me carrying that rifle. She said, 'If you try anything, I'll kill you.' I said, 'I don't have any doubt in my mind lady.' I said, 'Besides that, I can't run very well with one arm,'" Joe said.

"I fed Luca and petted her and told her everything was going to be all right. I turned around and came back inside the house."

Afterward, Paulson began to talk about how he created wooden flutes, and then he gave one wrapped in a little bag as a gift to M.A.

Later that evening, Joe attempted to reason with Gregg Paulson.

"I was trying to talk Gregg Paulson into giving up. I said, 'You're not gonna win. You're not gonna get out of here without going to jail unless you're killed. Out here you're either gonna get killed, or you're gonna go to jail,'" Rowe said. "Gregg kept telling me 'I can't leave my men.'"

At about one o'clock in the morning on April 28, by telephone, Captain Caver negotiated the Rowes' release with Paulson in exchange for Robert Scheidt's release from the Marfa jail.

They planned for Scheidt to drive his van up the road past the Rowes' house and honk three times to signal the Paulsons and Keyes that he was headed back to the ROT embassy. Once Scheidt cleared the Rowes' property, the Paulsons and Keyes would follow.

One small problem with the plan remained: Keyes earlier had shot out the tires on the Paulsons' Jeep Eagle. Paulson had decided Keyes' Volkswagen bug wouldn't suffice to carry them all and their gear up the hill to the ROT headquarters. Rowe remembers listening to the two ROT members argue about their escape plan.

At the top of the stairs, Paulson started stuffing duffle bags—seven total, with all of their gear—and he began delivering orders. Rowe offered to document the fact that they were leaving him alive by videotaping their departure, and Paulson agreed.

Then, because Keyes' Volkswagen bug would not start, Paulson asked Rowe if he could borrow his 1987 Ford 150 pickup truck. The Paulsons and Keyes planned to drive Rowe's pickup up the hill to a country store where Scheidt would be waiting in his van. There they would leave Rowe's pickup locked with the keys inside. Then they would load all their gear into Scheidt's van and drive on to the ROT embassy.

9

Day One
Standoff at the ROT Embassy

WHEN THE media stopped bothering Jo Ann Turner, she felt perplexed. She wondered why so many journalists had seemingly lost interest in her just hours after their constant pestering with requests for interviews.[1]

The answer revealed itself on April 27, 1997, inside the Travis County Correctional Complex in Del Valle. She and her fellow prisoners watched a small television mounted near the ceiling of the common room in the women's cellblock. In disbelief, Jo Ann observed as the scenes unfolded in a series of graphic and sensational news reports broadcast live from the Davis Mountains.

Before that day, the daily news had provided her with a mental escape from her cell in the rundown housing unit that suffered from recurring electrical and plumbing issues.[2] The vapors emanating from her unwashed fellow inmates, who lacked basic hygiene supplies such as shampoo and tampons, had become constant offenses to Jo Ann. She suffered in silence while her eyes attempted to focus on the broadcasts.

On camera, reporters held their microphones aloft while interviewing a feisty sheriff with gray hair and a gray mustache as he described his arrest of a member of the Republic of Texas (ROT) militia. At the mention of the ROT group, Jo Ann began to feel woozy. Immediately, she employed a tactic that she had learned as a child whenever she had to deal with difficult situations: she mentally traveled to another place. She allowed her memories to transport her from her present surroundings, back in time to one of the Turner family's only vacations taken outside of the country. She visualized Las Brisas, the resort built on a lush forty-acre tropical island paradise overlooking Acapulco Bay. Her daughter, Kelly, at that time had been just six months old, so Jo Ann, Bill, and their son Jeff had left in silence baby Kelly behind in Texas for a couple of weeks to be cared for by a professional babysitter.

The Turners had stayed in one of the little casitas at the famous hotel built on the site of an old fort. The cottages each provided its own private pool, cabana, and courtyard filled with hibiscus flowers. Outside their hotel room each morning, the staff had set up a breakfast table filled with deliciously strong coffee and goat's milk and all kinds of delicate pastries that looked almost too good to eat.

One day, Bill had rented a pink Jeep, and although the owners of the rental store had warned him not to drive outside of the city limits, he ended up getting the family lost in the suburbs. He accidentally drove to another town just outside Acapulco. When Bill finally realized his mistake, he turned the Jeep around. However, as they returned to their hotel, the jungle-like vegetation on both sides of the road, together with the huts and poorly constructed housing on the town's outskirts, frightened the Turners. That trip out of the country would be the last for any Turner family members for the next twenty-two years.

A raucous response by the other inmates in the cellblock at the mention of her name during the television broadcast brought Jo Ann back to reality. The women around her began shouting, "Jo Ann, Jo Ann, Jo Ann," in unison. Suddenly, the severity of the events being reported in the Davis Mountains delivered a new overwhelming fear to her. Secretly, she promised herself that should she ever be released from jail, she would convince her family members to flee the United States in order to escape prosecution.

■ ■ ■

On Sunday morning, April 27, 1997, the phone rang at around ten thirty in the Fort Davis home of Jeff Davis County Sheriff Steve Bailey[3] as he prepared waffles and pancakes for his family.

"I was gettin' ready to go to church," Bailey said.

Joe Rowe had telephoned Bailey to tell him that he had seen members of the ROT militia armed with automatic weapons in the hills across the road from his house. Rowe often had reported to Bailey about the group's comings and goings.

As soon as he hung up with Rowe, Bailey dressed and jumped into his sheriff's car and drove toward town. Just outside of Fort Davis, Bailey stopped a white van driven by Robert Scheidt, then a known member of the ROT, on State Highway 17 near its intersection with State Highway 166.

"He was probably nervous because I had my M-16 out,[4] full rock 'n' roll, and I was telling him what all I'd do to him and his mother and all his relatives and everything else because—the main reason was—because I didn't want to get killed and them guys was a bunch of nuts," Bailey said.

Inside Scheidt's van, he had left several guns exposed, including an SKS, a classic semiautomatic rifle, and an AK-47, a Soviet assault rifle.[5] Immediately, Bailey handcuffed Scheidt and radioed the Presidio County Sheriff's office dispatcher that he had made an arrest. About that time, the police radio began broadcasting some three-way chatter between the dispatcher and Texas Highway Patrol officer Mike Campbell, whose responsibilities covered Jeff Davis, Presidio, and Brewster counties.

At the time, Campbell told Bailey that he had been en route to investigate a fatal accident that had occurred the day before when a car driven by a retired Border Patrol agent ran off the road south of Marfa. He asked Bailey if he could borrow a camera to photograph the accident scene.

Just as he prepared to load Scheidt into his patrol car, Bailey used his police radio to call the Jeff Davis County dispatcher when he simultaneously happened to overhear a female voice break into the dispatcher's broadcast. The woman's loud voice rang clear in the ambient background sound of the dispatcher's office although it came from a telephone speaker. Bailey listened intently as she identified herself as a resident of the Davis Mountain Resort (DMR) and told the county dispatcher that someone had been shot inside her home. Bailey recognized the voice on the phone's speaker as Margaret Ann Rowe, known locally as "M.A."

"M.A. was on the phone screamin' at me and the dispatcher, sayin', 'They're breakin' in, and they've already shot Joe,'" Bailey said. "She was screamin', 'Get my sheriff out here; get my sheriff.'"

While this confusing three-way cross-communication occurred, Buster Mills, owner of the Limpia Creek Hat Shop in Fort Davis, happened to be driving down the same stretch of road where Bailey arrested Scheidt on State Highway 17 near its intersection with State Highway 166.

When Mills stopped to ask the sheriff if he needed some help, Bailey gave him his AR-50, a single-shot bolt-action rifle,[6] to guard Scheidt until another Texas Highway Patrol officer arrived. Bailey told Scheidt to sit down inside the bar ditch located just off the roadway. The sheriff then deputized Mills on the spot.

"I said to Buster, 'If Scheidt or anybody else gives you any problems, kill 'em all.' I said, 'Just pull the trigger,' and I was dead serious too," Bailey said.

Bailey also handed Mills a couple of twenty-round clips, or "banana clips," slang for a curved large-capacity magazine taped together and loaded with ammunitions for an automatic weapon.

Once back on the road, Bailey passed Texas Game Warden Randall Brown who also had just overheard the county dispatcher's broadcast. Bailey dispatched Brown to assist Mills, and Brown then proceeded at high speed onto State Highway 166. With his vehicle's lights flashing on top of his game warden pickup, Brown drove toward the spot where Mills still held a gun on Scheidt. Next, Bailey contacted Jimmy Lujan, who drove a wrecker/tow truck for Jeff Davis County. Bailey asked Lujan to pick up Scheidt's van.

After Brown secured Scheidt, he transported his prisoner to the Presidio County Jail in Marfa because Jeff Davis County did not have a jail. All the law enforcement agencies within the Fort Davis area, including Jeff Davis, Brewster, and Presidio counties at that time, shared the same frequency on their radio repeaters. Three Texas Rangers stationed in West Texas provided coverage in several counties that total an area about the size of South Carolina.

Texas Ranger David Duncan of Alpine had been en route to an accident site north of Presidio when he heard some of the same radio conversation about the home invasion on his state pickup radio. Duncan had intended to respond to a call by Presidio County Sheriff Danny Dominguez regarding a retired Texas Border Patrol agent who had died just north of Presidio. The agent had been hauling a load of pipe and had run off the road the night before on US 67.

Duncan never made it to his destination near Presidio. As soon as he heard about a home invasion in Jeff Davis County, he called Dominguez and told him that he had a change of plans and would be heading over to the Rowes' house.[7]

When Duncan arrived at the scene, he found that Campbell, a Texas Highway Patrol officer stationed in Marfa, had already positioned himself along Friend Ranch Road just south of the DMR cattle guard fence line, out of sight from the Rowes' house. Within minutes, Bailey pulled up behind the two men. Campbell told Duncan that there he discovered an abandoned and disabled car blocking the road in front of the Rowes' house.

Duncan telephoned his supervisor, Captain Barry Caver, in Midland because he knew that Caver had some experience commanding an armed siege. Caver previously had worked as an investigator of the scene following a fifty-one-day standoff (February 28 to April 19, 1993) between law enforcement and the Branch Davidians outside their compound in Waco.[8] Caver's primary job in Waco initially through telephone interviews with various Branch Davidians had been to help investigate the murders of four ATF agents before the Branch Davidians' compound burned to the ground.

"The fact that having been there and seeing how it eventually turned out was a 'black eye' on the federal government, especially with the FBI—my main goal was not to allow my situation in Fort Davis to end that way. It needed to end peacefully and solve the problem and for all of us to go home at the end of the day," Caver said.[9]

At thirty-nine years old, Caver was the youngest person ever to have served as a Texas Ranger captain, a job he had held for only six months before the Fort Davis siege began. On that first day in the Davis Mountains, Caver himself conducted all of the initial negotiations with ROT members by phone or by police radio before assigning the task to another Texas Ranger, Jess Malone. Afterward, Caver would become the commander of the siege.

The Rowes' house stands just inside the DMR, about four miles north of State Highway 166 on Tomahawk Trail and just a few miles beyond a home owned by former Texas Border Patrol agent Johnny Wofford and his wife, Mary Lynn, on the Paradise Ranch.

After losing his battle to claim the Woffords' land a few years earlier,

Richard McLaren focused his attention instead on the Rowes' property. The distance from the Rowes' house to where McLaren's ROT headquarters spans a good five miles along a road that winds and twists northward from a lower to a higher elevation.

Members of the ROT had long suspected that Joe and M.A. Rowe had alerted local authorities of their daily operations. The ROT members likely also blamed the Rowes for Scheidt's arrest and his suspected death at the hands of Sheriff Bailey.

"He [McLaren] thought that I had killed Robert Scheidt, and I think that he told Karen and them other guys to attack the 'headquarters,' as he called it, which was M.A. and Joe Rowe's house," Bailey said.

Bailey said he hired a reserve deputy, Joaquin Jackson, who had made a name for himself during the previous twenty-seven years as a Texas Ranger fighting against drug smugglers, rapists, and murderers. In 1993, when the Texas Department of Public Safety for the first time began hiring women to serve as Texas Rangers, Jackson, in protest, had quit his job, a position previously held only by men.[10] Jackson's career as Bailey's reserve deputy would be short-lived.

"He was arrogant, smoked a cigar, cussed, was a chauvinist, and was rough around the edges, but he was there when I needed him. I mean, I could call him and he would be there as quick as he could get there. He would work on a class C case like a parking ticket all the way up to a murder," Bailey said.

However, the reserve deputy quit his new job on that first day of the siege following an argument with Bailey. Jackson would eventually work as a self-employed private investigator until September 2016.[11] Before Jackson's death, former Texas governor Ann Richards would endorse his 2005 autobiographical book, *One Ranger. A Memoir*.

On the evening of April 27, Bailey phoned his three sons and his wife, Barbara, to let them know he wouldn't be home that night for supper. Then he called his mother, Audrey Laverne Bailey, to ask her to drive from her home in Monahans to care for his family. The sheriff told them all that he expected to sleep very little in the next twenty-four hours, but he promised to take short naps in the back seat of his patrol car.

Captain Caver and Midland Highway Patrol Captain David Baker flew by helicopter from Midland and landed at a ranch a few miles west of the DMR. They did not fly directly to the DMR because McLaren and some of his followers at Joe and M.A. Rowe's house had demanded that aircraft be kept out of the area, Duncan said.

US Deputy Marshal Paula Evans had previously arrested McLaren on outstanding warrants prior to this incident so she and the Texas Rangers anticipated all possible scenarios. Because they had already conducted background and intelligence work regarding the ROT group, they advised against provoking McLaren.

Caver also recognized Bailey as the Jeff Davis County Sheriff who had sought his help three months earlier when the local lawman had made a special trip to Midland out of feelings of frustration. Previously, Bailey alone had been tasked with dealing with an armed militia in Jeff Davis County, an area of land with more than 2,265 square miles inhabited by just 1,946 registered residents.[12]

"It was just a matter of time before something blew up," Caver said. "ROT people were coming in there to the resort at Fort Davis on the weekends to do their target practice, and groups would assemble to discuss their antigovernment beliefs. He knew something was in the works."

Immediately, Caver and other Texas Rangers set up a command post at the Woffords' house. The Texas Rangers used the Woffords' front yard and spare bedrooms along with a landline phone to begin negotiations with ROT members.

Department of Public Safety media chief Mike Cox soon arrived in Fort Davis to serve as a liaison between the press and law enforcement officials. Representatives from CNN, NBC, ABC, KTRH Radio in Houston, WBAP Radio in Dallas-Fort Worth, Channel 4 in Dallas, WOAI Radio in San Antonio, and National Public Radio contacted Cox to get the scoop on happenings in the Davis Mountains.

"From the media standpoint, this was a dream story: everyone was talking—the bad guys (with plenty of threatening rhetoric), the good guys (we weren't saying much, of course), and virtually everyone else reporters could get in touch with who had some kind of take on the situation. Neighbors and various other county residents freely offered their comments," Cox states in his book *Stand-Off in Texas*: *"Just Call Me a Spokesman for DPS."*[13] The media soon mobilized at a roadside picnic area known as the Point of Rocks.[14]

Caver sent Duncan and two other Texas Rangers, Johnny Allen from

Del Rio and Coy Smith from Uvalde, to retrieve Scheidt from the Presidio Jail in Marfa where he was being held. By phone, Caver contacted the ROT members in McLaren's trailer and began negotiating with them to exchange Scheidt for the Rowes. In the short time it took to deliver Scheidt to the command post, the number of law enforcement representatives at the siege had doubled.

"We put a stocking cap over his head (Scheidt's) so he couldn't see if we were really going to release him or what we were going to do. I think we kept it over his head as long as he was out and around," Duncan said. "He [Scheidt] couldn't really see what kind of response had been assembled or how many assets we had."

They planned to make the exchange sometime between midnight on the first day and two in the morning on the second day, April 28.

Cox mentions in his book that McLaren spoke that night on WOAI Radio in San Antonio, a Clear Channel, fifty-thousand-watt AM station that broadcasts nationwide. McLaren told reporter Tracee Evans that the "prisoners of war" would be released if two ROT prisoners were freed.

McLaren identified Robert Jonathan Scheidt and Jo Ann Turner, who had been arrested in Austin the week before. He said that the ROT group had taken the Rowes hostage in retaliation for Turner's and Scheidt's arrests.[15]

The radio show served to further sensationalize the events unfolding in the Davis Mountains. Wofford recalls that his then sixteen-year-old son, Jake, shared in the growing excitement about what was happening in the family's front yard. "My son came in and he said, 'Dad, there's two helicopters with a rope and ninety-seven police cars parked out here,'" Wofford said.

Almost immediately, the Texas Rangers kept the media far away from the entrance to the DMR at the Point of Rocks roadside picnic area. Located seventeen miles south of the DMR, at an elevation of 5,560 feet, Point of Rocks often attracts rock climbers and serves as a destination for rappelling because of its unusually large boulders.

Within hours, the Wofford Ranch took on all the hallmark signs of a military command post as AT&T workers arrived to install fifteen drop lines for communications between the Texas Rangers, Border Patrol, the FBI, the DPS, and the State Guard and the National Guard, as well as elected local officials. The Texas Forest Service provided tents and other resources.

Then–US Attorney General Janet Reno[16] telephoned with a mandate for all federal and state law enforcement officers to clear the scene. "Janet Reno sent word down here that the US Border Patrol was to pull out. Well, we didn't work for Janet Reno; we worked for the Justice Department," Wofford said.

Wofford convinced the Texas Rangers to contact Governor George W. Bush as well. A series of phone calls resulted in an immediate response from the state's highest office. "I called our regional office in Dallas and had one of the associate regional commissioners contact the governor. In about forty-five minutes, the Border Patrol rolled right back in here," Wofford said.

Johnny Wofford had worked as a Border Patrol agent since 1980 and looked forward to retiring in 1998, at age fifty, from the Marfa Border Patrol Sector. The Marfa station covered forty-five hundred square miles, sixty-eight border miles, and spanned the northern portion of Presidio County and nearly all of Jeff Davis County. The Marfa Border Patrol Sector became known as the Big Bend Sector. US Customs and Border Protection did not exist when the Fort Davis event occurred; the department's creation arose from the 9/11 attacks in 2001. At the time, in 1997 the US Border Patrol served within the US Department of Immigration and Naturalization Service (INS) and under the US Department of Justice. The US Customs and Border Protection, created in 2003, today maintains the boundary between the United States and Mexico and ports of entry.[17]

Wofford's authority extended from the Rio Grande all the way through North Texas to the Panhandle, including the state of Oklahoma. Within the Border Patrol, his unit's responsibility included the capture and prosecution of illegal immigrants upon entry or re-entry after deportation as well as vehicle seizures under INS law. US Immigration and Customs Enforcement (ICE) would not be created until 2003.

10

Day Two
The Media Creates "Satellite City"

FROM INSIDE the Travis County women's complex, as Jo Ann watched the day's television news reports, a woman who earlier had identified herself only as Natasha approached Jo Ann. In her hands Natasha held the most recent edition of the *Austin American-Statesman*. From the expression on the woman's face, Jo Ann surmised that Natasha was not merely delivering the day's crossword puzzle as she usually did.[1] The newspaper's headline stopped Jo Ann's breath. For several minutes as she read, she seemingly could not exhale.

On page A6 of the newspaper appeared Jo Ann's own headshot photo taken days before in booking at Travis County Jail. As dark and imposing as her image looked, the headline above it capsulized the story for readers: "Militant separatists take 2 hostages."[2] Reporters for the *Austin American-Statesman* present at the standoff in the Davis Mountains described the scene as a war zone. A printed quote from Rick McLaren confirmed that depiction: "When they arrested her, (Turner) they enacted a declaration of war," McLaren reportedly had told a radio station WOAI announcer live on the air.

■ ■ ■

Captain Caver[3] called Texas Ranger Jess Malone[4] to assign him the title of chief negotiator at the siege. However, in the meantime, Caver decided to swap his ROT prisoner for the Rowes who were being held as hostages in their own home.

"There's an old saying that 'commanders don't negotiate, and negotiators don't command.' Captain Caver was the commander, but he negotiated briefly and very successfully and very brilliantly with Rick McLaren and the people inside of the Rowes' house," Malone said. "Normally in negotiations, you don't do prisoner swaps, but Captain Caver brilliantly—and I can't overemphasize that word—requested that the sheriff go ahead and release Scheidt early."

According to Malone, if the ROT members had avoided taking the Rowes' house, Scheidt likely would have been released by Bailey the next morning on a personal recognizance bond; he referred to any charges against Scheidt as "trivial." However, because the takeover of the Rowe house had occurred, McLaren had little choice but to agree to the terms set by Caver to swap both the Rowes for Scheidt. Under the terms of their agreement, however, Jo Ann Turner would remain jailed in Austin.

In the meantime, Captain Caver sent Johnny Allen, a Texas Ranger from Del Rio, and David Duncan to Marfa to pick up Scheidt to exchange him for the Rowes.

"We put a stocking cap over Scheidt's head so he couldn't see if we were really going to release him or what we were going to do. I think we kept it over his head as long as he was out and around so he couldn't really see what kind of response had been assembled or how many assets we had," Duncan said.[5]

When the Rangers released Scheidt, he went to his van and drove it into the DMR and stopped briefly at the Rowes' residence. He honked to alert the other ROT members inside the house to follow. Within seconds the Paulsons and Keyes followed Scheidt in Joe Rowe's pickup the ten or twelve miles up the road to McLaren's trailer.

As part of the plan, the Paulsons and Keyes had agreed to clear the Rowes' premises on one condition: "We sent an ambulance crew up there and they, the ROT members, insisted that ambulance personnel be stripped down basically to their underwear to make sure that they weren't a tactical squad or unit who went up there," Texas Ranger Jess

Malone said. "So, we swapped prisoners—Scheidt for Mr. and Mrs. Rowe—with some very good ambulance folks in their underwear."

Within fifteen minutes after the Paulsons and Keyes left the Rowes' home in the DMR, an ambulance driven by Mike Ward[6] and Cathy Beemann Ward pulled up just outside the Rowes' property. Mike Ward said that he stopped because he immediately noticed a Jeep Eagle with four flat tires blocking the road. Behind the ambulance, deputies Tom Brown, Matt Adams, and George Grubb[7] had followed. Ward recalls feeling tense when he arrived outside the Rowes' house. He saw M.A. talking on the telephone just inside the kitchen. He exited the ambulance and rushed through the Rowes' mudroom door immediately.

"I grabbed her and pulled her outside the door and off to the side with me, to behind the rock wall of the house," Ward said. "M.A. was obviously pretty shaken up."

Once the deputies entered the house to declare it all clear, both Mike and Cathy Ward entered to further tend to Joe Rowe's injuries.

"He was an old codger that night, and he was pissed about the whole thing. Other than that, he was in good spirits that everybody had left and that they were both safe," Ward said.

Ward then drove Joe and M.A. to the Big Bend Regional Medical Center in Alpine. There Dr. James D. Luecke treated Rowe's wounds. Dr. Luecke told Rowe he had defied medical science, first by surviving a heart attack and then by not bleeding to death during a gunfight. Luecke was the doctor who had prescribed Coumadin for Joe just months before.

Rowe[8] recalled the pain he felt watching the news broadcast from a television in his hospital room hurt worse than being shot. With M.A. beside him, Rowe watched CNN reports about the day's events. Some reporters said Rowe had not been shot; instead, they said that pieces of the door had cut into his arm when Paulson fired his gun. The scar left from a bullet-sized hole in the muscular area of Rowe's upper right arm remains exactly where it entered and then exited out the other side.

"What really hurt the most was a piece of shrapnel that hit the bone. It really hurt and hurt for a long time—that hurt worse than anything, probably," he said. "Then the small pieces of shrapnel in my face and in my chest hurt and stung like bee stings, I guess. That's a good analogy probably—each one of them felt like an individual bee sting."

Luecke kept Rowe at the hospital for twenty-four hours for observation but allowed him outside his hospital room occasionally to take cigarette breaks. Joe soon felt well enough to be discharged.

Jeff Davis County Sheriff deputies Tom Brown, Matt Adams, and others began calling residents throughout the DMR to ask them to evacuate, said former Jeff Davis Deputy Sheriff George Grubb.

After Keyes and the Paulsons retreated to the ROT embassy, the deputies started a house-to-house search throughout the resort between the Woffords' house and the fire station, Grubb said.

Upon his release from the hospital, Joe and M.A. would stay two days as guests in the home of Constable Jack Bell and his wife Elaine, who lived on Sleeping Lion Mountain.

■ ■ ■

Meanwhile, throngs of media began gathering in the Davis Mountains, once affectionately called "the Texas Alps," about ten miles west of Fort Davis on April 28, 1997, the second day of the standoff with the Republic of Texas militia.

Reporters and camera crews soon claimed the landmark granite outcrop of boulders devoid of trees or grass known as the Point of Rocks. The newly established communications hub had once served as the ancient campgrounds of Mescalero Apache, Comanche, and Kiowa tribes. The spot also once marked a stop along an old Spanish trail route for the Butterfield Overland Mail stagecoach line that ran from St. Louis to San Francisco during the late 1800s.[9] Its southeast boundary also abuts a historic military outpost defended by the famous, blue-coated African American Buffalo Soldiers during the Civil War.[10]

As the media assembled in trucks, tents, and travel trailers near the entrance to the Point of Rocks picnic area off Highway 166, Sheriff Bailey began to refer to the encampment as "Satellite City."

Carl Covington,[11] owner of Covington Enterprises, recalls installing West Texas Utility powerlines at the site for local and national media uplinks to network satellites. He said NBC, CBS, ABC, and CNN followed law enforcement officers to the scene. "They didn't have any power. There's no power anywhere—line voltage wise—so they were all using their generators," Covington said.

After twenty-four hours, members of the media had contacted West

Texas Utilities (WTU), the owner of most of the powerlines throughout the area. WTU hired Covington to set a pole in the midst of the parking lot at Point of Rocks to temporarily provide breaker boxes so that the media vehicles could connect to satellite cable and electricity.

Covington remained late into the evenings to offer his expertise onsite just in case the newly installed power source created any glitches.

"So, I got to sit in the satellite truck as the producers were all talking to newscasters, or the people who were on the mic. I got to see all of that taking place and conversations going on between – I think it was the NBC van – and the conversations going on between them and folks in New York, as the national broadcast was going out for the nightly news," Covington said. "It was pretty cool."

As members of the FBI arrived, Sheriff Bailey surrendered his authority willingly.[12] Four years earlier, on a seventy-seven-acre compound outside Waco, seventy-five men, women, and children had died at the end of a fifty-one-day standoff between federal agents and the Branch Davidians led by David Koresh.[13] Gary Noesner, a well-known FBI hostage negotiator who was present at Waco[14] and served as a remote consultant at Ruby Ridge[15] and the Montana Freemen[16] incidents, arrived at the DMR to voluntarily offer his services. Noesner would later write about the Fort Davis events in his book *Stalling for Time: My Life as an FBI Hostage Negotiator*.[17]

"The biggest impact Waco had on Fort Davis was it enabled me, having been there, to say to the [Texas] Rangers: 'Don't make the same mistakes we made.' You know, the FBI is not noted for its self-reflection or admission of fault. So, when they heard an FBI agent say, 'Hey, here's where we screwed up, and I want to make sure that you don't do the same thing,' I think it carried a lot of weight with them," Noesner said.[18]

Local law enforcement showed tremendous patience from the beginning of the siege, starting with Texas Ranger David Duncan who arrived on the scene first, Noesner said.

When Caver arrived, Duncan filled him in about the events leading up to the siege. Duncan had served in Fort Davis for nearly his whole twenty-plus-year career in law enforcement. Though he is somewhat older, Duncan had no qualms about allowing Caver to command the siege. In turn, Caver depended on Duncan's knowledge of the area, its residents, and the surrounding history involving the McLarens.

Caver realized from the start that McLaren and his followers might not give up without a fight despite any attempts to deescalate the situation.

"He [McLaren] felt very passionate about his interpretation of Texas having never been part of the United States, and the US government, and paying taxes were something they didn't have to pay attention to," Noesner said. "He surrounded himself with like-minded individuals who were passionate but not very well informed or educated. That can be a dangerous combination."

Two months earlier, Bailey had invited both Noesner and Al Brantley, an FBI profiler, to the Davis Mountain Resort (DMR) to assess what he considered a hostile situation developing in the Davis Mountains. Brantley had earned a reputation for analyzing criminals who suffered from mental illness and who had been identified as serial killers.[19]

At that time, the FBI knew little about McLaren, and Texas had not yet enacted laws to criminalize the type of bogus liens that he had filed against his DMR neighbors.

"That was part of the problem. We didn't have any legitimate charges we could use to arrest him until this particular thing happened," Caver said.

Noesner said that Caver and the Texas Rangers welcomed his advice.

"One of our pieces of advice—also learned from Waco—was 'Don't go in there and arrest these people. If you're gonna serve papers against them or undertake an arrest, wait until they come off the property. Don't create a siege,'" Noesner said.

McLaren had obtained three underdeveloped lots five miles up from Limpia Canyon Trail north of the Rowes' house by filing false property-claim liens on prior landowners at the Jeff Davis County Courthouse.[20] Once he began referring to his trailer and a lean-to on the property as his "embassy," McLaren also began attempts to reclaim the state of Texas. His followers, many unemployed, quickly began moving onto McLaren's property in trailer houses, ramshackle structures, and tents.

"He began to believe that he had more people supporting him than he did and his legal case was more righteous than it was, and that other countries would recognize his claims. I'm not saying he was psychotic, but he certainly was self-deluding himself of his importance and the power of their cause," Noesner said.

Instead of launching a full assault on McLaren's compound, Noesner suggested to law enforcement officials that they should attempt to discredit the ROT's leader by publishing a press release in the Marfa newspaper, *The Big Bend Sentinel*.

"It basically said that 'hey, the people that believe in McLaren's ideology always boast about the sanctity of someone's home as being their castle and sacrosanct,'" Noesner said. "'And here we have these people, taking over the home of a Texas family, invading the home and holding people hostage. The people of Texas demand that the government step in and prevent that.' So, it kind of put it in our perspective."

Ordnance disposal folks together with a bomb squad from Odessa and El Paso's Fort Bliss soon arrived. Arvin Kilpatrick, a retired Department of Public Safety (DPS) officer from Lubbock who specialized in auto theft investigations, offered to guard Bailey's home and family. Neither Kilpatrick nor Bailey trusted ROT members—they feared retaliation for the arrests of Scheidt and Turner.

For years, McLaren had represented a figurative thorn in the sides of DMR residents, and they wanted him gone. "I'd had run-ins with him," Bailey said. "All kinds of stuff. Everything from trespassin' to traffic tickets and they made their own license plates—the Republic of Texas—and he would call me 'the so-called sheriff.'"

Other residents had often complained to Bailey that ROT members fired live ammunition on McLaren's land. Several expressed anger at Bailey and told him they thought him to be ineffective in his attempts to protect them. "There's nothing I could do. In Texas, if you've got property, you can shoot whatever you want on it," Bailey said.

With the Rowes' exchange completed, Malone began to assume all negotiations with the assistance of Noesner and another member of the FBI, Carlos Conejo, then a bureau negotiator for the El Paso Division.

"The FBI had been through a lot of events, and he was giving me the legion of success stories and a legion of not-so-much success stories—just 'Do this. Don't do this—do this.' They gave us some really great advice," Malone said.

Prior to the DMR siege, Malone had never before worked as a negotiator in the eighteen years of his previous employment with the Texas Highway Patrol. However, he became a quick study by telephone.

"I began to talk to the people inside of the [ROT] compound to see how many people's voices I could hear so that I could tell how many people were in it, to try and get a head count. We did not know if we had five people in there or fifty people, or how many people," Malone said. "I was a little bit concerned at one point that we might be a little bit undergunned or understaffed."

Soon, hundreds of Texas Highway patrolmen joined Caver and Malone on the scene, including Robert Braxton "Bobby" Holt,[21] an oilman and a DPS commissioner who owned the Holt Ranches north of Midland.

"He flew down and came out there and just gave me a hug and asked, 'What do you need?' And I said 'Have you got any way to get me fuel down here?'" Bailey recounted.

Holt acted as a liaison with law enforcement as he remained in constant telephone communication with Governor Bush.

"Bobby Holt treated my wife and I like royalty while he was here," Wofford said. "Nearly every day, Governor Bush would call to check on my wife."

Jean Parrott, the Jeff Davis County treasurer, called Bailey on the phone crying because Bobby Holt had just handed her a check for nine thousand dollars to cover fuel expenses incurred by local law enforcement.

Meanwhile, Bailey dealt with his normal day-to-day responsibilities as sheriff in Cherry Creek, Fort Davis, and Valentine. Johnny Wofford's wife, Mary Lynn, began cooking meals for everyone. Bailey's mother and his wife, together with Jeff Davis Judge Peggy Robertson, also prepared food. Other residents set up barbecue pits or brought in food from restaurants in Marfa and Alpine. Law enforcement officers stayed overnight in the local Alpine and Fort Davis motels.

"They were eatin' everything in sight with that much goin' on. I would just sleep, lay over in the back seat of my patrol car, and sleep for thirty minutes or so until somebody woke me up, and then go again for a couple more hours," Bailey said.

The Federal Aviation Administration restricted air traffic within five square miles over the Davis Mountains as helicopters operated by DPS and Border Patrol began reconnaissance operations in and out of the area.

Houston attorney Terence O'Rourke[22] arrived just before midnight to act as a liaison between law enforcement and the ROT group. O'Rourke offered his assistance in any way that he could to help resolve the siege. He suggested that Caver issue warrants for the arrest of members of the ROT while O'Rourke worked as a liaison to encourage the group's surrender.

"At that point in time, we were willing to do whatever it took to resolve the thing peacefully without us having to go in after them, so he [O'Rourke] negotiated with them," Caver said.

ROT members at several different times had sent out to the Texas Rangers diplomatic pouches that contained legal documents. O'Rourke helped Caver to interpret McLaren's demands.

O'Rourke had served twenty years in the Harris County Attorney's Office. From 1986 until 1996, O'Rourke served under County Attorney Mike Driscoll. At one time, he was employed as the first assistant county attorney and as a special assistant. In 1997, he operated a private practice in Houston.

O'Rourke had met McLaren years earlier when O'Rourke and Driscoll had traveled to West Texas to research some projects performed by the Civilian Conservation Corps in the Big Bend area during the Great Depression. They were investigating sites that had incorporated labor using low-technology equipment, hoping to produce similar projects in Harris County to be performed by prisoners.

The two hoped to resolve a significant overcrowding problem at Harris County Jail by putting people to work on constructive projects instead of just cutting weeds, painting over graffiti, or picking up trash along the highway. During Driscoll's and O'Rourke's meetings with residents of Fort Davis, McLaren had stopped by. O'Rourke found the ROT leader charming because of his study of Texas history. At that initial meeting, O'Rourke shared his business card with McLaren, never expecting to hear from him again. However, when his phone rang on April 27, 1997, O'Rourke recognized with surprise McLaren's voice on the other end of the line.

"I remember saying to him, 'Rick. I've been watching TV. It appears to me that you are surrounded by the Texas Rangers and that you have hostages there with you,'" O'Rourke said. "And he said, 'Yeah, that's why I'm calling you.' He said, 'I want you to arrange a cease fire for me with the Texas attorney general and the New World Order.'"[23]

O'Rourke had suggested to McLaren that he hire himself an attorney. As it happened, that's just what McLaren did.

"I said 'Hey Rick, I have a recommendation for you, I think you ought to renegotiate those hostages that you have with you and get yourself a lawyer because there is a high likelihood that the Texas Rangers are going to kill you in a very short period of time,'" O'Rourke said. "I had the belief that if I didn't do it, that there was no one else who was reasonably going to handle it and that the Texas Rangers would kill him and would kill his wife and would kill everyone there."

McLaren said he would convene a special meeting of the Congress of the Republic of Texas in order to officially retain O'Rourke. However within minutes, McLaren faxed over a signed copy of the retainer for O'Rourke.

Once O'Rourke's name appeared on the official negotiations list provided by the Texas Attorney General's office, he immediately made plans to fly to Midland and then to rent a car to drive to Fort Davis. O'Rourke called McLaren to tell him the news. In the meantime, O'Rourke also called his friend Dick DeGuerin,[24] the famous attorney who had represented David Koresh.[25]

DeGuerin provided O'Rourke with plenty of advice and insight about standoffs in general. He suggested that O'Rourke head to Fort Davis to negotiate his future defendant's surrender and safe transfer into custody so that afterward he could defend McLaren. DeGuerin surmised that it would be impossible to defend McLaren from a hostage situation. Over the next few days, the two men would confer often by telephone.

Used to dealing with Houston police, O'Rourke found the reception he received at midnight in Fort Davis surprising. Jess Malone, introduced himself to O'Rourke as the negotiator, and Captain Barry Caver, as the commander of the siege.

"Caver said, 'Mr. O'Rourke, it's so nice to have you here. It's wonderful,' et cetera. And 'Let me explain our position. We have studied the reality of this, and I want you to relax. This is not going to be another Waco,'" O'Rourke said.

"Then he said, 'We have studied it; we're not going to wait around forever like the FBI did, and we're not going to make mistakes like the ATF did at Waco.'"[27]

Caver told O'Rourke that he intended to serve some felony warrants to McLaren and to execute those warrants. Knowing the types of weapons McLaren's bunch likely possessed and that the ROT members might resist arrest, O'Rourke understood that the Texas Rangers held the upper hand. They could use their authority to use overwhelming deadly force to take possession of the property through an attack.

O'Rourke had assumed that they would rather kill than negotiate a surrender. Instead, O'Rourke observed that the Texas Rangers showed remarkable restraint; Malone especially proved extraordinarily skillful at negotiating with the ROT.

O'Rourke spoke to McLaren that evening using a pay phone located on a dude ranch where the attorney stayed overnight in Fort Davis. As McLaren talked, O'Rourke listened. McLaren filled O'Rourke's head with detailed information, including theories about the standoff. However, McLaren had not considered that his days as the leader of the ROT were numbered.

11

Day Three
Texas Rangers Move Closer

AS SHE WATCHED the live television news broadcasts sent from the Davis Mountains grow more intense, Jo Ann Turner began to assume a somewhat celebrity status among her fellow female prisoners in the Travis County women's cellblock. As the ambassador of the Republic of Texas (ROT), Rick McLaren of course was discussed frequently during the news broadcasts—and his name was often followed immediately by her own.

Members of the media also began to identify Jo Ann Turner as a catalyst whose arrest had helped to start the ROT's war. However, in Jo Ann Turner's mind, her own battle with Texas had begun years before and likely would not end any time soon. During the eight days since her incarceration, she had become convinced of one very important fact—no one cared what happened to her. Then, the local media began reporting rumors of her possible jailbreak.

Travis County officials suddenly moved Jo Ann Turner into an isolation cell after rumors spread that the Republic of Texas militia might attempt free her. As a result, Jo Ann became an enemy of the state. Four guards, two on each side, escorted Jo Ann to a cell in solitary confinement.

"Again, they shackled me around the waist and around the ankles. When they escorted me to lock up, I asked, 'Why does it take four people to take me to lock up?' They had no comments," she said.[1]

Chapter 11

In solitary confinement, one window allowed Jo Ann a view to the outside where she could see and hear helicopters overhead. She began to fear that McLaren and his ROT group might make things much worse for her if they tried to break her out of jail. She did not wish to be rescued; she just wanted to go home.

■ ■ ■

On day three of the siege, April 29, 1997, Texas Ranger Barry Caver[2] moved his command post several miles up Friend Ranch Road to an old volunteer fire station located within a half mile of McLaren's trailer.

Trees and brush obscured the Texas Rangers' view of the trailer. Whatever lay unseen between the fire station and McLaren's trailer also presented a challenge. Woodlands scattered among the rocky crests in the Davis Mountains provide a home to deer, elk, bears, mountain lions, and rattlesnakes. In addition, dangerous unmarked openings to former mineral mines overgrown with sage, greasewood, prickly pear, yucca, and ocotillo[3] provided an obstacle course to surveillance teams.

Texas Ranger Jess Malone[4] continued his negotiations by telephone with the ROT members who remained inside their so-called embassy.

Together, Malone and Caver came up with a plan to man a vantage point from atop the six-thousand-foot ridge located directly behind the ROT headquarters. Meanwhile, Malone quickly learned that patience pays when negotiating with suspected domestic terrorists.

"People go on emotional rollercoasters. When they're at the peak of an emotional rollercoaster, you're not gonna negotiate with them, but when they come to the bottom of that emotional rollercoaster is when they are more rational and you can talk to them and they can hear you," he said. "You have to empathize with them, but you can't light into them. Once you empathize with them, you have to tell them the barebone facts and say, 'I understand what you're saying, and I respect what you're saying.'"

Malone said he never lost control and attempted to keep whoever answered the phone talking, to listen for other voices in the background. While talking to people inside of the ROT compound, he hoped to determine how many people were present and to come up with a head count.

Within hours, however, he dismissed any worries about being outgunned when additional law enforcement converged on the scene. "It's a pretty sight when you get up at, like, six o'clock in the morning and the sun's comin' up and you look down this long dusty road in the middle of nowhere and there's basically a hundred and fifty black-and-white highway patrol cars with two troopers in each one of them. They had sent us approximately three hundred state troopers."

Malone slowly began to prepare for a worst-case scenario as he also called in members of the National Guard. During his negotiations with ROT members, talk became tense while speaking with Robert "White Eagle" Otto, who failed to keep discussions civil. Otto often used profane and foul language.

"I said, 'Look, the only thing standing between you and death is me. All I have to do is look over at Captain Caver and say 'pull the trigger,' and we'll come in there and overwhelm y'all. Your lives will be lost, and we'll lose lives, and of course we don't want to do that. At the end of the day, why are you talkin' to me with such foul language?'" Malone said.

Otto continued his tirade of obscenities until Malone finally hung up on him. Then he turned his attention to a National Guard member from Camp Mabry in Austin who commanded an M88.[5]

"I asked him, 'What exactly can you do with that tank?' And he said, 'I can destroy everything except the residence.' So, I said, 'Go up there. There're about fifteen or twenty cars—you run over everything up there that is not a residence,'" Malone said.

The M88 armored recovery vehicle was designed to support fighting tanks by refueling and repairing them and is much bigger than a normal tank. The driver soon leveled the ground by flattening about fifteen of the ROT's cars within an area of about three hundred yards surrounding the residence.

"I mean literally, we're talking, these cars were no more than eighteen inches tall when he got through with them," Malone said.

The M88 driver left untouched McLaren's embassy, essentially an Airstream trailer with some wooden structures attached to one side of it. During the demolition, Malone's phone rang once again. When he answered, he heard several high-pitched voices screaming on the other end.

"It sounded like everybody there was in the midst of puberty. A very high-strung voice said, 'My God, you're gonna kill us all,'" Malone said.

Malone remained calm, determined to impress upon the group the seriousness of the standoff. "I said, 'No, I'm not going to kill anybody, but

I'm making a point to you that we need to talk and negotiate, and you don't need to be addressing me in such vulgar terms. It's derogatory. It's not going to get us anywhere. I want to remind you that your lives are in my hands.' It pretty much set the tone for going downhill from there, because it was a very overwhelming show of force," Malone said.

Caver also advised Malone that he did not want negotiations to escalate. In the meantime, they began airlifting armed men onto the vantage point, the ridge behind the ROT headquarters.

US Attorney General Janet Reno ordered members of the FBI to leave the compound, saying that if they stayed and the standoff escalated, it could result in another "black eye" for the department, as had happened at Waco and Ruby Ridge.[6] However, at least one member of the FBI defied Reno and remained on the scene.[7] FBI negotiator Gary Noesner voluntarily began serving as a consultant at the Davis Mountain Resort (DMR) siege.

Noesner recalls that Texas Ranger senior captain Bruce Casteel approached him with the idea of making a full tactical assault on the compound.[8]

"I voiced my opinion that ROT members would most likely respond with violence," Noesner said. "Given our lack of specific knowledge, I was concerned that we were moving toward a 'linear approach' to incident management, which could lead to another debacle."

Instead, the Texas Rangers tried a "parallel approach" by negotiating in good faith while at the same time preparing for the worst.

Caver met with forty-year-old district attorney Albert Valadez, at the new command post set up at the fire station. Valadez told Caver that he had met McLaren a few years earlier at his law offices located in Fort Stockton. At that time, McLaren had asked questions about real estate and ownership deeds.

"I didn't do anything for him in my capacity as a civil attorney. I realized from talking to him that what he was asking me to do was beyond my ability. He was attempting to acquire property through adverse possession," Valadez said.[9] "He was trying to gain ownership of land because the people who owned it were absentee landowners. We had a pleasant conversation, but I didn't do anything to help him. He went on his way."

The Republic of Texas Embassy, 1997, owned by Richard Lance McLaren, consisted of a trailer and a lean-to attached without indoor plumbing. Photo by Jess Malone.

A former volunteer fire station for the Davis Mountain Resort served as a Command Center for the Texas Rangers during the standoff against the Republic of Texas militia in 1997. Photo by Jess Malone.

Joe Rowe stands at his home's glass front door where Republic of Texas militia member Gregg Paulson fired three shots at him on April 27, 1997. Photo by Jess Malone.

The white van driven by Republic of Texas member Robert Scheidt, April 27, 1997, prior to his arrest by Jeff Davis County Sheriff Steve Bailey. Photo by Jess Malone.

The Volkswagen driven by Richard Keyes before he and Gregg and Karen Paulsen held Joe and Margaret Ann Rowe hostage in their own home and incited a standoff between the Texas Rangers and the Republic of Texas militia on April 27, 1997. Photo by Jess Malone.

One of the hound dogs from the James Lynaugh Unit Prison that had been shot but survived while tracking two Republic of Texas members who had escaped into the Davis Mountains on May 3, 1997. Photo by Jess Malone.

The arsenal of firearms owned by the members of the Republic of Texas militia was surrendered to Texas Rangers on May 3, 1997. Photo by Jess Malone.

One of the cannons used by the Republic of Texas militia and seized by Texas Rangers following the standoff on May 3, 1997. Photo by Jess Malone.

View of the living room inside the Republic of Texas Embassy in the Davis Mountain Resort as it appeared when it was seized by Texas Rangers on May 3, 1997. Photo by Jess Malone.

View of the kitchen inside the Republic of Texas Embassy in the Davis Mountain Resort as it appeared when it was seized by Texas Rangers on May 3, 1997. Photo by Jess Malone.

View of the eating area inside the Republic of Texas Embassy in the Davis Mountain Resort as it appeared when it was seized by Texas Rangers on May 3, 1997. Photo by Jess Malone.

One of the Republic of Texas militia posters seized by Texas Rangers following the standoff on May 3, 1997. Photo by Jess Malone.

One of several how-to books found inside the Republic of Texas Embassy, May 3, 1997. Photo by Jess Malone.

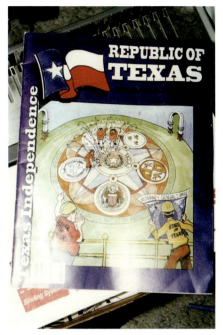

The official arm patch worn by members of the Republic of Texas militia at the time of their arrests on May 3, 1997. Photo by Jess Malone.

One of several magazine issues printed by members of the Republic of Texas militia in 1997. Photo by Jess Malone.

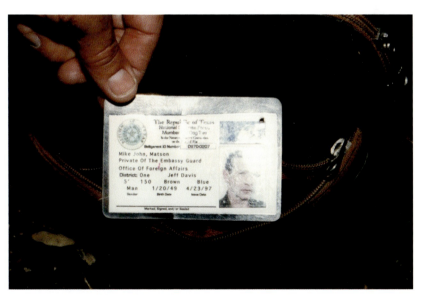

The ID card found on the body of Mike Matson, shot by Texas Rangers in the Davis Mountains on May 5, 1997, following the seven-day standoff with the Republic of Texas militia. Photo by Jess Malone.

The US Army Explosive Ordnance Disposal squad found twelve gasoline containers, thirty to forty crude pipe bombs, a five-pound propane tank filled with explosives, and a myriad of tripwires connected to booby traps on the grounds of the Republic of Texas militia compound during seizure by Texas Rangers on May 3, 1997. Photo by Jess Malone.

At left, Texas Ranger David Duncan stands with DPS Motor Vehicle Theft Agent Roy Parrack and an unknown Texas Game Warden together with FBI senior special resident agent Terry Kincaid following the 1997 standoff of the Republic of Texas Embassy. Photo by Jess Malone.

One of two armored personnel carriers loaned by then Sheriff J. B. Smith from Smith County Sheriff's Office in Tyler, Texas, used in the standoff at the Republic of Texas Embassy in the Davis Mountains, April 27 to May 3, 1997. Photo by Jess Malone.

A Texas Department of Public Safety SWAT and surveillance team watched Richard Lance McLaren and the Republic of Texas militia from a 6,000-foot ridge overlooking the Republic of Texas Embassy in the Davis Mountains during the seven-day standoff in 1997. Photo by Jess Malone.

Jo Ann Canady Turner interviewed with the author once a week for more than two years, including on her birthday May 29, 2018, in a private Southwest Austin home. Photo by Donna Marie Miller.

Bill Turner, the late first husband of Jo Ann Canady Turner, played bass and led a jazz combo known as the Bill Turner Combo at various nightclubs around Austin in the 1950s and 1960s. Photo by Jo Ann Canady Turner.

Former hostage Joe Rowe held by the Republic of Texas militia today still lives in the house he built on Tomahawk Trail located in the Davis Mountain Resort where he met with the author on March 17, 2019. Photo by Donna Marie Miller.

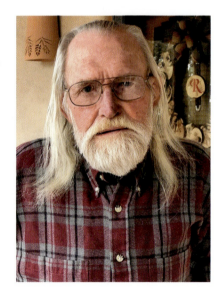

Former Texas Ranger Captain Barry Caver commanded the seven-day siege of the Republic of Texas Embassy in the Davis Mountains in 1997, and he currently serves as the assistant chief deputy at the Denton County Sheriff's Office.

Courtesy photo of Jess Malone, former Texas Ranger negotiator for the 1997 Republic of Texas standoff, who has since retired and operates a family ranching and hunting business in West Texas.

TEXAS DEPARTMENT OF CRIMINAL JUSTICE
Institutional Division

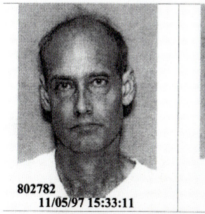 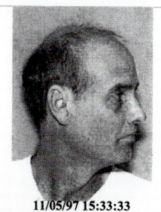

802782
11/05/97 15:33:11

11/05/97 15:33:33

ID Number: 802782
Date: 11/05/97
Name: RICHARD LANCE MCLAREN

At the time of his arrest on May 3, 1997, following a seven-day standoff in the Davis Mountains by the Texas Rangers, Richard Lance McLaren served as the ambassador and unofficial leader of the Republic of Texas militia. Courtesy of the Texas Department of Criminal Justice.

Evelyn McLaren, the common-law wife of Republic of Texas militia leader Richard McLaren surrenders to Texas Ranger and negotiator Jess Malone at the end of the seven-day standoff, May 3, 1997, in the Davis Mountains. Photo by Barry Caver.

The former ambassador for the Republic of Texas militia, Richard Lance McLaren, as he appeared in an interview with the author on May 15, 2018, inside the William P. Clements Unit in Amarillo, Texas, where he is serving a ninety-nine-year sentence. Photo by Donna Marie Miller.

Republic of Texas militia member Robert Scheidt surrendered May 2, 1997, to Texas Rangers in the Davis Mountains. Photo by Barry Caver.

Texas Ranger Captain Barry Caver greets Richard Lance McLaren, the ambassador for the Republic of Texas militia, following his arrest May 3, 1997, as Texas Rangers Coy Smith and John Allen restrain him. Photo by Jess Malone.

Jo Ann Canady Turner stands beside her son, Jeff Turner, in June 1970. Photo by Bill Turner.

Jo Ann Canady Turner holds her daughter, Kelly Turner, in a swimming pool in July 1973. Photo by Bill Turner.

Kelly Turner holds a portrait of her mother, Jo Ann Canady Turner, in an undated photograph inside their former home in Westlake, Texas. Photo by Jo Ann Turner.

Texas Department of Public Safety Corporal Johnny Anzaldua of Lamesa, Texas, welcomes former hostage Joe Rowe outside the house Rowe built at the entrance to the Davis Mountain Resort. Members of the Republic of Texas militia took Rowe hostage at the start of their seven-day standoff with Texas Rangers in 1997. Photo by Barry Caver.

Robert "Mac" McLaren holds his infant son, Richard Lance McLaren, shortly after the child's birth on August 18, 1953. Photo courtesy of Chuck Samson.

Front right, Robert "Mac" McLaren sits at the table across from his wife, Mary June Samson McLaren, who holds their son, Richard Lance McLaren, beside cousin Chuck Samson Jr. and his father, Chuck Samson Sr., and uncle, Bob Baumbach, at the Samson family table in 1953. Photo courtesy of Chuck Samson.

Richard Lance McLaren's father, Robert "Mac" McLaren, stands beside his father-in-law, Chuck Samson Sr., outside the family's Missouri homestead in 1953. Photo courtesy of Chuck Samson.

Mary June Samson holds her infant son, Richard Lance McLaren, beside his uncle, Bob Baumbach and grandfather Chuck Samson Sr., and cousin Chuck Samson Jr. and his grandmother Gertrude, at the Samson family table in 1953. Photo courtesy of Chuck Samson.

FBI agents captured Republic of Texas militia member Richard Keyes III after his four months on the run, September 19, 1997, in the Sam Houston National Forest near New Waverly, Texas. Photo by Barry Caver.

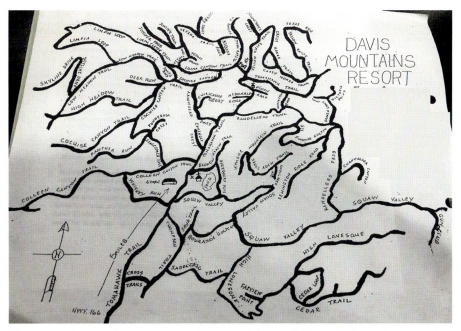

The Davis Mountain Resort consists of a series of dirt roads through about fifty acres of rough woodlands in the Davis Mountains where as many as one hundred fifty residents live among deer, elk, bears, mountain lions, and rattlesnakes. Drawing by Joe Rowe.

The Samson family homestead at 2109 Westview in Kirkwood, Missouri, where former Republic of Texas leader Richard Lance McLaren lived with his single mother, Mary June Samson McLaren, and her parents. Photo courtesy of Chuck Samson.

May 3, 1997, members of the Texas Rangers, Company E, pose with the captured flag of the Republic of Texas in front of the militia's embassy. Left to right back row: Jerry Byrne, Jess Malone, Buster Collins, Joe Hunt, John Allen, John Billings, Captain Barry Caver, Calvin Cox, Gerry Villalobos, Bobby Gruggs, Curtis Becker, and Gene Kea. Kneeling: Lieutenant Joe Sanders and David Duncan. Photo by Barry Caver.

Texas Ranger Captain Barry Caver holds the captured flag of the Republic of Texas militia, May 3, 1997, in the Davis Mountain Resort following a seven-day standoff. Photo by Jess Malone.

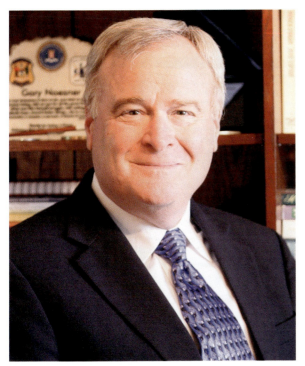

Former FBI Agent Gary Noesner, an investigator, instructor, and negotiator for standoffs for 30 years, served as a consultant at the Republic of Texas standoff in 1997 in the Davis Mountains.

Robert "White Eagle" Otto, after serving 24 years for engaging in organized crime during the 1997 standoff of the Republic of Texas militia and the Texas Rangers, earned an early release on August 3, 2020 under mandatory supervision.

Republic of Texas militia ambassador Richard Lance McLaren and eight other followers attempted to distribute worthless paper documents resembling state cashier checks and defrauded credit card companies out of thousands of dollars before being charged with federal bank and mail fraud in 1998. Photo by Barry Caver.

An aerial view of Joe Rowe's house where it sits at the entrance to the Davis Mountain Resort, a loosely developed subdivision outside Fort Davis and the site of a seven-day standoff between the Texas Rangers and the Republic of Texas militia during the spring of 1997. Photo by Jess Malone.

Texas Ranger David Duncan arrived first on the scene at the Republic of Texas militia standoff on April 27, 1997, while three members held hostages in exchange for the release of Robert Scheidt. Photo courtesy of David Duncan.

At center, former Jeff Davis Sheriff Steve Bailey stands with then-retired sheriff Harvey Adams and Texas Department of Public Safety Captain Arvin Kilpatrick during the Republic of Texas standoff in the Davis Mountain Resort in 1997.

On horseback, dog handlers from the James Lyndaugh Unit of the Texas Department of Corrections, including Sergeant Ralph Hager, left; Warden Terry Foster, right front; and Gene Kea, back right, track escaped Republic of Texas militia members in the Davis Mountains, May 4, 1997. Photo by Jess Malone.

A Texas Ranger in silhouette stands guard at a roadblock in the Davis Mountains during the standoff with the Republic of Texas militia, May 1, 1997. Courtesy of the Associated Press; photo by Jon Freilich.

By implementing the Law of Adverse Possession,[10] McLaren took over ownership of much of the property and made small improvements. The land he acquired served as his base of operations for the ROT headquarters. McLaren gained additional property through similar courses of action.

"Some people refer to it as squatting," Valadez said. "That dates back to the Republic of Texas before we were part of the Union. It was a way of encouraging people to become landowners in Texas. Back then, they had their reasons and primarily there were Native Americans that were living on those properties and they, the Texians, wanted them off. So, in order to encourage people to fight off the Native Americans, the government would give land to the settlers."

The laws remain in effect in Texas to this day.

Valadez had first learned about the siege on the very first day of the standoff when he received a phone call from one of two investigators who worked for him at the time. Within twenty-four hours, Valadez had packed up his gear and headed to Fort Davis. With few places to stay overnight, Valadez daily commuted the ninety miles between Fort Stockton and Fort Davis to be present and to observe the standoff.

"They [the Texas Rangers] wanted to make sure that the procedure they employed was within the law. Being the elected DA, they wanted my legal opinion on everything that might involve legal questions. That was my role," Valadez said.

The Texas Rangers allowed Valadez to listen to negotiations for the release of Joe and Margaret Ann "M.A." Rowe. As a result, Valadez began to praise the work provided by Jess Malone.

"He did a marvelous job. I didn't do anything to help him, but he and Barry Cavers and the rest of the Texas Rangers that were involved did a marvelous job securing the release of Joe and Margaret Ann Rowe," Valadez said.

From the beginning of the siege, Valadez understood that eventually he might likely prosecute the case against the ROT separatists. "I felt good about being there and felt it would be beneficial to all of us," he said. "I don't know how unusual it is, but we had a static rule back then if anytime there was a homicide or a crime of any nature that required experts, they would call my office."

Caver also met with McLaren's attorney, Terence "Terry" L. O'Rourke, who arrived at the standoff inside the DMR about nine o'clock on the third morning.

O'Rourke noticed that Bobby Holt,[11] a wealthy rancher and oilman who had served on the Department of Public Safety (DPS) Commission, kept a vigilant physical presence at the scene. The attorney held the belief that Holt, not Caver, maintained a silent command of the standoff.

"This guy [Holt] was a real player, and he was there to make sure that if it all went well, then the governor would take the credit, and if it didn't, he [Holt] would take the heat," O'Rourke said.[12]

O'Rourke described his witnessing of the standoff and siege of ROT headquarters as "a fascinating experience." He noticed that Holt dressed in a tailored suit, as elegantly as any aristocrat. The delegate for the DPS held the most modern cell phone O'Rourke had ever seen—almost unknown among the general public during the 1990s; with the slim and elegant device he seemed to maintain a constant connection with Governor George W. Bush.

Meanwhile, in the evenings, O'Rourke utilized his downtime by socializing with members of the press at Fort Davis's historic Hotel Limpia. The place served as the media's main watering hole. O'Rourke enjoyed listening to members of the press in order to get their understanding of the situation. Before long, O'Rourke began to suspect that Governor George W. Bush[13] had an interest in killing members of the ROT rather than negotiating with them.

"Remember that Texas was the leading state in the country in executions," O'Rourke said. "I mean we led the state and Texas led the nation. I believe at one time there were more people executed in Texas than the rest of the country put together."

In the year 1997 alone, Texas performed a record number of executions—thirty-seven, out of seventy-four executions performed in the US, or 50 percent.[14]

12

Day Four
Supporters Attempt to Join the Rebellion

JO ANN TURNER'S solitary cell seemed much worse than the one that she had formerly shared in the Travis County women's cellblock. She thought the inside walls of her new cell looked like a poor imitation of a Jackson Pollock painting, covered in swirls of blood and feces. However, no artful intent seemed evident in the anonymous painter's handiwork. Suddenly, and in broad daylight, a solitary rat appeared from behind her bunk. She put her feet up and watched as the creature just sat in the corner staring at her with its nose twitching. After several minutes it crawled along the floor and up the frame around the jail door to the cinderblock rim beneath the window.

Within solitary confinement she grew increasingly more anxious with each hour that passed. Suddenly, a female prisoner in the cell next door began talking to her through the air vents. Jo Ann felt terrified.

"The voice said, 'You must have done something pretty bad because everybody's talking about you,'" Jo Ann said.[1] "I could hear her as if she was in the same cell with me because I could hear every word clearly through the walls from the air-conditioning units. That was scary because I thought, *Oh my word, what if she gets out?* I didn't know why she was in lock up. Obviously, she could have been a violent offender or worse. She didn't know why I was in lock up either, except that I was the one mentioned in the TV broadcasts, and she wasn't. Perhaps she was just as scared as I was."

■ ■ ■

On day four of the siege, April 30, 1997, the Texas Rangers enlisted three hundred law enforcement officers and agents from across the state, including local volunteers to help them in their siege of the Republic of Texas (ROT) embassy. Vehicles of all makes and models spread unnaturally across every bare space of brown earth along the road and roadside near the command center that the Texas Rangers had set up in a former volunteer fire house.

"Media reports may have exaggerated the total as five hundred," former Captain Barry Caver said.[2]

Richard McLaren told negotiator Jess Malone by phone that as many as five thousand Texas militants would soon show up to lend their support to the ROT inside the Davis Mountain Resort.

"We felt like the longer we prolonged this, the worse it could possibly get. We wanted to end it as soon as we could," Caver said. "We knew that a lot of his supporters and followers would come into the area on the weekends to do target practice and training and such. So we were trying to avoid reaching another weekend."

FBI consultant Gary Noesner encouraged the local law enforcement agents to do everything within their power to deescalate the standoff. He discussed some verbal strategies for Texas Rangers to use when speaking to McLaren and his followers. He also briefed Department of Public Safety (DPS) media chief Mike Cox prior to each day's press conference.

"There was also some concern that there would be like-minded, quote/unquote, patriots come in to assist McLaren," Noesner said.[3]

McLaren and his group had broken off communications, so the Texas Rangers began a series of press releases in print and by radio broadcasts to bring them back to the table.

"Sure enough, I think we read McLaren pretty well—being the never-get-tired-of-hearing-his-own-voice kind of person that he was. He felt absolutely compelled to respond, and that opened up the dialogue again, which is what we wanted," Noesner said.

As suspected, McLaren and other ROT members had watched both local and national television news reports and listened to the radio broadcasts about the standoff. Though the Texas Rangers had cut the traditional telephone lines to the embassy, the ROT's communication with the media continued, leading to speculation that its members used satellite phones in addition to shortwave radio to talk to their sympathizers.

McLaren continued to make threats on the ham radios to gain support from the outside. The Texas Rangers felt if they prolonged the standoff, things could possibly become worse.

Noesner shared with the Texas Rangers his own experiences negotiating with right-wing militants and separatists. He characterized all antigovernment militia members as "undereducated, unsuccessful people who feel empowered by the attention they receive from a leader who gives them a cause or a reason to fight for a life that in general has not been kind to them."

"People like McLaren and [David] Koresh[4] and many others . . . kind of know how to exploit, whether naturally or they learn it," Noesner said. "They become the ones with all of the knowledge, all of the insight. They control every facet of a person's life, and there are people who either want, or need, or crave that kind of direction and control."

Noesner profiled members of the ROT as men who lived unstructured lives, never achieved notable success in their lives, and had mixed or nonexistent employment records. He further described McLaren's followers as men who likely had never experienced true happiness in their relationships at work or at home.

While preparing for a mass press conference, the Texas Rangers dropped off a written response to McLaren's demands that he had made the previous evening. O'Rourke included a letter in the package asking for McLaren's surrender.

At a press conference that day, Cox delivered a statement that provided points from several of Noesner's suggestions, including identifying the standoff as simply a State of Texas matter and clarifying the FBI's role as purely advisory as well as the following:

> The ROT claims that people should be free in their homes, yet ROT members violently invaded a home at gunpoint and took two people hostage. The people of Texas expect law enforcement authorities to investigate and prosecute such crimes. Texas authorities are

attempting to serve valid arrest warrants; they are not concerned about Mr. McLaren's political beliefs.[5]

The press release also indicated that Texas law enforcement would continue to show patience in their negotiations in order to ensure a peaceful resolution. The strategy worked. Members of the ROT quickly responded by using state and national media outlets, including one based in Tampa, Florida.

Then Texas Rangers arrested seven men at the Flying J truck stop near Pecos, Texas, and found a variety of weapons inside their vehicles.[6] Caver recalled that Texas DPS officials had alerted local law enforcement officers earlier in the day that a group of men associated with the ROT might be passing through the area. Pecos patrolman Cosme Ortega spotted two vehicles on I-20 at mile marker 43 just before five thirty that morning and followed them to the Flying J truck stop at US 285 and I-20. Ortega learned that the men had told a waitress inside Thad's Restaurant that they were going hunting.

As luck would have it that day, several Texas Rangers, including Captain Carl Weathers of Lubbock Company C, together with Gary Henderson and Larry Gilbreath, visited the restaurant to eat breakfast before reporting for duty. After finishing their meal, they heard the police broadcasts about possible ROT supporters in the area. While leaving the restaurant, the Texas Rangers spotted the vehicles and the suspects. The Rangers spent the remainder of that morning questioning the seven suspects in Pecos.

"It was what you call one lucky day," Caver said.

During a search of the suspects' 1983 Oldsmobile Regency and a 1980s model Chevrolet Suburban, Texas Rangers discovered approximately two pounds of marijuana inside their vehicles. The Rangers also found weapons, ammunition, explosives, camping gear, and the ROT's propaganda pamphlets. They quickly arrested James Leslie Williamson Jr. on an outstanding warrant for theft.

They also confiscated two SKS 7.62 semiautomatic assault rifles, one with two 30-round clips, another with a 30-round and a 40-round taped together. Other items found in the suspects' cars included a quart of blasting powder, two military helmets with ROT Defense Police insignia, one bulletproof vest, rounds of rifle ammunition, printed ROT propaganda, instructions on how to create false identification, thirteen microcassette tapes labeled Republic of Texas, and a Confederate Army cap.[7]

Meanwhile, back at the DMR, during a direct call between the ROT members and Texas Ranger Jess Malone, Quantico FBI consultant Jim Duffy suggested a "summit meeting," hoping the idea would likely appeal to ROT members who believed that they represented a separate independent nation. The ROT group agreed on a scheduled time for the summit, at seven thirty on the evening of April 30. However, before that meeting could take place, an unidentified person in the law enforcement entourage cut the phone lines to the ROT embassy.

About that time, Terence O'Rourke began executing a plan for Evelyn McLaren's daughters to send a letter to their mother to plead for her surrender. O'Rourke said various law enforcement representatives who had been burning up time and money with motels and food bills seemed a bit anxious for a peaceful resolution.[8]

O'Rourke also heard from members of the ROT who worried that they might be lured into a trap and killed if they surrendered. McLaren told O'Rourke that he wished to be protected under the Geneva Convention for Diplomats,[9] like an "enemy combatant," as the Japanese had been labeled after Pearl Harbor.[10]

Whenever O'Rourke prepared diplomatic documents, the Texas Rangers cautiously placed them in pouches in an armored personnel carrier (APC)[11] and delivered them to a designated spot in the dirt road located directly in front of McLaren's trailer. The two APCs were on loan from then Sheriff J. B. Smith from the Smith County Sheriff's Office in Tyler, Texas.

"We would put down the diplomatic pouches as close to the gate to the resort as possible—as far as we could get down in there without having to get out of the APC, because we didn't know if it was an ambush-type situation or what," Caver said.

Members on both sides of the standoff began to fear that the worst was yet to come.

13

Day Five
The Texas Rangers Show Restraint

From a small window in her isolation cell at Travis County Correctional Complex, Jo Ann Turner occasionally spotted a helicopter flying so close that she could hear its whirling blades as it hovered close to the roof. She wondered if Rick McLaren manned the helicopter and if ROT members possibly lay in wait just beyond the jailhouse walls.

In the beginning of her association with the ROT, Jo Ann had felt drawn to McLaren, but his common-law wife, Evelyn, had sealed the friendship. Jo Ann saw Evelyn as a very levelheaded, longtime US Post Office employee. If Evelyn believed in McLaren, Jo Ann had decided that she would too.

Admittedly much of what Rick McLaren had told Jo Ann about the Republic of Texas had seemed beyond her level of understanding. She had questioned him, but only once.

"I did ask him 'Do you think this will work Rick?' And he said 'Yes, Jo Ann,'" she said.[1]

McLaren had convinced her that filing a lien would prohibit Stewart Title from processing any Texas mortgages, including her own. So, she had typed and delivered Rick's lien against Stewart Title, without asking any questions.

"In a sense. I was afraid of finding out too much. I began to think maybe this [ROT] wasn't really a legitimate organization," Jo Ann said.

She also began to worry about what might happen to Bill. Her husband had never attended any of the ROT meetings.

"We never talked about the ROT or what I saw or what we did at the meetings. I don't think Bill wanted to know. I think he felt like 'Let her take care of it.' I wore the pants in our relationship pretty much. He would go along with whatever I said. It had always been that way," Jo Ann said.

■ ■ ■

By day five of the siege, on May 1, 1997, Texas Ranger Lieutenant Richard Sweeney in Garland Company B began gathering up body armor to distribute for a full assault on the ROT headquarters in the event that a complete surrender failed. Texas Ranger Barry Caver had expressed his concern that a mass number of ROT supporters might attempt to join the ROT in the Davis Mountains, especially now that the media had leaked specific events about the siege.

"So, we had issues on both sides of the barricade really," Captain Caver said.[2]

Meanwhile dozens of Texas National Guardsmen had arrived in the Davis Mountains to join the siege against the ROT embassy. As a result, McLaren began refusing to talk to anyone, including his retained attorney, Terence L. O'Rourke. The Department of Public Safety (DPS) media chief, Mike Cox,[3] suggested to Caver that he and O'Rourke should appeal to McLaren in a live radio broadcast from the Alpine station KVLF/KALP because they knew McLaren would be listening. At eleven thirty that morning, they aired a special program about the siege by answering questions from listeners. McLaren took the bait; about a half hour passed before he called to talk to Jess Malone.

Malone previously had served as a criminal investigator for DPS and at a distance had worked in Waco during the same time that Captain Caver had investigated the ATF's handling of the February 1993 siege. The two felt a familiar connection. Caver also made sure that Malone communicated frequently with DPS director Dudley Thomas and assistant director Tommy Davis.

O'Rourke recalls being impressed with the restraint local law enforcement officials showed during the siege. "The Texas Rangers from what I saw did a remarkable job of restraint, and I would say that Caver, at least of the ones I dealt with, and especially Jess Malone was extraordinarily skillful. And of course, so was the FBI guy, Gary Noesner," O'Rourke said.[4]

He said that the Texas Rangers seemed willing to do whatever they could to avoid any incidence of violence.

"They said this was not going to be another Waco," O'Rourke stated. "They weren't just going to go kill them is what I got. I mean, when they made up their mind, there was not going to be any fair fight or anything else like that. They were not going to lose anybody."

Meanwhile, McLaren sent a letter to Caver asking all law enforcement officials to surrender to him as the leader of a sovereign country. O'Rourke suggested to Caver that Evelyn's daughters, Lisa Rutledge and Julie Hopkins, should write a letter to their mother asking for her surrender.[5]

Later that evening O'Rourke read the women's letter aloud to the media gathered at the Point of Rocks picnic area. It read, in part:

> Dear Mom, when I talked to you on the phone Sunday, I told you that from watching the news it was clear that you were not home baking cookies. You joked with me and said, 'No, but I am baking chicken,' and you said you weren't anywhere near what was going on and not to worry. Mom I would sincerely rather have ya'll in prison and not in the line of fire. This is no joke![6]

O'Rourke had arranged for the Texas Rangers to deliver the women's letter to Evelyn McLaren as part of the regular daily delivered diplomatic pouches. ROT member Robert Scheidt would retrieve the packets for the ROT and bring them inside the embassy.

That night, some of the residents of the DMR began complaining to Cox that they were fed up with the standoff and wanted to return to their homes. At least one local resident tried to avoid one of the roadblocks set up by the Texas Rangers. They caught Ron Beames driving along a back road in attempt to sneak back into the DMR so that he could care for his horses.

"We told those people who lived there, it was their prerogative to leave, but once they left, they would not be allowed back in," Caver said.

Several residents who had chosen to stay behind inside their own homes throughout the siege complained to Caver before the Texas Rangers cut all of the phone lines inside the DMR in order to thwart

McLaren's communications with his supporters. The Texas Rangers also attempted to cut electrical power to the residences inside the DMR. However, they quickly learned that the ROT embassy operated its own backup generator. The delay in creating "a blackout" inside the DMR caused the Texas Rangers to rethink a bit more creatively about how best to end the standoff.

"We told McLaren that we there to serve the warrant and we were there to make the arrest and we were going to do it one way or another and with whatever means were necessary. I didn't really go into specific details, but he knew that time was becoming short," Caver said.

14

Day Six
Robert Scheidt Surrenders

JO ANN TURNER felt anxious as she watched the news broadcasts about Evelyn McLaren's impending surrender, although the local law enforcement authorities had promised to keep her friend safe and unharmed. However, Jo Ann feared the worst awaited Rick McLaren.[1]

McLaren had truly seemed to want to help Jo Ann, yet she could not help but think about some of the other men in the Republic of Texas (ROT). They all carried guns, and they often talked about protecting themselves with their weapons. She felt sure that if any law enforcement officer had confronted them during a meeting, a showdown would have resulted. She knew that members of the ROT felt willing to do whatever it took to reclaim the independent nation of Texas.

She didn't own a gun, and she certainly could not envision herself shooting anyone, but she had perceived that some members of the ROT might, given the chance. Over the past two years, Jo Ann had carefully avoided mentioning to her husband that members of the ROT carried guns. He never would have approved.

While in 1889 Texas had become the first state in the Union to ban the carrying of concealed handguns,[2] by 1995 the state's legislators changed the law to allow its citizens the right to lawfully carry them.[3] Jo Ann had no doubt that McLaren would freely demonstrate that right.

Chapter 14

■ ■ ■

On day six of the siege, May 2, 1997, Fort Worth residents Julie Hopkins, age twenty-nine, and Lisa Rutledge, age thirty-three, arrived by private helicopter at the Point of Rocks picnic area in the Davis Mountains. Several times, the women spoke by telephone with their mother, Evelyn McLaren, to ask for her surrender from inside the ROT embassy.

Photographers and videographers from all over the United States shot images of the two sisters huddled together with Lisa's husband, Rob Rutledge, and the couple's two-year-old son, Christian. The images and their names ran in local newspapers and were distributed nationally by the Associated Press. National television affiliates broadcast the same images of the women in that evening's reports. The women's very public images and their story also appeared in newspapers internationally as far away as Canada, including in the *Edmonton Journal*.[4]

The sisters had surprised nearly everyone with their sudden appearance at the siege—everyone except McLaren's attorney Terence O'Rourke.

"They showed up at just the right time," O'Rourke said. "They were angry at the FBI or the Rangers because they thought that they had been lied to on some matters."[5]

When Evelyn's daughters arrived at one of the initial checkpoints in the Davis Mountain Resort (DMR), the Texas Rangers prohibited them from visiting the command post or entering the ROT embassy property. However, Texas Ranger Captain Barry Caver hoped the two women would turn the negotiations around for at least one of the ROT's members.

"We felt like Evelyn was the weakest link at that point in time. If we could convince her to come out, then perhaps she could in turn convince Rick McLaren as well," Caver said.[6]

O'Rourke felt the pressure mounting, and he counseled the women about how to speak to the Texas Rangers and how to calm themselves before and during appearances in front of the media. "At the time that I met them, it could have been minutes or hours before their mother or sister was going to be killed by the very cops that they were talking to," he said. "So that's really a strange universe that you're in; you're talking to the people who are going to go kill your mother."

When O'Rourke first met the daughters at the Point of Rocks picnic area, the women expressed a variety of extreme emotions. "I explained to them, 'You have got to set your anger aside; I understand how angry you are, but you have got to at this point be charming,'" O'Rourke said. "If the world could see that these were attractive, articulate, intelligent young women who just wanted their mother to come out alive, then I was going to buy time."

He also consulted with his colleague and famous Houston attorney Dick DeGuerin, recognized as one of Texas' best lawyers.[7]

"The most important thing to do in situations like this is to buy time and stretch it out so that the government doesn't just go in," O'Rourke said. "You stretch it out from your perspective, buy time, and create some space for negotiation as opposed to—there's a momentum in the government that they build a certain set of forces and when they're ready, they go. They were all ready at what I would call 'go position,' so there's just these last-minute things that they do on the checklist before literally the tanks roll."

O'Rourke said he advised Evelyn's daughters just how they should plead for mercy for their mother.

"I said, I want you to appeal to the governor of Texas, George W. Bush, and say 'Governor Bush, please do not kill my mother.' Ask for mercy, ask for time, ask that your mother can come out alive. Do that. Because, see, even the Rangers in their code of ethics don't kill women unnecessarily," O'Rourke said.

"Evelyn wasn't a gun-toting crazy; she was just crazy enough to fall in love with Rick by the story. That's the story that we were telling: 'Evelyn's just a woman in love. Are you going to kill a woman in love?' Her daughters just wanted her back. That was my position. I told them, 'Just hold your horses, literally. Take your fingers off the trigger. Let's just breathe a little bit guys.'"

Caver recalls thinking at the time that if anyone could make a difference in the siege, Evelyn's daughters might. "I was hopeful. I believed that they could make a difference once they started talking to their mother and telling her how much she meant to them and the grandkid and so forth. We were hoping that would be a good leverage for us," Caver said.

Meanwhile, the Texas Rangers began to take a more aggressive position on a six-thousand-foot ridge[8] overlooking McLaren's trailer, after John Brannon, a helicopter pilot, volunteered to fly in and land some military snipers.

"During this whole process, we would get several different phone calls from different people and different organizations or companies offering their assistance and equipment that they had. We had gotten a call from Raytheon out of Dallas offering us the thermal imaging night vision equipment that they had available," Caver said. "They offered at no cost to us to allow us to utilize that to observe that site during the night hours as well."

Soldiers armed with assault rifles rotated in and out by helicopter throughout the day and night, so they had a very clear view of activity outside the embassy. DPS media chief Mike Cox noted that one evening an ROT surveillance team watched as McLaren and his colleagues cooked steaks outside of their embassy.[9] Caver confirmed the scene. "That's typical of him [McLaren] and his attitude towards us and in general. I think it kind of speaks volumes about what kind of person and what kind of character he was," Caver said.

At one point, Caver still believed a full assault on the ROT might happen. "We were certainly getting prepared to do that because eventually, had they not surrendered when they did, it would have led to that," Caver said. "Probably three or four people were assigned to that ridge to keep a lookout for us and to let us know what all they could and what was going on in and around the compound," Caver said. "We used that as a vantage point in what we called, in our language, 'an observation post.'"

Rancher Johnny Wofford[10] said he observed law enforcement officers often aiming their rifles at McLaren whenever the ROT leader walked outside his embassy. "McLaren was a walking target the whole time the last few days up there," he said. "There were snipers within easy range of him at any time."

Both the financial costs of staging the siege and the threats that McLaren continued to make to the local media began to wear thin, Caver said. "It had gotten so drawn out to the point that we were finally willing to do whatever it took to get them to cooperate and surrender."

Local ham radio operators picked up transmissions believed to have originated at the ROT embassy:

> "Mayday! Mayday! Mayday! Hostiles are invading the Republic of Texas Embassy," McLaren yelled into a radio. "We have hostiles in the woods. This is a Mayday call for any nation in the world... We are being invaded!" Then his tone became taunting: "I guess you boys didn't learn anything from Waco or Ruby Ridge... and you fools are going to come here and kill me, huh, and overrun this mission. Well, be prepared to take the fall... you're dead meat!"[11]

At nine o'clock that morning, Robert Scheidt appeared on the road near the DMR gate entrance where an armored personnel carrier and SWAT team member had just dropped another diplomatic packet. To Caver's surprise, Scheidt, dressed in camouflage, just kept walking past the team toward the Texas Rangers to surrender.

"Of course, it very much surprised us in that we didn't expect it to happen. We didn't have a clue. He didn't give us any kind of warning," Caver said. "It shocked everyone. We weren't real sure of who he was or what he was doing. He finally identified himself, and of course, having talked to him, we knew who he was and took him into custody at that point."

Immediately, the Rangers asked Scheidt to change out of his camouflage clothes because he resembled many of the law enforcement agents on the scene that day. The Texas Rangers gave Scheidt a Texas Department of Corrections prison uniform to wear instead. Caver said he immediately realized the impact of Scheidt's surrender.

"He could kind of see the 'handwriting on the wall' and felt like he knew what was about to happen and he didn't want any part of that," Caver said.

McLaren then typed a 174-word letter addressed to ROT member Carolyn Carney of San Antonio and the Tenth ROT Congress, together with handwritten wills signed by Mike Matson, Robert "White Eagle" Otto, Gregg and Karen Paulson, and himself.

Next, the Rangers' command post received a fax from Boyce Eugene Halbison, identifying himself as president of the ROT as of April 19, 1997. Halbison ordered McLaren's surrender. ROT Major General Melvin Louis

Kriewald also had signed an order for McLaren and his companions to lay down their arms and to surrender. The Texas Rangers delivered that message to the embassy by way of a diplomatic package drop.

McLaren announced at 3:44 p.m. that he would not comply with Halbison's commands. Much of McLaren's written reply could not be deciphered.[12]

"It's just really strange when you try and read that and try to decipher it and figure out exactly what he means by some of that stuff," Caver said. "It was news to me. I didn't really understand what he was talking about."

Then McLaren announced he would relieve attorney Terence O'Rourke of his duties. That action also bewildered Caver. "I had a hard time trying to figure him [McLaren] out. I'm not sure I ever did or ever will. He just has a strange way about him and his philosophies," he said.

While no one suspected McLaren might try to take his own life, Caver thought the ROT leader wanted fame. "I personally thought that he wanted to go down in a blaze of glory. I think he wanted to basically make us kill him. Based on his actions, that is what I felt was going to happen," he said.

At four thirty that afternoon, Evelyn McLaren announced in a telephone conversation with Jess Malone that she would surrender. Before she did so, she told him that she had some preparations to make. Law enforcement would wait nearly twenty-four hours.

15

Day Seven

The McLarens Surrender as Two ROT Members Escape

ONE DAY about mid-morning, without any explanation, the guards removed Jo Ann Turner from her isolation cell and returned her to the women's cellblock in the Travis County Correctional Complex.

"I asked, 'Why have I been here?' One guard said, 'We're not allowed to tell you. You can ask your attorney.' I asked, 'What attorney?' They were just so vague," she said.[1]

"I just couldn't imagine because I was fifty-four at the time. I wondered what a younger person might be going through. They had yet to experience any joy in life. How could they handle all of that?"

Once Jo Ann was back inside the cellblock, her fellow inmates asked if she knew why she had been kept in solitary confinement. She offered only one reply: "I told them, 'Read the newspapers and watch the news on TV. You'll find out why they think I'm in here, but it's not the truth.' The truth was that I was a scapegoat," Jo Ann said.

From the television in the common room of the complex, Jo Ann watched the broadcast about the arrest of Robert "White Eagle" Otto and Rick McLaren streamed live from the Davis Mountains. Otto wore overalls and a T-shirt, like a farmer about to go to work in the fields. McLaren, gaunt with his balding scalp and wild hair sticking out from the sides of his head, looked just as unruly as ever. He carried a briefcase and wore jeans, a western shirt, a sports coat, and boots, but Jo Ann thought he looked somewhat like an unkempt used car salesman.

Evelyn, on the other hand, looked well-coiffed. She had curled her bleached blond hair and dressed in her Sunday-best dress as if headed to church instead of jail. Jo Ann imagined that Evelyn had prepared well in advance for her media close-up. The media's cameras seemed to photograph and videotape the McLarens' faces from every angle in celebrity-like profiles, though they referred to the two ROT members as "paper terrorists." Jo Ann recalled that, two years earlier, her friends the McLarens had offered what seemed like sound advice following her home eviction. They had suggested that she telephone the owner of Alar Moving Company to ask for the return of some of her possessions taken during the Turners' eviction. McLaren had told Jo Ann that Texas' property laws required the company to return some of her basic furnishings.[2]

That day, after she had called and spoken to the owner of Alar Moving Company, a truck had arrived at the Turners' apartment. Movers returned her bed, kitchen table, and some mismatched dishes but none of her mother-in-law's crystal or china or the Turners' expensive furnishings. Nearly everything else the Turners owned had been auctioned and sold to the highest bidders. She had lost everything else, including boxes of her children's baby photos.

She recalled how one day a woman who purchased the anonymous unmarked and unopened box at auction had telephoned Jo Ann and asked to meet with her in the parking lot at the Arboretum. "She had this one box that she had purchased that had the baby pictures, but not all of them," Jo Ann said. "She just kept saying, 'I'm so sorry for you. I am so sorry,' and then she left."

Now Jo Ann wondered what words of comfort she might offer to Rick and Evelyn McLaren if she might be allowed to talk to them. They likely also would lose everything they owned following their arrest and incarceration. At the very least, each of them had lost their dignity. Silently, she said a prayer for her friends.

■ ■ ■

On day seven of the siege, May 3, 1997, Evelyn McLaren prepared to surrender to law enforcement officials by washing and styling her hair and applying face makeup.

"She was supposed to have met us at eight o'clock that Saturday morning, but it was several hours later. I want to say it was about ten p.m. before she finally came out," former Texas Ranger and commander Captain Barry Caver said.[3]

Meanwhile, McLaren began drafting a peace treaty for his common-law wife to deliver to the Texas Rangers along with the terms of his surrender. Caver consulted with Fort Stockton district attorney Albert Valadez as well as with Texas Ranger Chief Bruce Casteel about whether he should sign McLaren's cease-fire agreement.

"We were all basically in agreement that I would be signing it under duress based upon the stipulations, in that I could go ahead and sign it and it wouldn't be binding in a legal courtroom," Caver said.

The Texas Rangers allowed Evelyn to walk from the trailer, where she and other ROT members had been holed up for six days, to the Rangers' command post. Negotiator Jess Malone met her on the dirt road and brought her inside the former fire station to introduce her to Captain Caver.

As part of their agreement, Evelyn called McLaren to tell him that she had arrived safely at the command post and that the Texas Rangers had treated her with dignity and respect.[4] She used their secret "Code 99" to indicate to her husband that she was telling the truth.[5]

Within minutes, McLaren exited the ROT trailer as if he were merely walking outside for a stroll. He was followed by Otto. The latter ROT member pointed his sharp nose and pursed his lips in the air in defiance. Gregg and Karen Paulson walked to a little shack not far from the trailer where all the guns owned by the ROT had been stored. The couple sat down in their camouflage fatigues beside the ROT compound's flagpole to surrender in military fashion. In the midst of the activity, two other ROT members, Mike Matson and Richard Keyes, escaped into the mountains on foot.

"It was sort of all happening at the same time. Again, the spotters we had up on the ridge could see everything going on because it was out in the open. They could see that Matson and the other guy Keyes went out of the trailer the other way—the back way—and up through the canyon and into the woods," Caver said.

A handful of snipers who had held a vantage point on a six-thousand-foot ridge behind the trailer watched as the ROT members escaped into the mountain terrain.

"We didn't have any choice at that point because we already knew that there were some booby traps and some IEDs [improvised explosive devices][6] set around," he said. "It was a dangerous situation at that point. We needed to take everyone into custody that was willing to give themselves up, and then once we got those people handcuffed and in custody, then we would pursue the other two."

The homemade bombs had been constructed using many different forms of common materials, such as pipes, nails, glass, and metal fragments, and they had been intended to destroy any trespassers. The IEDs were designed to be ignited by a mix of flammable fuels and a power source. ROT members had concealed the explosives, along with tripwires, in the dirt surrounding their embassy.

The Texas Rangers decided to pause their pursuit of Keyes and Matson, who had escaped into a canyon in the Davis Mountains after the sun had set and temperatures had dropped to close to freezing. Caver said the local wildlife contributed to the possible threat for anyone who pursued the escapees.

"There were rattlesnakes everywhere. It was just a dangerous situation between chasing these people in the dead of night and the terrain and the type of environment we were in. We just decided to call it off until the next morning," Caver said.

16

Day Eight
Deactivating Explosives in the DMR

WATCHING THE television broadcasts from inside Travis County Correctional Complex, Jo Ann Turner[1] spied her first glimpse of the Republic of Texas (ROT) headquarters that the McLarens had boastingly referred to as "the embassy." She had never seen the structure in person, but on television, the trailer appeared to her to be as raggedy as a homeless shelter.

The people arrested at the compound appeared briefly on the television monitor. She only vaguely recognized Gregg and Karen Paulson, whom she had met once at a ROT meeting held in Austin; she had not considered them acquaintances, let alone friends. She could not remember ever meeting the strange-looking man outfitted in military garb that the media identified as Robert "White Eagle" Otto. His face held an ominous look. However, watching the arrest of her friends Rick and Evelyn McLaren, Jo Ann wondered if perhaps she had made a mistake in trusting them. The thought caused her to reminisce about all of her past acquaintances. However, the names and faces of her other former friends had grown faint over the years, and memories of them only brought Jo Ann sadness and regret. She had at one time rubbed elbows with some of Austin's most respected and elite members of society.

Jo Ann's circle of friends had once included Bob and Margaret Kelly, who held tremendous prestige in Austin's Junior League. The Kellys had orchestrated the renovation of the 1900s classic revival home, the Daniel H. Caswell House.[2] However, she had not heard from the couple in years.

She recalled the summer of 1966 as a happy one when Jeff had made friends with two little boys in their neighborhood. Life seemed idyllic then as the Turners regularly entertained Bill's friends from the Texas DMV. Before school began, Bill and Jo Ann took Jeff and his best friend, Marty Pagnozzi, to Six Flags Astroworld[3] in Houston. They invited along Marty's parents, Pag and Barbara Pagnozzi, who owned a mechanic's shop near the old Robert Mueller Municipal Airport.[4] During their outing to the amusement park, the children rode the Texas Cyclone rollercoaster and the Wagon Wheel ride, and afterward they ate hotdogs and cotton candy and drank sodas along the park's midway.

In the 1970s, Jeff made friends with Gary Depew, a boy his own age who lived just down the street. Gary's parents had told the Turners about the Austin duplex when they transferred back to Austin from Houston. Winston Depew also worked with Bill in the same DMV department. He and his wife, Susan, and their son, Gary, had become fast friends with the Turners. The two families had entertained often at one another's homes.

Bill also had invited his fellow members of Ben Hur Shriners to their home. Jo Ann too had belonged to the Ladies Oriental Shrine of North America as a charter member of Austin's chapter. She had climbed the organization's social ladder to acquire the position of high priestess, the equivalent of its president. She had worn that crown proudly.

Throughout the 1980s, Jo Ann had befriended several of her coworkers at Shoal Creek Hospital, including the doctors and nurses who lived in affluent Bryker Woods, a historically elite neighborhood.[5] Despite the Turners' indebtedness, Jo Ann threw a lavish party for Nancy Townsend, the Shoal Creek Hospital administrator, to celebrate her upcoming promotion to another position in Nashville, Tennessee. Jo Ann had hosted Townsend's party with professional caterers and spared no expense in decorating.

The Turners had invited everyone they knew, but only one couple from their own neighborhood had joined the Turners' party, Kenneth and Mickey Hannes. Kenneth had previously worked as a machinist with Cameron Iron Works in Houston before they moved to Austin and bought a lake house. The Hannes had often invited the Turners onto their large flat-bottomed party boat complete with a tarp cover. Jo Ann recalled how Kenneth had enjoyed decorating his boat for different events, such as parades on the lake.

They lost touch with the few friends they had made after Jo Ann began spending more time working outside the home. Subsequently, she missed most if not all of her daughter Kelly's PTA meetings, open houses, and school events. Bill continued to favor Kelly and to spend time with her alone; he would take her shopping at Barton Creek Mall or to the movies. Other times, he would drop Kelly off at a friend's house. Kelly became popular among a group of students at Hill Country Middle School, and she kept those friendships later while she attended Westlake High School in the wealthy Eanes Independent School District. Yet, the parents of Kelly's schoolmates never once had visited the Turners' home or invited the family over to dinner.

Throughout the 1980s, Kelly spent many of her free evenings alone watching popular TV shows, including *Dallas*,[6] a fictitious tale about a wealthy family of Texas ranchers that was filmed at Southfork Ranch in Parker, Texas. However, she preferred *Charlie's Angels*, a scintillating fictional series about three women who dressed in bikinis, evening gowns, or other sexy clothing while working for a private investigation agency. Kelly had developed a more conservative and somewhat tailored sense of fashion. She wore a lot of skirts and blouses; sometimes she wore a sweater tied around her shoulders. Jo Ann noticed that her daughter did not wear much makeup; she was a natural beauty with dark arched eyebrows, perfect skin, and long eyelashes. Occasionally, but not very often, Kelly wore a little bit of lip color.

When Kelly began dating close to the end of her junior year of high school, Jo Ann noticed that her daughter's boyfriends were all good-looking. Jo Ann insisted on meeting the young men whenever they came to the house. Jo Ann's favorite of Kelly's suitors was Brian O'Halloran,[7] an Austin guitarist, and she made every effort to make him feel welcome. When Kelly expressed to her mother that she might be a little overbearing, Jo Ann dismissed the comment without a thought.

After graduating from Westlake High School, Kelly earned an undergraduate degree in psychology in 1995 from the University of Texas. Despite being deep in debt, the Turners held a large graduation party for their daughter at their lake house. A few of Kelly's high school and college friends who owned cigarette boats,[8] high-powered speedboats, parked them side-by-side in the lake channel beside the Turners' house. All day long they took turns providing rides for Kelly's guests up and down Town Lake. No one, including Kelly, likely had suspected that a foreclosure lurked in the Turners' future.

Now Jo Ann wondered if any of her friendships and associations in her life had served her well. It seemed to her that she had always given more than she received. Certainly, now she felt that she did not have a real friend left in the world.

■ ■ ■

On day eight of the siege at the Davis Mountain Resort (DMR), May 4, 1997, the Texas Rangers began the arduous task of searching hundreds of miles of mountainous terrain for two missing separatist members of the ROT: Richard Keyes and Mike Matson.

The Davis Mountains encompass the southern segment of the Rocky Mountain range that dominates most of western North America.[9] From Marfa northward, the range extends forty-five miles. Volcanic activity more than 25 million years ago formed the unusual landscape that features spectacular canyon walls made by the outcrops of bedrock that rise to elevations of more than eight thousand feet. Mount Livermore, also known as Mount Baldy or Baldy Peak, at 8,382 feet marks the highest peak.

Within Davis Mountains State Park, eleven miles of hike and bike trails meander along narrow cliff edges hundreds of feet tall. However, off trail, even the most experienced nature lovers find the remote and rugged terrain challenging, especially during inclement weather. Navigating the mountains can prove dangerous for humans, as rattlesnakes and mountain lions increase the risk.

The Texas Rangers knew Matson to be a trained survivalist who had once served in the United States Marines. They knew less about Keyes, the ROT's twenty-one-year-old follower. Both men had escaped a trailer that had served as the group's headquarters just one day earlier.

McLaren would one day tell a newspaper reporter that he gave Keyes and Matson a choice that day either to surrender or to escape, by comparing their experiences to the dramatic last moments of the

Battle of the Alamo.[10] Five ROT members taken into custody that day included Rick and Evelyn McLaren, Gregg and Karen Paulson, and Robert "White Eagle" Otto. After the arrests, a US Army explosive ordnance disposal (EOD)[11] team arrived on the scene.

"We had personnel to try and deal with any kind of bomb issues—which we had a lot of," Captain Barry Caver said.[12]

Gregg Paulson agreed to stay behind to help state bomb technicians locate and disarm all the ROT's explosive devices one-by-one, and the process took hours.

The EOD squad found twelve gasoline containers rigged with fuel ready to be ignited and rolled downhill, thirty to forty crude pipe bombs, a five-pound propane tank filled with explosives, and a myriad of trip wires connected to booby traps.[13] Once the bomb squad had secured the outside perimeter of the trailer, they cautiously searched inside for more weapons and evidence. Wofford remembers the day very well.

"They deactivated a bunch of homemade bombs that they [the ROT] had scattered around the periphery of his little place there," Wofford said.[14] "Propane bombs and pipe bombs with nails in them and stuff like that, supplies that Rick's wife had carried into him—that was the scary thing."

The siege at the DMR ended without one loss of life on the law enforcement side of the standoff.

"All of us in law enforcement that day would have preferred that after day one they all would have put their hands up and walked out and said, 'We're through,' instead of doing what they did," Wofford said. "You know we didn't want to see anybody killed up there, but at the same time, we weren't going to let any of our people on the law enforcement side of the house be killed either."

Law enforcement agents began dispersing from the scene, including members of the local Jeff Davis County Sheriff's Department, the Department of Public Safety, the FBI, and Border Patrol—all of the more than three hundred officers who had been present since the siege began. Only one federal entity had not been invited to participate: the Bureau of Alcohol, Tobacco, Firearms and Explosives (ATF). US Attorney General Janet Reno had prohibited the ATF from participating in the standoff at the DMR, fearing similar mistakes to those made by the organization at Waco.[15]

FBI negotiator Gary Noesner[16] suggested to the Texas Rangers that, rather than act with force, they use the press in a positive way to get the ROT members to do what law enforcement wanted them to do.

"That's the disagreement that led us to so many problems in Waco. Of course, David Koresh also was a very different figure; McLaren was kind of self-deluded and had an overinflated sense of himself and was sort of a bombastic guy. Koresh had some of those characteristics, but Koresh was also very, very manipulative and self-serving," Noesner said.

Noesner said he never wholly figured out McLaren's motivation behind his attempts to reclaim Texas for his ROT members—other than perhaps financial gain and power. "His was more about sovereignty, and you know, he was more like this patriot movement kind of folks than he was a cult-type. There's no shortage of either kind, but certainly McLaren felt very passionate about his interpretation of Texas as having never been part of the United States and the US government and paying taxes were something they didn't have to pay attention to," Noesner said.

A certain political ilk will take a very complex issue and make it very simplistic and use a buzzword or trigger word to inflame their followers, he said.

Throughout the siege, McLaren constantly summoned followers of his ROT cause to join him in the standoff. Law enforcement officers believed that he used a variety of radio communications gear, including Citizens Band Radio Service,[17] satellite radios, as well as local radio station broadcasts.

DPS media chief Mike Cox also spoke to the local media during the siege in an attempt to deescalate the standoff. Noesner collaborated with Cox about the wording of the statement.

"One of the points we made was, 'We're trying to take the big, bad federal government out of this, and we were saying this is a State of Texas matter. This has nothing to do with the federal government,'" Noesner said.

The Texas Rangers took charge of the siege, and representatives of the federal government served only as consultants.

While US government officials previously had refused to negotiate with anyone who took hostages, Noesner supported the decisions made by Caver to swap Robert Scheidt for the Rowes early in the negotiations.

Noesner supported the swap as a very successful turn of events in the DMR standoff.

"I will tell you our [government] negotiation orthodoxy is, 'You don't trade hostages,' but in this case, it was a smart and wise move because the Rangers were getting innocent people out," Noesner said. "It was a good trade in my opinion. The Rangers got a little criticism for that, but I defended them on that as having made what I thought was a great decision."

Also on May 4, the Texas Rangers decided to bring tracking dogs out to hunt for the missing ROT members, Matson and Keyes. Dog handlers from the James Lynaugh Unit in Fort Stockton released sixty dogs provided by the Texas Department of Corrections. As darkness fell, the Rangers attempted without success to track the two missing ROT members through the Davis Mountains.

That night, both the dogs and their handlers camped out on the mountainside, sleeping on the ground unsheltered, with plans to start a fresh search the next morning when daylight broke.

Governor George W. Bush released a formal statement regarding the ROT standoff at a press conference on May 4, 1997, held inside the governor's mansion in Austin.[18] Bush's statement read:

> "It is fine for people to come together and air their grievances," Bush said. "But it is not good for people to be carrying all kinds of weapons and threatening innocent citizens."
>
> "And if that were to happen again, the state of Texas would take appropriate action and the people would be brought to justice just like happened out in Fort Davis."

17

Day Nine
Mike Matson Dies

FROM INSIDE the cellblock, Jo Ann Turner[1] watched the evening news feeling a pang of sympathy for a tracking dog that the media had identified with a still photo and the name Sugar. The dog had likely died tracking two Republic of Texas (ROT) escapees in the Davis Mountains.

Jo Ann had always liked dogs. The Turner family once had rescued a large mixed-breed dog from the Austin Animal Shelter that her son Jeff named Rusty. That dog had provided years of affection for Jeff. Jo Ann recalled at bedtime she often would find Rusty curled up at the foot of Jeff's bed. In the mornings, whenever she woke Jeff, Rusty always licked her son's face to rouse him out of bed. The two would romp around the kitchen playing chase with a ball or another toy before breakfast. After school, Jeff often came home to an otherwise empty house, but as always Rusty wagged his tail to greet him.

Her son and his dog had developed a symbiotic relationship. Following those times when Bill had given Jeff a severe beating with a belt for what he determined was "smart talk" or disrespect, Rusty had refused to leave her son's side. Afterward, if Jeff chose not to come to the table to eat dinner, neither would Rusty. Ultimately, the dog chose Jeff over everyone and everything else.

At age sixteen, after Jeff had moved out of their house they did not hear from him for more than a year. Twelve long months of living without

Jeff took its toll on Rusty; eventually, the dog died of grief. She found Rusty one morning lying still on Jeff's bed. Jeff's faithful companion had proved loyal to a fault.

Jo Ann's thoughts snapped back into the present when a man's photo momentarily appeared on the television. Below the image a caption with a name appeared; the media identified the suspect as one of the escapees from the ROT compound. She did not recognize the man pictured and consequently felt nothing at all for him.

She did wonder briefly what in the world had happened to another missing ROT escapee that the media had identified in a photo; she thought Richard Keyes looked about her son's age. She felt a tinge of empathy for the young man's parents, although she did not know him or his family. She wondered how he had seemingly disappeared from the face of the Earth.

■ ■ ■

On day nine, at about two o'clock in the afternoon of May 5, the leader in a pack of eight tracking dogs from the James Lynaugh Unit Prison tracked two ROT members who had escaped from the embassy in the Davis Mountains.

At the foot of Mount Livermore[2] near a small man-made cave, one of the Lynaugh dogs, Sugar, spotted Mike Matson, a forty-eight-year-old former Marine from Colorado Springs. The mixed-breed blue tick Beagle and Bloodhound, with mostly black coloring except for her tan belly, weighed about thirty-five pounds. She had long floppy ears and soft brown eyes that made her appear both loveable and affectionate, but she had been trained only to track. As always on this day, Sugar had demonstrated her training for all work and no play.

"Prison dogs are trained to track you. Once they track you and find you, it's over for them. They're not attack dogs; they won't bite you. They'll track an inmate or a prisoner and then they'll lick him, play with him, and stand there with him," said Texas Ranger and negotiator Jess Malone.[3]

"Sugar finally caught up to Matson. The dog was just gonna go up to him and stand there like, 'Hey, I found you; tag, you're it.'"

Usually, the Lynaugh dog handlers followed their tracking dogs on horseback. However, the rugged terrain of the Davis Mountains had deterred them from bringing their horses. One of the dog handlers, Sergeant Ralph Hagar, had tracked Matson and Keyes on foot all morning.

By noon, the dog pack changed as Eric Pechacek, a thirty-two-year-old field lieutenant for the Lynaugh Unit Prison System sent eight of his Texas Department of Corrections tracking dogs through the mountains to chase down the two ROT suspects.

"It was so rough that we had to go in on foot," Pechacek said. "Horses couldn't keep up with the dogs in that rocky country. We had to just leave them, or else we were going to end up crippling them."[4]

Within two hours, Pechacek's five-year-old lead dog, Sugar, located Matson traveling alone on foot in the mountains. "She was one of the older dogs in the pack and had more experience, so she was one of the go-getters," he said. "They all had a job to do and a purpose, and theirs was tracking. Each dog was different; some were good trackers, some were good 'treers,' and some were aggressive, and some weren't aggressive. She was a good tracker, but she wasn't really an aggressive dog. She would go right to where she was supposed to; usually she was the first one to get there, but she wouldn't be the first one to get hold of 'em if she had to."

Sugar stopped Matson in his tracks that afternoon, but within seconds, the ROT member shot her at close range. She likely died instantly. Pechacek sensed immediately that something had happened to her. The dogs had tracked Matson to a spot beyond Pechacek's and Hagar's view; the two men heard high-pitched barking followed by a series of gunshots. After hearing the gunshots fired, Pechacek called back his dogs. Only seven dogs returned, two with non-life-threatening gunshot injuries.

When Sugar did not return, Pechacek headed into the area where he had initially heard his dogs barking. "The dogs were well ahead of us. You can't keep up with them on foot once they get on track; they're going to get ahead of you and leave you. You're just going to have to follow by sound," Pechacek said. "Sugar wasn't real vocal. She wasn't the last one, but she was going to be the one that stayed on the track because her nose didn't lie to you."

Texas Rangers stationed on the ground nearby held their positions for forty-five minutes waiting for additional help to arrive. Others traveling by military helicopters flew low through the mountains overhead to discover Matson's location and immediately commanded him by megaphone broadcasters to surrender.

Chapter 17

"I knew one of my dogs had been hurt because all seven of the others were all laying against my leg and the tree I was standing behind. Whenever I called to them, they all came to me," Pechacek said. "Sugar was the only one of them who did not return, so I was pretty certain that she was one of the first casualties of the gunshots when he [Matson] first started firing."

Instead of surrendering, Matson began shooting at the helicopters. About then, Texas Ranger Coy Smith opened fire on Matson with an AR-15 sporting rifle.[5] To cover Smith, Ranger Gene Key also fired a Mini-14 Ruger Ranch Rifle[6] at Matson from the helicopter.

"When he [Matson] started firing at the helicopters, with friends of mine standing on the rungs—that was his [Matson's] choice, nobody else's," Pechacek said.

Taking aim at Matson from fifty-six yards away, Pechacek fired his grandfather's .270 Winchester bolt action rifle.[7]

"I fired twice, and the first time I hit him right where I was wanting to—in the arm. That turned him a complete flip. Then he came up the second time and had the pistol in his other hand shooting at the helicopter. That's when I took a second shot at him," Pechacek said.

"It entered in just below his left shoulder, because he was facing away from me shooting up at the helicopter. It went in just underneath the shoulder blade, but it came out under the front pocket of a T-shirt he was wearing. It was a heart shot."

He saw Matson fall immediately, but Pechacek continued to hold his position in the brush for another forty minutes as a precaution in case the other ROT escapee, twenty-one-year-old Keyes, might appear. However, the St. Mary's, Kansas, native seemed to have disappeared. When the Texas Rangers arrived on the scene, Pechacek moved up the mountain to the location where he had seen Matson go down, and he found Sugar's body lying about ten feet away.

"She was right there up on him when he fired point blank at her chest. He just had a little .22 pistol, but it was effective," Pechacek said. "Her death was likely immediate."

Texas Ranger supervisor Carl Weathers also arrived on the scene with other Texas Rangers, Captain Barry Caver and negotiator Jess Malone. Soon afterward, Justice of the Peace George Vickers pronounced Matson dead.[8]

They found Matson's body prone and still clutching a flashlight that had been camouflaged with some leaves and secured to his arm with rubber bands. Though his body had been recovered during the daylight hours, Matson likely had used the camouflage overnight to reduce the flashlight's emissions to no more than necessary while traveling on foot through mountainous terrain.

As sunlight faded on the horizon, the team of trackers and Texas Rangers decided how best to transport Matson's body out of the mountain canyon. "I'm an old country guy raised on a ranch, and I kept telling Captain Weathers that I could pack Matson's body out of there on a horse because we had horses—kind of like an old Western, where you can strap somebody over the saddle," Malone said.

"Captain Weathers told me, 'I've got a helicopter comin' out of El Paso,' which was six hours away, and we had been out there eighteen or twenty hours. Everybody was tired. He kept saying, 'No son, we don't want to do that.'"

Instead, Weathers suggested to Malone that they airlift Matson's body by helicopter out of the mountains beyond the media's view. "He said, 'Son, come here. Let me explain something to you.' He said, 'You strap him [Matson] over that horse, and we take him down this mountain, and we get down there to Satellite City, and how's that going to look on every major news station in the United States?'" Malone said.

Later, when helicopter operators ran a cable down through the pine trees with a soldier attached to the end of it, the Texas Rangers insisted on a specific and highly unusual protocol: "We told that helicopter pilot, 'When you land, as a matter of respect, that dog comes off that helicopter first, and then he's [Matson's body] dumped off, and they did it," Malone said.

Pechacek said he took a photograph of one of the Texas Rangers carrying Sugar in his arms as they were lifted together into the helicopter. Afterward, the guards buried Sugar outside Fort Stockton, on the grounds of the James Lynaugh Unit. Meanwhile, the Rangers continued their search for Keyes.

"I actually thought he [Keyes] had gone back in there and died. I'm sure he probably got some help from somebody locally—either intentionally or unintentionally," Malone said.

Ralph Matson would later tell a reporter for the Associated Press that

Richard McLaren had "duped" his brother, Mike Matson, into thinking the ROT ambassador was a freedom fighter.[9] As a result, the younger Matson willingly gave his life fighting for the ROT.

As the saying goes, the apple does not fall far from the proverbial tree. Ironically, after the siege in the Davis Mountains ended, police in Newark, Ohio, arrested Gregg Paulson's sixteen-year-old son, John Paulson, and charged him with planting a fake bomb on the campus of Newark High School. The teenager would later admit in court that he planned the bomb scare as a prank. The threat caused the school to close for three days while police searched for other possible explosives.[10] Gregg Paulson and his ex-wife, Mary Paulson, had four children together, including John, before they divorced in 1975.

Meanwhile, the Texas Rangers gave up their search in the Davis Mountains for missing ROT member Richard Keyes.

18

Day Ten
The Search for Richard Keyes Ends in the Mountains

JO ANN[1] felt that no matter what became of her, she had already paid the ultimate price many times over for her association with the Republic of Texas (ROT) militia. She wondered what more anyone would attempt to take from her; she had nothing left to give. As darkness descended in her jail cell, she hoped that she might sleep a deep and dreamless sleep, never to awaken. Death to her seemed like a welcomed end to her tortured life.

However, after watching the evening news on television about the ROT standoff, she did manage to fall into a fitful sleep in her bunk. As she slept, she dreamed that she had escaped into the desert terrain high atop the Davis Mountains. Texas Rangers and tracking dogs followed close behind her in quick pursuit. Breathlessly, she searched the horizon for any sign of refuge and found none. Wandering through her ethereal surroundings, she found herself seemingly lost in the forest of suicides that she imagined to be the seventh circle of *Dante's Inferno*.[2]

Deep within her nightmare, a rattlesnake appeared wearing her husband's face, a mountain lion resembling Richard McLaren pounced at her, and a hawk with Evelyn McLaren's voice soared high into the sky calling Jo Ann by name. Terrified, she ran naked and barefooted across hot sand, sharp stones, and fire while scorpions attempted to sting her feet. Then she awoke with a start.

■ ■ ■

On day ten, May 6, 1997, the Texas Rangers gave up their search for missing ROT member Richard Keyes in the Davis Mountains. Though they had spotted plenty of wildlife and rattlesnakes, they had found no sign of Keyes.[3]

"We decided again that the terrain was just too rough. We were putting ourselves in more harm's way than we thought we should. It was kind of like trying to find a needle in a haystack," Barry Caver said.[4] "We had no idea where he was or which way he was headed. There's rattlesnakes and all kinds of wildlife, coyotes, mountain lions—and we just felt like the danger was too great to continue."

The number of law enforcement officers on the scene dwindled to less than half of the number from the previous day; about one hundred fifty agents remained. The Texas Rangers also began to allow about forty residents of the resort to return to their homes. Meanwhile, they informed the local residents to be on the lookout for Keyes in case he tried to flag someone down or to ask for a ride.

"I think it was quite an accomplishment for us to have gone through this whole ordeal for seven to ten days with only having to fire the one shot and everyone else eventually surrendered or captured later. So, when you look back overall, we accomplished everything that we set out to do," Caver said.

Feeling relieved after the siege ended, fatigue finally attacked Caver's body. His wife, Tammy, had worried about him daily throughout the siege, although they had talked by telephone regularly. Their boys, eleven and eight years old at the time, looked forward to having their dad back home in Midland.

Daryl Johnson writes in his book *Right Wing Resurgence: How a Domestic Terrorist Threat is Being Ignored* that Texas Department of Public Safety (DPS) officers had obtained a search warrant for the ROT compound and found several confidential government documents marked "For Official Use Only."[5] The officers learned that members of the ROT had planned to attempt to evict foreign military personnel and equipment from both Fort Bliss and Holloman Air Force Base in Texas. In their investigation of the ROT compound, officers had never been able to determine how the government documents had been obtained.

Together with several other Texas Rangers in June 1997, Caver and Governor George W. Bush would celebrate the surrender of the ROT militia. The reunion became an annual event and would continue well through 2009 when Bush's term as the nation's forty-third president ended and he and his family moved to a ranch in Crawford, Texas. Caver would grow even better acquainted whenever the Bush family visited the president's mother-in-law Jenna Hawkins Welch, a resident of Midland. Bush and Caver also participated in a few public events, including a fundraiser in Austin.

"I have a photograph of he [President Bush] and I running down Congress Avenue at a Special Olympics fundraiser—he was a big jogger back in the day, and so was I, so we were there to help protect him. I have some very fond memories of him," Caver said.

The Davis Mountain Resort (DMR) siege would highlight Caver's career as a Texas Ranger for more than a decade. About a month before his retirement from the Texas Rangers, Caver would work at another siege, in Eldorado, Texas, from April 3 through April 10, 2008, on a compound led by polygamist leader Warren Jeffs, who already was being held in prison on other charges.[6]

FBI agents finally arrested Richard Frank Keyes after his nearly four and a half months on the lamb, outside Sam Houston National Forest, September 20, 1997.[7] FBI agent Chris Swecker, together with Texas Rangers and a DPS special crimes unit, surrounded Keyes and arrested him by surprise.[8]

Agents captured the fugitive in the middle of the afternoon as Keyes walked alone and unarmed along FM to Market Road 1375 about fifty-five miles north of Houston. Agents later discovered Keyes's campsite and supplies that he had left behind in the nearby national forest. Through the use of physical surveillance specialists flying a Cessna airplane, plus maps and computer databases available at the time, the FBI team spotted Keyes.

"He just kind of played right into our hands. It could have been problematic. We had to make sure there was nobody else around. We wanted to take him down in an area where we had full control," Swecker said.⁹ "We just fully expected him to resist arrest. So, we wanted to get him at his most vulnerable point."

Keyes might have realized he was under surveillance and decided to give himself up to authorities. "He probably also knew how vulnerable he was, and he made the choice to not be armed and to live," Swecker said.

The fugitive had created a campsite near a public park where he left several supplies. Swecker compared Keyes to far right extremist Eric Rudolph,¹⁰ arrested in October 1998 in North Carolina. Rudolph had executed the bombing in Centennial Olympic Park in Atlanta, Georgia, midway through the 1996 Summer Olympics.

"These people are survivalists. They feel more comfortable away from society. They also know that at some point they're going to be on the run, so they're prepared for it. This is their way of preparing for that moment. They have campsites, stashed supplies, and they think society is going to disintegrate at some point," Swecker said. "A lot of them are what we call 'preppers': preparing for a sort of Armageddon. So that goes along with that type of ideology."

Though Keyes had not spoken with his relatives since before the time of his escape, his grandfather, Dr. Richard Keyes of Vincennes, Indiana, had communicated with members of law enforcement regularly throughout the summer. The FBI also had conducted surveillance operations at the residences occupied by several of Keyes's family members over the more than one hundred twenty days that he spent hiding from authorities. His grandfather had taken a leave from his job at North Knox High School in Vincennes to help search for his grandson. The separatist's father, Richard Keyes Jr., remained in St. Marys, Kansas.

Agents booked Keyes into the Harris County Jail by early evening on the same day of his capture and arranged to return him to Jeff Davis County. Texas Rangers, in May, had given up hope of ever finding the fugitive alive in the desolate Davis Mountains though they had correctly theorized that he might have escaped with the help of other unknown separatists.¹¹

Caver would discover exactly what happened to Keyes when the fugitive spoke to Joe Dyer, then an editor at the *Boulder Weekly* newspaper in June 1997.¹² Dyer provided a lengthy account of Keyes' escape and a plot to avenge the death of his late ROT friend and comrade Mike Matson.

Keyes told Dyer that once he escaped from the spot where the Texas Rangers killed Matson, he telephoned a friend with a New Mexico militia group. Members of that group moved Keyes into hiding by transporting him to and from a series of safehouses.[13]

Another article by Dyer ran in *Mother Jones* on June 25, 1997.[14] In that interview's transcript, Keyes described how he could feel the blades of the helicopters "slash the air just a few yards above his head" during the day-long mountain search led by the Texas Rangers.

Dyer and Keyes had met a year earlier while the writer researched the antigovernment movement growing in the Davis Mountains. The two had spoken by phone on the very day that the West Texas standoff began. *Mother Jones* printed Keyes's verbatim account about what he said happened on the morning of Sunday, April 27, 1997, following Robert Scheidt's arrest.[15]

> "[Richard] McLaren and White Eagle [Robert Otto] come running out of the embassy saying that they heard on the [police] scanner that Bob Scheidt had been picked up. Gregg Paulson made the immediate decision on the spot to take a portion of the embassy guard right into Fort Davis, capture the courthouse, and free Bob Scheidt. I argued against that because I said that if, as we had suspected, Joe Rowe, who was located at the entrance of Davis Mountain Resort, had told Sheriff Bailey that Bob was leaving the resort area, then he would also call Sheriff Bailey and say we were leaving too. Bailey would have 15 minutes' advance notice that we were coming.
>
> "We started to leave the embassy perimeter in White Eagle's car; we being Gregg Paulson, Karen Paulson, and myself. We were about a mile away when White Eagle called us back on the radio." The orders had changed. "Instead of going into Fort Davis, we were told to capture the Rowes' house, hold the Rowes as prisoners of war."[16]

Dyer also authored a book about the growing underground domestic terrorist movement he referred to as the "alternate America."[15]

A jury convicted Keyes of aggravated assault on June 20, 1998,[17] and today the forty-four-year-old is still serving a ninety-year sentence at the Barry B. Telford Unit in Texarkana, ineligible for parole until 2087.

Throughout the 1980s and 1990s, FBI agents dealt heavily with domestic terrorism. The Fort Davis standoff had followed others at Ruby

Ridge, Idaho, in 1992;[18] Waco, Texas, in 1993;[19] and in Jordan, Montana, in 1996.[20]

"The FBI was very focused on domestic terrorism because of Oklahoma City[21] and because of all the standoffs around the country that had occurred. We had some violent incidents and some violent standoffs," Swecker said. "Probably the Texas group was one of those that led with violations in stockpiling weapons, occasional breakouts of violence, targeting government people, especially law enforcement. We were very focused on that. This was sort of the tail end of that era."

On May 8, 1997, Texas Attorney General Dan Morales filed a state lawsuit against Carolyn Carney, a ROT member, claiming she had failed to pay thirty-two thousand dollars in sales taxes to San Antonio and to the state.[22] A Bexar County constable arrested another ROT member, Donald Varnell of St. Hedwig, and charged him with two counts of contempt for disobeying a summons by State District Judge Joseph Hart, who charged him with issuing false liens to Texas businesses.

On May 9, 1997, Representative Allen Hightower (D-Huntsville) authored a bill that made writing phony liens a state crime punishable by up to two years in jail and a ten-thousand-dollar fine. The same bill also identified the issuance of false court complaints, judgments, or summons as a Class A misdemeanor.[23]

Part III

After the ROT War

19

State Trial for the ROT, and the Worst of Times for the Turners

TRAVIS COUNTY jailers suddenly released Jo Ann Turner on May 27, 1997. She immediately telephoned her husband, Bill, at home. The guards offered no explanation for her release but simply told her that she was free to leave.

"'Come get me,' I told Bill. 'I'm a free woman,' but I felt anything but free from suffering," she said.[1]

Jo Ann had spent a combined forty days in both the Travis County Jail and the Travis County Correctional Complex and had lost twenty-five pounds as part of what she would someday jokingly refer to as "my prison diet." However, her humor had evaporated long ago; instead, Jo Ann felt only shame and humiliation.

She dressed in the same clothes that she had worn on the day of her arrest, although she noticed that her pants and blouse looked slightly soiled and wrinkled. She placed the same sandals on her feet and stood just inside the doors of the facility while clutching her purse and patiently waiting for Bill to arrive.

When Bill picked her up a half hour later, Jo Ann felt relieved but numb. He drove to their favorite restaurant, Red Lobster, on South Lamar Boulevard. After they ordered, they spoke very little as they ate their meal.

"It was a little strained because I didn't particularly care to share too much about my time in jail with him. I could tell that he was disinterested in it and in me," she said. "He was bothered by the fact that I had caused all of these problems. He blamed me for getting involved with the ROT and for going to jail and [for] him having to be at home fixing his own meals with no one to do it for him like I used to. I was to blame for everything."

Bill really did not need to verbally blame Jo Ann because she felt a tremendous amount of guilt. "That's when I think I finally broke down. I said, 'I'm sorry that all of this happened. I'm sorry that I caused you so much trouble,' and all he said was, 'Okay. Well, let's not go through this again,'" Jo Ann said.

Back at their apartment and already tired after a full day, they retired early because Bill had to report to work at Leal Trucking by seven thirty the next morning. That night, the Turners slept back to back in the same bed, just as they always had, but in silence. Neither felt a need to read, nor did they care to discuss the day's events. The same scene would play out night after night in their two-bedroom apartment over the months to come.

The next morning, Jo Ann awoke anxious to read any ongoing coverage in the *Austin American-Statesman* about the arrests of the Republic of Texas (ROT) members in the Davis Mountains.[2] She expected to see a report about her jail release somewhere in the paper, but she found no mention.

Since her release, none of the members of the media had attempted to ask her how a former businesswoman from Westlake had found herself penniless and incarcerated. Had anyone asked, Jo Ann might have shared her long and sad story. However, twenty years would pass before she would have the chance.

During the days that followed, after Bill left for work in the mornings, Jo Ann busied herself by cleaning the apartment and by searching all the job listings in the *Austin American-Statesman*. Eventually, she contacted Kelly Services, an employment agency, to work as a temporary receptionist or a secretary around town.

Summer passed without much celebration. The Turners kept to themselves and did not entertain, and they did not leave their apartment except to go to work or to buy groceries. Unlike they had in the past,

Bill and Jo Ann did not host a cookout on Memorial Day or watch the fireworks show at Zilker Park or from Town Lake on the Fourth of July. Bill also worked all day on Labor Day and came home to eat a meatloaf that Jo Ann had prepared.

During that time, Jeff lived in Tahoe with his live-in girlfriend Melissa Chamberlain and their son Chance Turner. Southwest Airlines had assigned Kelly to a permanent base in Los Angeles, California. Thanksgiving arrived without celebration, and for the first time ever in their married lives, Bill and Jo Ann ate their holiday dinner alone. Jo Ann prepared a small lunch with traditional items—cornbread dressing, green beans, and cranberry sauce, but she roasted a whole chicken instead of a turkey.

Jo Ann missed her familiar china, crystal, and sterling silver place settings. The Turners ate their meal on a few melamine plates she had purchased at Target. They did not bother to eat at their stainless-steel kitchenette with its Formica tabletop. Instead, they ate at the kitchen counter on barstools. She wondered where else in the city someone might be eating a holiday meal using her former table settings. Finally, she called her sister, Lillian Mae Lehman, as she always had, to wish her a happy Thanksgiving. However, Jo Ann kept the conversation light and uninformative.

"I let Lillian know that I was 'out' of jail and that I was home. She knew I had been in jail, but I don't think she ever knew why. She never asked. I don't think she would have understood if I had told her," Jo Ann said. "Nobody talked about my arrest, though it was all over the television news and in the newspapers."

She did not call her youngest sister, Becky Canady. The two had never been close because of their age difference; they were born seventeen years apart. She also didn't want to worry Becky.

■ ■ ■

The state trial against Richard McLaren and Robert Otto had moved to Brewster County Courthouse[3] in Alpine on a change of venue. The regal courthouse provided a beatific backdrop to an otherwise less blissful event in November 1997. Public animosity toward members of the ROT remained high despite the change in locale twenty-six miles southeast of Fort Davis.

Ancient pecan trees surrounded the two-story historical building constructed of red bricks, cream-colored wood trim, and limestone mortar. The site also served a dual purpose because of its matching gazebo as both a community center and a favored wedding site. Across from 201 West Avenue E, inside a matching jailhouse, two ROT defendants remained secured behind bars awaiting court.

Looking out the window from inside his jail cell, McLaren likely had a picturesque view of the grounds, including mounted artillery that stands on the east lawn. The courthouse appears on National Register of Historical Places and has been a Texas Historical Landmark since 1965.[4]

The 394th District Court of Brewster County in Alpine tried McLaren and Otto together. Their trial lasted just one week as the jury heard evidence presented against the two defendants, said former state prosecutor Albert Valadez.[5] However, other than a spectacle they created while representing themselves at the trial, McLaren and Otto spent very little time inside the courtroom.

McLaren and Otto had insisted on representing themselves even though 394th State District Judge Kenneth DeHart had provided them with court-appointed attorneys. DeHart removed McLaren and Otto from the courtroom nine times because they refused to follow courtroom procedures by often interrupting the proceedings with loud outbursts and political statements.[6]

Their own defense arguments hinged on the belief that they represented the Republic of Texas as a sovereign nation and that the state held no jurisdiction over them as foreign nationals. The two members of the ROT stated repeatedly that the United States had not properly annexed Texas in 1845.

DeHart asked a guard to remove both men from his courtroom and to place them in a separate viewing room with camera surveillance after attempts to control their interruptions went unheeded. More than once, DeHart invited the defendants back into his courtroom to participate in the trial. However, both McLaren and Otto stood and delivered defiant declarations that fractured every courtroom protocol.

"It was very annoying to everyone, and it was disruptive to our proceedings, and the judge gave them many warnings, but they wouldn't stop," Valadez said. "They were brought back into the courtroom for the purpose of cross-examining the witnesses. Instead of cross-examining the witnesses, they would go into the same tirade, so the judge said enough, and we ended up having to do that with every single witness."

In an adjoining room with a monitor providing a livestream feed, the two defendants watched and listened to their trial proceedings and to the testimony of the state's witnesses. The ROT members, who had attempted to control the courtroom proceedings, consequently forfeited their chance to be heard.

"It was a show for them. I don't know how serious they thought this was going to turn. I don't think they thought that their lives were going to end up being spent in prison. They soon found out it wasn't a joke," Valadez said. "They were going to have to answer for their crimes, and the courts would figure out whether Texas is or is not part of the Union. We knew that wasn't an issue. It made us think that Rick was a person who was really just out of his mind."

Only Valadez called witnesses; no one spoke on behalf of McLaren, although several ROT members sat in the audience watching the week-long trial. Neither McLaren nor Otto made any attempt to speak in his own defense. Three witnesses testified on Otto's behalf.

"Rick had enough knowledge to read the law, but unfortunately, he didn't understand it. Because he spoke well and the others were not as educated as he was, this group listened to him. It made sense to them because it sounded right, but of course it wasn't. So, the premise was flawed from the very beginning," Valadez said.

Witnesses for the prosecution included Joe Rowe, formerly held as a hostage inside his own home in Fort Davis for thirteen hours beginning April 27, 1997, by ROT members Gregg and Karen Paulson and Richard Keyes. The trial proved for Rowe to be a strange reunion of sorts.

On October 28, 1997, in less than two hours, a jury found both McLaren and Otto guilty of conspiracy and kidnapping. Jurors had been selected from little more than five thousand people in the county seat, also home to Sul Ross State University.

On November 4, 1997, DeHart sentenced McLaren to ninety-nine years in prison[7] and Robert "White Eagle" Otto to fifty years and attached a ten-thousand-dollar fine for plotting a kidnapping.[8] The state never charged Evelyn McLaren, but she was held without bond while she and her husband and several other ROT members awaited a federal trial on charges of bank and mail fraud. A second federal trial on charges of violating the National Firearms Act also awaited Richard Lance McLaren and other ROT members.

In 1998, three remaining members of the ROT who had been present at the standoff—Gregg and Karen Simon Paulson and Richard Frank Keyes III—would face separate state trials in 311th District Court in Marfa.

■ ■ ■

Just as they had muddled through Thanksgiving, the Turners also suffered through Christmas 1997 in isolation. Memories of their former home beside Town Lake and the large mahogany dining-room table with beautiful place settings for as many as twelve people haunted Jo Ann.

To make their small apartment festive, Jo Ann had purchased a tabletop tree, hung some string lights from the boughs, and added a few colored bulbs.

"I felt so empty in the Shepherd Mountain apartments. It felt like I was just going through the motions just to try to make Bill happy. I just tried to set the stage for the holiday, but it just didn't feel realistic or [feel like] something I really wanted to do. I felt like I was living a nightmare," Jo Ann said.

Christmas came and went without gifts. She cooked a ham and some sweet potatoes and made a German chocolate cake, Bill's favorite. Afterward, they sat in front of the television watching holiday specials in silence. When Bill slipped off to bed, Jo Ann sat alone in the dark living room wondering what the new year might bring.

Early in 1998, the Turners moved into a duplex owned by Earl Fields located off Lakeshore Drive. Fields also owned a two-slip boathouse on the lake where the Turners docked their boat, which had escaped auction. In the months that followed, they continued to spend their weekends in solitude, boating on the water.

"We could have entertained, but we didn't. At that point, I think that we both were—more so myself—embarrassed about our situation. I just was reluctant to talk to anybody. Besides that, I didn't know if anyone would want to talk to me," Jo Ann said.

She closed her real estate and networking office at Wind River Office Park on Angus Road that she had shared with Mary Magel. From the office, the Turners removed a beautiful coffee table with four cushioned chairs on rollers to furnish their new duplex. Jo Ann purchased other furnishings at local consignment shops. Soon their duplex began to look like a home, but Jo Ann did not feel satisfied.

"Bill was happy to be back living beside the lake near the water," Jo Ann said. "I had nice things again, but they were nothing like the irreplaceable and priceless things I had owned before. It wasn't enough."

Jo Ann soon began looking for an attorney to represent her in a lawsuit against Alar Moving Company. She remembered the name of attorney Nick Milam, who had represented her in court hearings in Travis County, and she called him.

"Nick took our case on consignment. No one else would even consider representing us," Jo Ann said. "We felt lucky to have him on our side."

Milam represented the Turners in court, and they were awarded two hundred thousand dollars as compensation for the loss of their personal possessions. She and Bill considered the amount that they received inconsequential considering the lifetime of cherished possessions they had amassed over the years and lost at auction. Approximately fifty thousand dollars of their financial award went to Milam. That left the Turners with little more than one hundred fifty thousand dollars.

Jo Ann learned by watching the news and reading the newspapers that Rick McLaren and Robert "White Eagle" Otto, had been tried on charges of conspiracy and kidnapping in a state court in Alpine.[3] The two, together with Evelyn McLaren and several others, also would face federal charges of mail and bank fraud in Dallas.

Worried that she might be indicted on any number of crimes related to the McLarens' cases or to those related to other ROT members, she began to feel an urgent need to hide. She also began trying to convince Bill to leave the United States with her.

"We were just sort of in limbo," she said. "I thought it was in my best interest and my time to just start packing everything and deciding what we were going to take and what we were going to sell. I started selling all that stuff in the duplex."

Then fellow Austinites Robert "Bob" Hughes and his wife Kay befriended the Turners. The Hugheses invited them to dinner at the Austin Country Club to talk about a vacation home that they owned in Honduras. Jo Ann thought Bob looked a bit like Ernest Hemingway and Kay resembled a gracefully aged Hollywood starlet.

Over cocktails, Jo Ann shared with the Hugheses her own tragic summary of the past two years. That night, the Hugheses suggested that her story might make a good screenplay. So, the next day, Jo Ann purchased a Brother WP-5600 MDS,[12] a hybrid type of typewriter. The word processor provided a little window at the center of the device located just above the carriage return that allowed her to see whatever she typed. The genius of the self-correcting apparatus was its ability to save to digital memory everything she typed and to print single sheets of standard typing paper simultaneously. Although not nearly as nice as the new computers being released on the market at the time, the Brother brand word processor to Jo Ann seemed both lightweight and affordable; the price was right too at just under four hundred dollars.

She also purchased several books about screenwriting, including *The Screenwriter's Bible: A Complete Guide to Writing, Formatting, and Selling Your Script*.[13] by David Trottier. Jo Ann read them cover to cover and soon felt self-taught in the craft of screenwriting. She had convinced herself that she could write her own compelling story and that it would make a great Hollywood film documentary someday.

The Turners did not throw themselves a going-away party in Austin. Instead, they purchased airplane tickets and made plans to secretly disappear out of the country.

"I didn't want anybody to know that I was leaving," Jo Ann said. "I just wanted to get away from it—as far away from it as I could. I didn't want any more involvement, or reminders of all that stuff that had caused me to go into jail to begin with."

One of the saddest chapters in my life has come to end. Jo Ann thought. The courts had stripped her of her dignity, but she hoped to leave the country with her self-respect intact. Bill told Jo Ann that he held second thoughts about leaving the United States because he feared that he would miss his musician friends, playing live music, and driving his boat on the lake.

"I just said, 'Why don't we go try it out and see how we like it, and if we do, we'll stay, and if not, we'll come back,'" Jo Ann said.

Jeff returned to Austin from Lake Tahoe about that time; he and Melissa had agreed to separate. Not long afterward, he decided he would make plans to leave the country together with his parents. He told Jo Ann he felt remorse about leaving behind his son, Chance Turner. Jeff had hoped to earn an advanced scuba diving license and to find opportunities to teach classes in Honduras.

"I think Jeff was just so frustrated with life himself, with the fact that we had the bankruptcy there in our past. I think he was interested in just getting away from it all too," she said.

"I was thinking we would try to retire there if it worked out. I felt like we had enough in our savings plus the money from the lawsuit. Plus, our Social Security checks were still going into the bank. I felt like we had enough to live on because it was so much cheaper to live there than back here in the states."

Kelly told her mother that she would never move to Honduras. She told Jo Ann that she wanted to remain in the United States and continue living in California and working for Southwest Airlines. Besides, Kelly's lifelong friends still lived in Austin, and she wanted to visit them often.

Jo Ann accepted Kelly's decision. After all, she thought, Kelly could always hop on a plane to visit them.

20

The Turners Leave the Country at the End of the ROT's First Federal Trial

THE TURNERS began making final plans to move from Austin to Honduras. Jo Ann[1] had feared that she might be arrested again during the interim between the state and federal trials of several Republic of Texas (ROT) members. So, the Turners had packed up, sold what they didn't need, and put what little else they owned into storage.

Because neither Jo Ann nor her husband Bill had ever been formally charged with a crime, their US passports and visas remained unrestricted, they could legally leave the country. Some Dallas friends had suggested that the couple relocate to Honduras. Former 302nd Family District Court Judge Bob Hughes[2] and his wife Kay owned a couple of businesses in Honduras. The Hugheses invited the Turners to spend a couple of weeks as guests in their three-story condo built on the island of Roatan.[3]

Kay had retired as a secretary for the Texas Senate. The Hugheses often commuted back and forth from their Dallas home to another house in Austin and to their exotic vacation condo in Honduras. They told Jo Ann that they maintained two businesses in Roatan, mostly souvenir shops where they sold trinkets made by Hondurans.

■ ■ ■

Security at the Earle Cabell Federal Building and Courthouse in the Northern District of Dallas[4] during the April 1998 federal trial of Richard and Evelyn McLaren had never been tighter.

The building already possessed a controversial history. The late district attorney Henry Wade had prosecuted Jack Ruby in the courthouse at 1100 Commerce Street after the gunman shot President John F. Kennedy's killer, Lee Harvey Oswald, on November 24, 1963. Wade also lost one of the most controversial cases in judicial history when Norma McCorvey, or "Jane Doe," sued him for the right to have an abortion in Texas. After trying the case twice, in 1971 and 1972, the Supreme Court ultimately decided in McCorvey's favor in the January 22, 1973, landmark decision *Roe vs. Wade*.[5]

The east wall of the federal Earle Cabell building shares the west wall of the Santa Fe Building, which was built in Art Deco style in 1925. The 402,500-square-foot, and twenty-nine-story federal building, situated on granite with a brown brick veneer, towers above 1114 Commerce Street in Dallas. Outside its first-floor front doors, an imposing belt of concrete medallions provides alternating images of American eagles, heads of the Roman god Mercury, and lotus flowers. Five concrete supporting columns divide recessed window bays obscured by aluminum panels. The US government had acquired the building and completely gutted its interior in 1978, but inside, plenty of exposed concrete remains.[6]

Dallas County law enforcement officials had considered the McLarens and other members of the ROT threats to the safety of the general public throughout the highly publicized trial. "During the federal trial, the US Marshalls had the tightest security I've ever seen in twenty years in a federal trial in Dallas," US Prosecutor Mike Uhl said.[7] "They shut down streets in Dallas to transfer the prisoners from Dallas County Jail here to the federal courthouse, and it was extremely tight security because they had, because of the West Texas siege and the violence they demonstrated out there and the guns."

The trial lasted six weeks; afterward, a Dallas jury took three and a half days of deliberation to find seven ROT members, including Richard and Evelyn McLaren, guilty of mail and bank fraud. US District Judge of the Northwestern District Joe Fish announced sentences April 15, 1998.[9]

Five new defendants were introduced at trial; their names and faces had never been associated with the ROT or mentioned by the media. In fact, their sole connections stemmed from private agreements made with Richard and Evelyn McLaren. As a result, the newly accused men were charged together with the McLarens for conspiring to commit bank and wire fraud.

In court, the defendants each claimed that McLaren had promised them bank charters, jobs, and salaries as officers of the ROT in return for cash down payments. However, other than the McLarens, only Richard George Kieninger had previously gained much public attention. More than ten years earlier, Kieninger had authored the book *The Ultimate Frontier* using the pen name Ekial Kueshana[10] and claimed to have been contacted by a secret brotherhood. He also joined a spiritual group known as Adelphi, founded in the community of Terrell, Texas, about an hour east of Dallas. That group practiced self-sufficiency and had expected the world to suffer an economic and governmental collapse by May 5, 2000.[11]

Attorney Tom Mills represented McLaren at the federal trial and remembers taking the case pro bono. "I did it because it was so interesting—but I think there were people in the Republic of Texas group, probably one of whom, or more than one who knew me, or I helped them out, or something. So, I got into it probably just doing it for free rather than getting paid; I don't think I got court-appointed," Mills said.[12]

However, Mills had a difficult time building McLaren's defense on several points. The defendants built their defense case around a claim that the FBI had planted an informant in their group in an attempt to entrap them. They identified the suspected informant as Arthur Griesacker, according to the *Texas Observer*.[13]

The FBI never officially identified Griesacker as an informant. However, he had been arrested just one month earlier, on March 22, 1998, while attempting to pass off five hundred thousand dollars in worthless checks in Wichita, Kansas.[14] Griesacker also had been previously observed by surveillance videos as present during the time of the Oklahoma City bombing on April 19, 1995.[15] Mills identified an individual photographed on the grounds right outside the Oklahoma federal building following the explosion as Arthur Griesacker; the man had also attended ROT meetings.

"I was looking at videos of things that Mr. McLaren or other people had made regarding meetings of the Republic of Texas; there was Arthur Griesacker," Mills said.

According to Mills, Griesacker also had been arrested and held in an Oregon jail together with other members of a group protesting the legality of that state's laws. Mills subpoenaed him and several US Marshalls traveled to Oregon, put Griesacker into custody, and brought him to stand trial in Texas. However, on the witness stand after Mills called him to testify, Griesacker refused to answer any questions and invoked his Fifth Amendment right to silence.

"So, we found him, we got him, but I really do think he was an informant, but you know he wouldn't testify, so I couldn't make him," Mills said.

Another problem with McLaren's defense stemmed from the fact that the ROT had collateralized the official Treasury of the State of Texas. The prosecution convincingly argued that members of the ROT had assigned themselves as heads of an independent nation, but that claim alone could not qualify as a legitimate defense.

"There's a phrase in trial law called 'jury nullification'[16] where you basically convince the jury or raise reasonable doubt that things were done wrongly and try to get them to vote 'not guilty,'" Mills said. "I totally believed in his [McLaren's] sincerity, and it was not illogical, but it was going to be an absurdly hard case to win."

Additionally, the prosecution provided evidence at trial that proved the ROT had printed money bearing the official State of Texas Treasury seal.

McLaren claimed to be an ambassador for the ROT, and he identified Texas as a sovereign nation. He claimed that the US judicial court system had no jurisdiction and that only an international court of law could try him as an enemy combatant. However, instead, McLaren would continue to testify on the witness stand about the most obscure things. For example, according to Mills, "He would state to the judge that the court had no jurisdiction because of the Texas flag and the fringe on the flag."

Judge Fish recalled Richard Lance McLaren's highly unusual defense that Texas had been annexed illegally in 1845 by the United States.

"I thought that the defendants, as best I can remember, presented a defense that was somewhat credible," Fish said. "McLaren, as I remember, testified in his own defense."

Fish had decided other bank and mail fraud cases, but McLaren's stands out among all the rest. "I've presided over other mail fraud cases, but none that had the kind of claim that McLaren made in this case, that Texas was still an independent nation," he said.

"The one part of that case that stands out in my mind is that it was difficult to fashion the jury charge in the case because of McLaren's contention that Texas never validly entered the Union. Legally, that position was unsound because I was bound by precedents from higher courts, and the US Supreme Court had decided in an old case—I think from the 1870s—that Texas had validly reentered the Union after it joined the Confederacy."

The judge referred to the 1869 Supreme Court case *Texas v. White* case that declared the United States "an indestructible Union."[17]

At the McLarens' 1998 trial, prosecutor Mike Uhl presented damning evidence against the ROT, including witnesses who provided testimony. The defendants had attempted to cash millions of dollars in bogus checks and used various credit cards to purchase merchandise that included the lease of a Lear jet and a three-hundred-dollar Neiman Marcus clothing bill.[18]

Former US Attorney Paul Coggins[19] provided witnesses at trial who were never able to recover payments from the defendants for goods and services. Roger Downs, owner of Print & Sign Designs of Fort Worth, testified that he printed five thousand ROT "passports" in November 1996 at a cost of $4,569.[20]

Kelly Smith, owner of Kelly's Jewelry in Austin, testified that he created seventy-five sterling silver badges for the ROT resembling those worn by Texas Rangers. However, Smith did not deliver the $3,496 order after a check written by members of the ROT bounced at his bank.

The indictment against the defendants claimed that each had attempted to cash bogus checks in Fort Worth, including $2,525,000 to Bank One, $525,000 to Nations Bank, $13,595.72 to First Class American Credit Union, and $19,895.72 to Omni American Federal Credit Union.

In addition, ROT members had attempted to pay for their monthly credit card charges of $7,835.78 to Visa and $333,000 to American Express using bogus warrants or checks. Charges included the purchase of airline tickets to Puerto Rico.

The defendants also had attempted to open a commercial checking account and to cash five million dollars in bogus warrants at Banco Bilboa in Guaynabo, Puerto Rico. Others filed liens against state agencies and officials, including then Texas Governor George W. Bush.[21] The ROT members had attempted to use funds from the State of Texas Treasury to pay their bills; they used counterfeit money, and they counterfeited documents.

"So, whenever they decided that they wanted to buy a tank of gas, or some groceries, or you know—whatever, they could just print out what they called 'the warrant' and make it fancy-looking and claimed that that was sufficient, and of course it wasn't," Uhl said.

In conspiracy cases, the law allows all individuals indicted on a similar charge to be tried together. As a result, the court charged all of the ROT members together on several counts of bank and mail fraud and also created an overall conspiracy count.

"These guys were bandits; they were outlaws, they were con men—they were trying to get something for nothing, and they were good salespeople. They may have told people that they believed it and this 'warrant' thing worked and all that, but it was nonsense, it was nonsense from the beginning," Uhl said.

"They really besmirched the good name of the Republic of Texas. It's unfortunate that they adopted that name, and it really has damaged the good reputation of what was the Republic of Texas. It's a shame that they did. I think in the end, it wasn't a surprise to them that they got convicted and that they got the sentences that they did."

Uhl had previously prosecuted similar cases in Dallas, but he said the ROT trial stands out as the most unique. "That was the only case I think I'd ever dealt with where a group or an association, or an organization or really just a bunch of conspirators, decided to print their own currency and claim that it was good and passed it around the state of Texas, really defrauding good merchants," Uhl said. "It's just a fraud—it's just a theft to present something that is counterfeit and claim that they could get it and not pay their bills."

His office had encountered others who protested tax payments to the United States government. Antigovernment protestors often share a preference for tax evasion.

"Tax protestors are kind of the same thinking; sometimes they will come up with some crazy ideas about the United States and whether the tax system is appropriate and say they're citizens of different countries and all kinds of things—so the federal government encounters these kinds of people frequently," Uhl said.

"Certainly, the Republic of Texas case was front and center, the foremost of these protestor-type groups that claim independence or claim that the law doesn't apply to them or frankly come up with their own laws."

The state pushed to prosecute its case against McLaren and members of the ROT before their trial on federal firearms violations was scheduled to begin. "My thought was, well, this is totally different, and he has to serve the state sentence, but he doesn't get a freebie on the federal charges either. He's ripped off a lot of companies here and would have continued to rip off companies by buying goods and services and not paying for them. The federal government takes a dim view of people printing their own money," Coggins said. "I think the judge was a little skeptical about why we were going forward with this federal prosecution, but as it turned out, you know, that state sentence was reversed."

The 12th Court of Appeals in El Paso, on August 26, 1999, reversed DeHart's conviction[22] against McLaren on kidnapping charges based upon insufficient evidence. However, McLaren was not released because prosecuting attorneys for the federal courts kept him in state prison pending another federal trial on charges of violating the National Firearms Act.

US District Court Judge for the Northern District Paul L. Friedman, on August 17, 2000, would affirm the court's earlier convictions and deny the ROT members' appeal.[23]

■ ■ ■

Twenty-two years later, during an exclusive interview at the William P. Clements Unit prison in Amarillo, McLaren did not express remorse when providing his own version of defense at the trial.[24] On the contrary, he said that "the shit hit the fan" only after an unnamed ROT foreign ambassador to the Middle East attempted to write a check to Israel for one hundred million dollars to buy military arms in 1997.

"Because when the US pulled out, we had to protect ourselves. That's when that ward [check] cleared IMF," he said. "It cleared the Federal Reserve Bank, but the way that they brought it in wasn't supposed to be granted through that type of system, so they went nuts and they put a hold on it and that's when everything went bad."[25]

In court, McLaren attempted to prove that because the Texas comptroller's office had paid some of the checks written by the ROT, that all remaining outstanding warrants were also legal.

"The Fifth Circuit Court of Appeals stated that the warrants were not used by anybody personally, but for debts of the Republic of Texas," McLaren said.

McLaren had planned to use the money from the official Texas state's treasury account as a business fund to operate his Republic of Texas. "The money in the state of Texas belongs to the Republic of Texas. They're just the trustees under the War Powers Act," he said. "There was no bank; there was no bank check ever written. The warrants went through the same process that the state of Texas uses."[26]

He said that he only spent what was necessary to operate an independent nation. "We went down there to Puerto Rico; we went through litigation—even the Fifth Circuits said that there was a dispute over who owned the money, but the court never resolved it."

"Those state assets were converted under international monetary law, okay? Then what we did was, we needed to draw funds from the appropriations that the Congress had appropriated as money. In a Congress assembly for certain payments, we turned around and wrote 'a treasury warrant.' It's not a check. It's a foreign bill of exchange."[27]

McLaren said he placed the official seal of the Republic of Texas on each of the warrants. He also gave others strict instructions about how to use the ROT checks.

"The appropriate person who was delegated to pay through the appropriations presented it. There were instructions with it: 'You do not go to the bank and cash this check. This is how you obtain the funds.' What happened is, they went to the bank and said, 'I need to make a special transfer of this warrant bill of war,'" McLaren said.

"So, what happens is, that warrant is sent by the bank with a special attachment that comes back to me. I put a counselor's stamp on it and certify that it is a withdrawal, that it is appropriated money. Then I mail it by certified mail to the Comptroller in Austin. Now the Comptroller has to issue a check or a conversion warrant and send it to that person, or me. This is what happened. What happened was, they don't know what to do because we just went to their own court and cleaned them out."

McLaren claimed he was "elected" the ambassador of the Republic of Texas, an independent nation. However, this private election discounted a majority of citizens who never voted. McLaren also failed to mention that a ROT member located outside of Fort Davis impeached him shortly before the standoff occurred.

"You are separated into two classes: the struggling class and the people who are not acting in the struggling class. Those are the people who come forward belligerently, who say, 'I'm a Texian; I'm claiming my rights.' They have access to the titled assets—not the twenty million sittin' on their asses doing nothing, or the people who never vote," he said.

"We were elected by over ten thousand people voting the second time, okay? Plus, the Eighth Legislature gave us the power in 1861."[28]

According to McLaren, the Federal War Powers Act[29] gave him the authority to appropriate funds held by the state of Texas.

"That's why we went through the court system to appropriate those funds. We went through the delegation of seizure under the laws of war. So, we went through the process to get the assets back. Then we had a meeting, and we appropriated funds to each department to carry out, just like a normal government does. It's called a 'provisional government,'" he said.[30]

Richard McLaren was sentenced to serve twelve and a half years on twenty-one counts of mail and bank fraud concurrent to his state conviction, and he was fined $24.25 million, a debt to date he has never paid. He remains in William P. Clements Unit prison in Amarillo serving a ninety-nine-year sentence. Evelyn McLaren served twelve and a half years and was paroled; she currently lives in the Dallas/Fort Worth area where she cleans private homes for a living.

Lihn Ngoc Vu, convicted in August 1998, served twenty-one months.

Jasper Edward Baccus, convicted in July 1998, served twenty-one months. Richard George Kieninger, convicted in August 1998, was sentenced to serve twenty-four years. Erwin Leo Brown, convicted in September 1998, served ten and a half years. Joe Lewis Reece, convicted in October 1998, served twenty-one months. Steven Craig Crear, convicted in October 1998, served twenty-seven months.

■ ■ ■

In October 1999, Bob Hughes met the Turners at the airport in Roatan, Honduras, picked up their luggage, and drove them to a vacant duplex he owned. After they unpacked, Jo Ann and Bill locked up and went next door to the Hugheses' condo, a big, single-story all-wood structure built with a patio clear across the back of the house facing the ocean. The Hugheses' condo, with modern décor, had all the conveniences of home, complete with air-conditioning and ceiling fans.

The Turners spent several days taking in their surroundings. They sat for hours on the back patio of the Hugheses' condo looking out at the sea, enjoying the sun and the scenery. They admired the scene, a paradise with a plethora of sun, palm trees, ocean, and sand. They often ate their meals in local restaurants.

"I was making a new life for myself. I didn't ever want to repeat everything that happened in my life prior, and I just wanted to live happily ever after," Jo Ann said.

The Hugheses continued to invite the Turners to their condo from time to time for a cookout or asked them to dine in any one of the local touristy restaurants. Two weeks after their arrival, the Turners moved to the West End of the island where they rented a house for eight hundred dollars a month, then considered expensive even for Roatan. The house on stilts supported a three-hundred-sixty-degree porch that overlooked the ocean, located down the beach from Anthony's Key Resort.

"It was a much better location than where we had been living in the Hugheses' duplex. The new location was where the cruise ships came in," Jo Ann said. "Jeff was living there with us the whole time except from time to time when the girls would come into port off the cruise ships; he would meet up with them. We wouldn't see him for days. They were girls from foreign countries, people who worked on the cruises. He was a ladies' man. I worried about that. A few of the girls wanted Jeff to go back with them—one was from Nova Scotia."

Jeff told his parents that he liked Roatan so much that he never wanted to leave. However, the poverty on Roatan impacted the Turners. Their poorly constructed new home offered little or no insulation, and Jo Ann remembers that she could see through foundation cracks that formed along the inside walls. Always an early riser, Jo Ann spent her mornings outdoors on the wooden deck that extended right over the ocean from her back door. Sitting in a tiny chair at a tiny table, she could see right down to the shoreline. At times she saw young people passed out on the beach from a night of revelry, alcohol, and drugs.

Within the first few months, the Turners suffered two break-ins at their residence. The thieves took two televisions and other personal belongings. When Jo Ann replaced the televisions, the thieves returned. Finally, Jo Ann and Bill began to keep a vigilant surveillance of their property. They took turns leaving the house, and if they left together for a short period of time, they left the lights on to make it appear as if someone was home. They began leaving only for trips to the grocery store for provisions.

American imports at the local grocery stores remained scarce. Jo Ann often had trouble finding items she needed to prepare their favorite meals. Fast food consisted only of items cooked by vendors in structures that she considered unsanitary. She also wondered about the price gouging; vendors sold several items at a price that the city's poor could never have afforded.

Jo Ann spent much of her days working on her screenplay. In the evenings, she, Bill, and Jeff sometimes walked down the road to the Anthony Keyes Resort for dinner. The resort provided a nine-hole golf course, but the Turners never played. The restaurant overlooked the ocean and a place well known as a popular hangout for marine life. The cruise ships often docked there, and the tourists swam with the dolphins in Coxen Hole and in nearby Mahogany Bay.[31]

Few Americans lived in Roatan; generally, foreigners visited from time to time or vacationed in large and luxurious homes. In the 1990s, the sleepy little tourist town was known only to cruise ship travelers, to others who owned property there, and to those who had previously visited the resorts. Today, Roatan marks the largest of Honduras' three Bay islands—though only five miles wide and forty-five miles long.[32]

Chapter 20

The Turners enjoyed the Caribbean and the island music, but Bill didn't perform music at all while they lived there. Instead, he took up another local hobby, snorkeling, with Jeff.

"This was the first time in many years that the two did something together. For a while, there was no fighting. For once in a long time, they got along," Jo Ann said.

After a few weeks, Jeff found a job working in the West End at Sueno del Mar, a diving resort. He soon earned his diving certification while working at Sueno, built on stilts above the water and ocean.

The family also frequented Half Moon Resort, an exclusive locale that offered ocean rides in glass bottom boats and unique diving experiences. Jeff began working nights and often did not arrive back at the Turners' condo home until about two or three in the morning. Life might have been idyllic except that Jo Ann observed Jeff falling in with a bad crowd, and she suspected that he was taking drugs. Working as fast as she could to complete her screenplay, Jo Ann felt burdened by her worries about Jeff.

"I thought to myself, *I need to get Jeff out of here. He's not going to go back by himself. Then what would we do? Would we stay here?* The more I thought about it, the more I couldn't see how we would stay there. What would we do? We would have been so bored. There was nothing to do. I thought we should just get out of there—just go back home," she said.

The Turners had managed to live well for an entire year in Honduras on money that Nick Milam had recouped for them as part of their civil lawsuit. However, during their stay in Honduras, they had saved just enough to pay for their three one-way airplane tickets back to The States. They arrived homeless at the gate inside the recently constructed Austin-Bergstrom International Airport. They rode an escalator downstairs to baggage claim in silence. There, among hundreds of people greeting loved ones, Jo Ann couldn't help but feel alone, as no one welcomed the Turners back to Austin

21

The Turners Return as ROT Members Await Another Federal Trial

THE TURNERS returned to the states in January 2000 and decided to stay temporarily in the home of Bill's daughter, Barbara Shannon, and her husband Freddy. For one month, the two families lived together in a doublewide trailer in Liberty Hill, Texas.

At the time, Barbara worked at Travis County Courthouse in administration. Freddy, an electrician, worked as a contractor. Their teenage daughter, Stephanie Shannon, also still lived at home and attended school.

Everyone quickly fell into a routine at the Shannons' home. Weekdays, Bill and Jeff awoke early and traveled to work in Austin. Jeff had found a job working for John Green, a general contractor who built custom homes. Jeff put up frames, attached dry wall, and painted. Meanwhile, the tension between Jeff and his dad seemed resolved for a while.

They saw very little of their daughter, Kelly, during this time, except when she visited town to see her childhood friends, Jancy Darling, Lisa Ann Wilson, and Lori Martin. Kelly would fly in from California, and all of the girls would meet for dinner somewhere in Austin.

One day while watching television at the Shannons', Jo Ann saw a commercial advertisement for truck drivers wanted at Schneider Trucking Company, then based in Mesquite, Texas. Jo Ann immediately called the phone number that appeared on the television screen. Within days, Jo Ann and Bill headed to Mesquite.

Training to become truck drivers required a two-week stay in a motel in Mesquite. Every morning, a driver came to their motel and picked them up and shuttled them to the trucking headquarters. The Turners reported to classes daily and were provided a sack lunch at noon. They passed all the oral and written tests and soon climbed into a semi-truck cab to learn how to drive on the road.

"I never got nervous. I couldn't believe it. Now it would scare me to death to get in one of those trucks—an eighteen-wheeler," Jo Ann said.[1]

Jo Ann surmised that staying mobile in a semi-truck would make it difficult for anyone to trace their whereabouts. She hoped that they could remain under the radar from federal investigators and other law enforcement authorities. She still feared possible prosecution related to her ROT affiliations years earlier.

For six months, the Turners drove a contracted tractor-trailer across the country and back again to Mesquite. Their first job involved driving to a pickup area in south Texas and hauling the load to New York. Next, they drove to Indiana to pick up a load of popcorn; it was the lightest load they ever carried. They dropped the popcorn shipment off at Camp Mabry[2] in Austin, Texas. Jo Ann felt apprehensive as she showed her Texas driver's license at the gate to the military base. She wondered if perhaps her face might have appeared on an America's Most Wanted poster.

With Jo Ann at the wheel, the Turners stopped their semi-truck and trailer rig at the entrance to Camp Mabry, and she presented the guard on duty with the proper paperwork. Without hesitation, the guard directed her to a building to dock and unload. Afterward, Jo Ann began to feel somewhat invincible.

The longest haul the two truckers ever took was from New York to Los Angeles, hauling a maximum load of eighty tons. The trip took several days. The Turners stopped only to refuel and at roadside truck stops where they slept in bunk beds inside their sleeper cab.

Still, Jo Ann failed to master the skills necessary to back up the truck. Bill often had to back it up wherever they stopped for the night. Jo Ann also found most truck stop food distasteful; on the road, they frequently ate fast food at McDonald's, Subway, or Denny's. When Jo Ann saw the calories beginning to show on her waistline, she began to reconsider her truck-driving career move.

Before long, they also heard complaints from the Schneider Trucking Company administrators who suggested that all their drivers should drive 24/7. They admonished the Turners, saying that while one person was driving, the backup driver was expected to sleep. However, the Turners found the demanding schedule daunting.

"Bill was not that good of a driver, and he was not that alert—not as alert as I was—so I couldn't go to sleep while he drove. I just stayed awake, or we had to park the truck at a truck stop and sleep there overnight and start out again in the morning," she said.

"Management didn't like that. They didn't like that at all. We were supposed to be on the road all of the time. So, I knew it was just a matter of time before they let us go."

Jo Ann thought the trucking job did not pay well enough and didn't like the physical demands, especially at weigh stations en route between states. Both Jo Ann and Bill possessed slight physiques in those days. Still, she mustered the strength needed to physically redistribute the weight inside the trailer. She lifted boxes with her bare hands at times to shift weight from one side of the trailer to another.

"I'd get out there and move those big ol' bars and shift that whole trailer. Back then, I could do it. That's a heck of a lot of weight; it's like moving a freight train," she said.

During driving assignments, Jo Ann and Bill often didn't speak to one another. She also didn't trust his driving. Once, they stopped at one of the multitudes of fast-food restaurants along the road; Bill accidentally drove their truck over a three-foot concrete wall.

"I was scared to death. I looked around at all those truck drivers who were there, and they were all looking at us, I imagine wondering how we were going to get that truck down off that wall," she said. "I'm surprised no one called the police or the DPS. Everyone else probably thought we were drunk or something. That's why I didn't want Bill to drive. He was not very intuitive, and he did not judge curbs and things like that very well."

Afterward, she never trusted Bill to drive the truck at night while she slept. They soon decided driving trucks was not for them.

After collecting their last paychecks, the Turners returned to the

Shannons' trailer and stayed until Jo Ann could figure another way for them to earn money. In the meantime, she leased a US Post Office box in Austin to begin receiving mail, mostly from her grown children. Jeff returned to Tahoe where he hoped to become a ski instructor. Kelly still lived in California and worked for Southwest Airlines.

■ ■ ■

Richard and Evelyn McLaren together with six other ROT defendants convicted on multiple counts of mail and bank fraud in Dallas appealed on the premise that the FBI withheld evidence during the trial about an informant. However, the Fifth Circuit US Court of Appeals for the Northern District of Texas judges Harold R. DeMoss, Jr. E. Grady Jolly, and David D. Dowd affirmed the original sentences on August 17, 2000.[3] Within one year Richard Lance McLaren and five other Republic of Texas members would face yet another federal trial for violating the National Firearms Act. In the meantime, they remained held in jail without bonds.

22

The Turners Become Home Stagers and ROT Members Imprisoned

THE TURNERS possessed little more than a hope and a prayer when they pulled into Austin's city limits in the fall of 2001. They began staging homes for Realtors throughout Austin. The couple lived in other people's homes offered for sale. The work provided them with a place to live temporarily as they kept their address fluid so no one in law enforcement would be able to find them.

Austin Realtors could not have been more eager to take advantage of Jo Ann and Bill, who were down on their luck. The Turners began paying a minimal rent fee to live in the most luxurious homes, which they staged while Realtors continued to show the properties to potential buyers. Jo Ann managed to keep their showcased homes so sparkling clean that no one could have guessed that anyone lived in them. The only problem with the arrangement was that sometimes the houses sold within weeks; the Turners then had to move again.

At first, the real estate representatives who sponsored the Turners provided them with a warehouse full of furnishings and décor on loan. However, gradually, the Turners accumulated enough furniture of their own to stage a five-bedroom house.

The Turners spent as little as one month and up to two years living in a house, and they staged as many as ten houses over the next fifteen years. Jo Ann quickly turned moving into a science. Depending on the size of the house they were moving into, she knew exactly what to pack and unpack. She knew just how much to unpack from various labeled boxes at each house and where to store the rest of their furnishings.

Many of the Realtors, with few exceptions, asked the Turners to pay rent while they lived in the houses they staged. When the houses sold, the Turners received a small percentage of the sales commissions. However, Jo Ann often spent a large portion of her sales commission at a few West Lake consignment shops. Her favorite houses included a very grand house with a pool off Canyonwood and US 290 West. The Turners considered the residence a bargain because the Realtors charged only six hundred and twenty-five dollars per month rent to live there. Jo Ann and Bill also enjoyed living in two other beautiful residences, including a house located off City Park Road and another on Prince William Drive.

She visited consignment stores so often to shop for furniture that the salespeople came to know her on a first name basis. While shopping, she tried not to think about all the personal possessions she had lost in foreclosure. No one likely suspected that the Turners lived from paycheck to paycheck and that they had started with nothing just four years before.

They never invited guests into any of the houses that they staged because they held such sparse furnishings. Jo Ann also worried about keeping each of the premises spotless in case a Realtor dropped by unannounced with prospective buyers. The echoes that often rang throughout the houses whenever the Turners spoke loudly to one another seemed to epitomize the emptiness Jo Ann felt inside.

"There was no meaning to life at that point. We were starting all over. I was just so distraught about everything," she said.[1]

However, in many ways, their lifestyle in Austin had improved since returning from Honduras. Jo Ann and Bill held jobs, earned money, ate well, and no longer were being robbed. During those years, the Turners kept in touch with few of their old friends.

"They were just happy to hear from us that we were okay. But we said, 'We're not partying; we're not doing anything socially—we're just working to get back on our feet over here.' It was very hard. It was very embarrassing and very humiliating, to say the least," she said.

She and Bill kept their daily routines while trying not to draw attention to themselves. Bill performed with a local band, but very seldom. Their daughter, Kelly, did not visit during those years but kept in touch with her parents by phone.

"I think she was just working quite a bit, and I didn't encourage it; I didn't suggest it," Jo Ann said.

Jo Ann had hoped that her job as a home stager would provide a temporary fix to their lives and would help her family once again earn the same social status that they had enjoyed before her arrest. Jo Ann also had hoped outsiders would never assume that anything bad had ever happened to her.

To supplement the family income, Jo Ann began working temporary jobs assigned by an employment agency. She found that she could adapt easily to any job, and she felt that her employers liked her. At the University of Texas, Jo Ann found a temporary position in the office transcribing tapes recorded during conferences. However, she missed regular interaction with people, so she took another job at Dell Children's Hospital. There she made only a few new acquaintances.

The Turners kept their lives fluid out of fear of staying in one place long enough that either state or federal investigators might find them. Jo Ann's problems with law enforcement and her incarceration seemingly had left her with an undiagnosed post traumatic stress disorder. "I thought they might be watching me to see if I was connected to the Republic of Texas group, though no one ever talked to me about it," she said.

Jo Ann also figured that neither she nor Bill would qualify for a home loan because of their credit history and her arrest record. The IRS also continued attempts to track the Turners down in order to collect back taxes and attached interest penalties.

By 2014, the Turners would rent an apartment off US 290 West at the Fox Hill apartments. Bill continued working for Leal Trucking, and Jo Ann began working part time at an H-E-B grocery store as a cashier at a branch in Oak Hill. However, the position required her to stand at the cash register for hours. When the standing caused severe back pain, she invested in a back brace that helped somewhat. Physical and emotional pain and suffering had become a familiar daily distraction in Jo Ann

Chapter 22

Turner's life. They would remain her constant companions for several years to come.

■ ■ ■

On August 26, 2001, in Midland, Texas, Gerald Carruth[2] served as prosecutor for the final federal trial of Richard Lance McLaren and five other Republic of Texas militia members charged in 1997 with violating the National Firearms Act.

US Western District Judge William Royal Furgeson Jr.[3] presided at the trial held in the courthouse originally named the George Mahon Federal Building. It had been built by architects Neuhardt & Babb and Covington, Shelton, Taylor in a modernist style in 1978.[4] The Texas Senate in 2012 had renamed the site the George H. W. Bush and George W. Bush United States Courthouse and George Mahon Federal Building at 200 East Wall Street.[5] Six years of local campaigning had culminated with the courthouse being renamed to honor both Bush family members who had spent decades living in Midland prior to earning their political fame. A rooftop terrace displays the lengthy name along the brownstone structure's facade as it looms over an entire block-long stretch of barricaded sidewalk.

McLaren, at age forty-seven, faced firearms violations along with five other defendants: Robert "White Eagle" Otto, age forty-nine; Jonathan Robert Scheidt, age forty-seven; Richard Frank Keyes III, age twenty-five; Gregg William Paulson, age forty-nine; and Karen Simon Paulson (formerly Karen Sperling,) age thirty-seven.[6]

The court charged all six defendants with using illegal weapons, such as modified machine guns and destructive devices, to commit crimes of violence at the Davis Mountain Resort (DMR) in April and May 1997. Charges stemmed from explosives that ROT members had installed on McLaren's property in the DMR as a means of keeping neighbors and law enforcement from trespassing.

Judge Furgeson had ordered a change of venue, moving the trial from Pecos to Midland for security reasons.

"They had more deputy marshals, and there was a lot of talk back in those days about someone trying to bust these people out and help them escape. So, security was of primary concern," Carruth said. "I remember the case quite well because it was an unusual case, to say the least, but also because I retired from the US Attorney's office in 2009, and I still get served with copies of writs every time one of these people files one."

Carruth recalled that over three days, each of the defendants pleaded guilty.[7] In the morning on the first day of trial, Karen Paulson, a native of Germany, pleaded guilty to one count of being an illegal immigrant in possession of firearms. On the third day of trial, five defendants, Otto, Keyes, Gregg Paulson, Scheidt and McLaren, pleaded guilty to conspiracy to violate the National Firearms Act. In addition, McLaren pleaded guilty to receiving and possessing unregistered firearms and those not identified by serial number, to wit destructive devices, namely, explosive devices including pipe bombs and components intended for making explosive bombs, Carruth said.

Furgeson had assigned standby counsel to each of the defendants but they all had asked to defend themselves. Attorney Robert Leahey[8] served as standby counsel only for McLaren.

"Obviously they were not particularly good advocates for themselves," Leahey said. "I mean in court, legal insanity is such a tough burden. Just having bizarre beliefs isn't enough."[8]

Leahey recalls that McLaren and the other ROT members were "frustrating to work with." McLaren would ask Leahey, as standby counsel, to look up cases for him or to do some legal research. McLaren didn't have access to the law library, but nothing he asked Leahey to research had anything to do with his case. Instead, McLaren asked Leahey to research "weird civil cases" and corporate cases that would help define corporations.

"I remember pretty vividly that his big tag line was 'the corporate states of America' and his saying, 'I've never agreed to be part of the corporate states of America.' Frankly, nobody could ever understand what he was talking about," Leahey said.

"There's wasn't any discussion with them. They had their beliefs, they had their theories, and nothing you could say or do was going to suggest to them anything they could do to examine their beliefs."

He said McLaren never entrusted him with the details about his own defense because he considered Leahey also part of the "corporate states of America."

At trial, Carruth presented hard physical and photographic evidence regarding the types of weapons and bombs used by ROT members during the 1997 standoff against three hundred law enforcement officers.

"Rifles and pistols—it looked like an armory in the courtroom," Leahey said.

ROT members broke Texas laws when they modified some of their semiautomatic guns by making them automatic and rapid-fire and by sawing off shotguns. ROT members also created homemade bombs on their property in the DMR.

"They didn't bring explosives into the courtroom, obviously," Leahey said. "But a lot of photographs and a lot of them looked like your typical propane tank from the barbecue grill. They weren't anything sophisticated."

By mid-trial, all six of the ROT members pleaded guilty without any need for a jury verdict.[9] Furgeson sentenced McLaren to ten years in prison to be served consecutively with the previous state sentence imposed in 394th Judicial District Court in Brewster County.

The judge also assessed McLaren a fine of one hundred dollars to be paid immediately to the United States and set nineteen mandatory and standard conditions upon his release. Under further conditions, Furgeson prohibited McLaren from living in any place where firearms are possessed or stored, including Jeff Davis County and/or near the residences of Joe and/or M.A. Rowe.[10]

Furgeson required all six ROT members to undergo three years of supervision following any served sentences and upon their possible release from prison.

All but McLaren waived their right to appeal; McLaren's federal appeal would be denied on December 6, 2001. Except for Scheidt, the other ROT members were already serving time for other state and federal crimes. In addition, all of the defendants were charged a maximum two hundred and fifty thousand dollar fine.[11]

By January 15, 2003, State District Judge Susan Larsen in El Paso would examine new evidence against McLaren and reaffirm the 12th Court of Appeals court's earlier conviction based on charges that the ROT leader had participated in organized crime in the 1997 standoff.[12] The court would uphold an earlier conviction and McLaren's sentence of ninety-nine years. He would appeal on April 10, 2003, but his request for another trial would be denied.

According to Robert Hurst,[13] public information officer for the Texas Department of Criminal Justice, the state paroled Otto on August 3,

2020, and he remains under mandatory supervision. Gregg William Paulson still serves a life sentence at the Preston E. Smith Unit in Lamesa, Texas; he is not eligible for parole until 2027. The state sentenced his wife, Karen, to serve thirty years for burglary of a residence, and in 2002 she received a separate sentence to consecutively serve fifty months after being convicted for possession of a firearm as an illegal alien. However, Karen was extradited to her home country of Germany in 2014, and her sentences were commuted. Keyes still serves ninety years for burglary of a habitation at the James V. Allred Unit in North Iowa Park, Texas.

Scheidt served five years in federal prison before being released and he died from cancer at fifty-eight years old on October 2, 2012, in Cortez, Colorado.[14]

23

Ninety-Nine Years Imprisonment for Richard Lance McLaren

FROM BEHIND a Plexiglas petition and seated inside an interview room at William P. Clements Unit prison in Amarillo, Richard Lance McLaren[1] looked tired from spending twenty-two years behind bars, most of that time in isolation. Tufts of white hair sprouted out from the sides of McLaren's mostly bald head and sparse eyebrows. Beneath his deeply sunken, dark eye sockets hung teabag-size folds of thin and mottled skin. His once periwinkle blue eyes now appeared as dull as two worn US nickels suspended in veined white orbs.

Holding an earpiece attached to a microphone, he smiled a bemused grin, somewhat concealing teeth that appeared in urgent need of dental attention. McLaren wore loose-fitting standard white prison garb and looked slight in build, slighter than depicted in vintage photographs taken upon his arrest in 1997 by the Texas Rangers.

For more than an hour during our exclusive interview, McLaren attempted to explain how he believes the American judicial system failed him for more than two decades as the leader of an independent nation known as the Republic of Texas.

McLaren recalled attacks on him and other ROT members, beginning with the arrest of Jo Ann Turner in Austin on April 22, 1997. "That's what kind of started the ball rolling, you know, that went from there into a military armed conflict," McLaren said.

He remembered Jo Ann Turner had called him from Travis County Jail. "She asked for some sort of help to get her out at the time," he said. "I told her we would try to do everything we could, and I think that was all I could tell her at the time."

McLaren said he remembers making some calls to verify Jo Ann Turner's status as a prisoner. He said he failed to locate an attorney who could manage her release from jail on a twenty-five thousand dollar bond.

"None of the lawyers would represent us. The thing was too hot to handle for any of the lawyers. Because the one or two lawyers that did try to get onboard, they got threatened by the [Texas] Bar Association," McLaren said.

He knew that because Jo Ann and her husband, Bill, no longer owned any valuable assets, they found it difficult to come up with the bond money to pay for her release. The Turners lost all of their personal belongings to foreclosure; McLaren and his wife, Evelyn, lost everything they owned as the result of their arrest and convictions.

In addition, he believes that much of his paperwork about the annexation history of the Republic of Texas has been stored or kept hidden by his political enemies. He places much of the blame for his incarceration on what he perceives to be corruption within the Texas court system.

Speaking unfiltered in a fluid stream of consciousness, McLaren shared his insights about the 1997 standoff and aftermath in what amounted to a series of mental calisthenics.

"I was lucky that my wife Evelyn got some of her stuff out. I lost a lot of my personal stuff after the siege. The county is still holding it up in the attic at the courthouse in Jeff Davis County," McLaren said.

"The problem of it is, you're dealing with a court system that is so corrupt that they don't even recognize law anymore. Things have gone so far even over the last twenty years; if you had seen the litigation and where we've been and the level of corruption in the courts, [it's] unbelievable. They don't follow their own laws. The problem being is, they are still operating under these 1860 War Powers."[2]

Since his incarceration, McLaren has lost touch with all his fellow ROT members. He hopes to file a suit soon with the International Court of Arbitration on the group's behalf.[3]

"We've got a universal claim through this whole process, and everybody directly affected as far as plunder of war and all that stuff—she's

[Jo Ann Turner] affected. She's one of the original people [ROT]. There are some people that were actually attached to the mission, and there is a sublet [sic] of people who are directly affected—like a hundred and something people. She was one of the ones in the lawsuit that we filed, one of the counteractions," McLaren said.

"All that has to go through arbitration now because the courts have said we can't deal with it anymore, because we can't resolve it. They are finally starting to admit that this was all political to begin with."

He remains unflappable in his belief that the United States illegally annexed the Republic of Texas in 1845.[4]

"I'll prove that Texas is still a Republic and illegally occupied, and they can't afford to give me the hearing because I have everything already cataloged and ready to go for the hearing. So whether they give it to me or the [Permanent] Court of Arbitration[5] awards the jurisdiction and enforces them ultimately—that's our next shot. She's [Turner] involved in that claims process along with the rest of us," McLaren said.

Former Texas Attorney General Dan Morales, in 1997, referred to ROT members as "paper terrorists" for filing false liens against city, county, and state agencies,[6] but McLaren still believes they acted within the boundaries of the law. By arresting Jo Ann Turner and serving subpoenas to ten Internet service providers[7] who conducted business with ROT members, Morales attempted to supplant Texas laws while running his race for governor,[8] McLaren said.

"Morales, he was corrupt as hell," he continued. "Morales made one mistake that's helping us now; he filed that stupid lawsuit, and they can't resolve it."[9]

Morales filed a state lawsuit in May 1997 against ROT member Carolyn Carney of Bulverde and her former business, Contract Microfilm Co./ Protek Archival Labs, alleging thirty-two thousand dollars in unpaid sales taxes.[10] Morales also filed a civil lawsuit against the ROT at about the same time to prevent twenty-five of its members from filing false liens against businesses and individuals. In that lawsuit, Morales accused Donald Varnell of Hedwig of issuing bogus documents to various financial institutions and requesting that the state's assets be turned over to the "treasury" of the ROT.

McLaren still has no idea of the fate of his former codefendants or how much personal property they lost in the process, but he hopes to someday reclaim whatever he can. He has not stopped filing petitions in the Texas court system.

"Once we win the petition for the jurisdiction of the court, it's filed on an amended claim on everybody. I did file the original one with Congress for the damages. Of course, they're not going to do anything, like they normally don't do. It has to be done before I can go into the arbitration court and go for the damages because they're all considered Texas war debt," McLaren said.

"This is the key: they're all Texas debts. This is what Governor Greg Abbott is hiding; he filed a second lawsuit over the first one that Turner was involved in and put his foot into it, and that opened the door for us to countersue and bring in an attachment to the original action. That's where we are at right now, is arbitration."

Even after being held behind bars for more than two decades, McLaren still considers himself wronged by the Texas judicial system. "I can't be in here. I'm an enemy combatant. The trial court certified me as an armed belligerent of war. They brought in the military. We had military. The court said it was a military siege. It had nothing to do with civilians. I have immunity from trial from the civil courts because I was involved in war. Committing an act of war is not a crime. You have to be charged with a lower crime or a violation of the Law of Armed Conflict," he said.[11]

He refers to himself as an "enemy combatant" based on a Supreme Court case involving an American-born Saudi, Yaser Esam Hamdi, captured in 2001 while the United States fought the Taliban.[12] McLaren claims that he has been denied a Combatant Status Review Tribunal.

"I never had a hearing," McLaren said. "The law says that they have to give me a hearing as a combatant before they can ever charge me with a crime."

McLaren plans to prove he was denied his rights under the Tenth Amendment[13] of the US Constitution. "The State Department is the responding agency for the United States, not the Justice Department; where when we countersued the state of Texas, we brought in the United States because that is the agent for the state of Texas, it's not the state of Texas under the Tenth Amendment," he said.

"It's the state of Texas under the Reconstruction Acts[14] or the military acts of President Abraham Lincoln. It has no tie to any legitimacy in the Union."

He said he planned to file an appeal with the Permanent Court of Arbitration (PCA), established in 1899, to seek a resolution. At the time of McLaren's PCA filing, Jo Ann Turner still lived, but the two had not communicated by any means since their arrests in 1997. However, in 2018, he said he still believed that Jo Ann Turner would join him in any future litigation he filed to legitimize his right to reclaim the Republic of Texas.

Furthermore, McLaren used the word "we" when referring to other former ROT members arrested in 1997 in the Davis Mountains; though he has had little or no contact with any of them except by US mail in nearly twenty-five years. McLaren did not clarify his use of "they" during the 2018 interview.

"We don't have to be recognized under international law; all we have to do is prove title. That's why they said the military was to kill us, so we could not continue to exercise title. That's what we did when I went to court. That's what I'll say when I go to arbitration court: I'll say, 'See, we have title, and they don't. We're a belligerent state power. We are exercising our rights out of the Laws of Occupation under the Geneva III and IV Convention.'"[15]

By occupation under the laws of war and under the prior acts of the Eighth Legislature that met at the beginning of the Civil War, McLaren claims to be the ambassador for the Republic of Texas. "They [legislators] gave us the power to do what we're doing. Texas law provides during war and occupation for a provisional government. That is Texas law, and it was in force in 1997," he said.

He admitted that he obtained land in the Davis Mountain Resort legally under adverse possession or by filing lawsuits against the landowners who had filed bankruptcy, and he claims that he still owns land there. He estimates that, before the 1997 siege, he owned nine hundred acres. However, he remains unaware that several of his former neighbors bulldozed the ROT embassy from its former site in 1998, according to Joe Rowe.

"I still have my claim on what they stole from me, that they don't have any title to because they can't, under the laws of war, use plunder as a title," McLaren said. "My vineyard is up in the same area where all the stuff came down."

McLaren identified his vineyard partner as L. D. Whitehead of Whitehead Real Estate Group in Dallas. However, that information could not be verified.

He said that as recently as the spring of 2018, members of the FBI visited McLaren in prison after he filed attachments against all the judges still living in Texas who have heard his cases and/or Turner's case. McLaren said he sought revenge on Jo Ann's behalf without her knowledge.

"The FBI agent just looked at me and just shook his head. I said, 'Look up the documents; look up all the documents in the lawsuit.' They got sued for libel," he said. "Those documents against Jo Ann [Turner] were libel under the laws of war and libel under Texas Law," McLaren said.

After Judge Joseph H. Hart charged Jo Ann Turner with contempt of court, McLaren filed a lien against him. The lien effectively, for a time, froze Hart's financial accounts.

"He was the first one to try and go get a loan for his wife and found out all of his credit had been attached. After I got the judgment, I put attachments on all those judges, including the one in DC. I got eighteen federal and state judges, including all of the criminal court of appeal judges," McLaren said.

McLaren believes that the ROT remains the same viable group that he and other founders created in 1994. "Everything that we're doing is still based on what we did in '94, '95, and '96. The [1997] Cease Fire Agreement[16] is what melded everything together," he said.

However, McLaren said that he feels sympathy for Ed Brannum, the current president of the Republic of Texas. "I feel sorry for him," he said. "He cut himself off from the original [ROT] initiative."

He does not recognize Brannum's status as president of the ROT, and likewise, Brannum and his membership no longer recognize McLaren as their ambassador.

"Do you know who the only real president of the Republic of Texas is? It's [Texas Governor] Greg Abbott, but Greg Abbott refuses to assume the title," McLaren said.

He also said he interviewed with Daniel Miller, the leader of the Texas Nationalist Movement.[17] Meanwhile, the movement to make Texas its own country rages on, promoted by various factions, while three of the founding members of the ROT remain behind bars.[18]

More than two decades of mostly solitary confinement have negatively impacted Richard McLaren and his ability to express his opinions in writing, said Dessie Andrews,[19] his former friend. She said McLaren has written a book in prison about his 1997 standoff experiences.

"Richard sent his 'book' to me and he really believed it would have all the answers and would be revolutionary, and it wasn't. He just went over the same old topics," she said. "He told me it was a revolutionary, 'set-everybody-free' document, and it wasn't. I just didn't have the heart to even tell him."

24

Kelly Turner's Murder

THE TURNER'S forty-three-year-old daughter, Kelly Turner, had worked for Southwest Airlines as a flight attendant stationed in Oakland, California, since graduating in 1995 from the University of Texas in Austin. She had remained in contact with several of her Austin friends, including Christian Sharpley, who once lived across the street from the Turners' lake house.

Kelly's best friend, Jancy Darling, also a 1989 Westlake High School graduate, had invited Kelly to visit her in Austin over the Halloween weekend beginning on Friday, October 31, 2014. Kelly decided to bring along her boyfriend, Joseph Frederick Karr. She and Karr, a self-employed metal artist from Oakland and ten years Kelly's senior, had not known one another very long.

Kelly and Karr flew together to Austin on a Southwest Airlines flight that Friday, the night before Halloween. Darling and her boyfriend, Michael Hammond, picked them up at Austin-Bergstrom International Airport. Once they arrived at Darling's two-story condo on McCarthy Lane in Austin's Oak Hill suburb, the women began changing into their costumes to wear for an outing on Sixth Street, Austin's renowned bar and entertainment district.[1]

Another friend, Lori Martin Reeves, arrived dressed as a ninja warrior. Darling dressed in a vintage airline stewardess outfit, a blue A-line suit, and wore 1960s-era white patent leather go-go boots. Kelly donned a

Spanish traditional Day of the Dead[2] costume complete with white skull makeup with dark black circles drawn around her eyes and a tiny rose heart painted on the tip of her nose. As part of her costume, she donned a tight-fitting black spandex body suit topped with a crocheted poncho. Karr did not wear a costume.

The group spent the night bar hopping along Sixth Street. They ate and drank their fill before Darling drove them all back to her condo, arriving shortly before midnight. At the condo, Darling and Hammond headed upstairs for bed. Kelly and Karr remained downstairs in the kitchen and den where they prepared a pullout sofa bed.

Austin Police Department reports reveal that within minutes both Darling and Hammond heard the loud sounds of angry voices coming from the kitchen, followed by Kelly's screams. When Hammond heard Kelly screaming, he told Darling to remain upstairs while he alone rushed downstairs to help. Hammond grabbed a handgun and ran downstairs. At the bottom of the stairs, he saw Karr covered in blood, standing over Kelly holding a knife in his hand. Blood covered the walls and the floor. Karr had stabbed Kelly thirty-seven times.

Hammond testified that he looked down at her lifeless body and saw Kelly's lips move. It appeared that she whispered the words "I love you" to Karr, who still stood over her body with a knife in his hand. Karr mumbled the words, "I killed her. I killed her." Suddenly, as Karr made a move as though he might come up the stairs, Hammond told him to stand down. At that point, Karr grabbed the keys to Darling's Jeep and ran out the front door of the condo. As he got into Darling's car and drove away, Hammond hollered upstairs to Darling to call 9-1-1.

Within seconds, an emergency medical services (EMS) team arrived at the condo, located just down the street from a fire station. Around one o'clock in the morning, on November 1, 2014, the EMS team arrived on the scene to treat Kelly's wounds, but she had died of her injuries.

Meanwhile, Jo Ann Turner had been living in a house at Canyon Lake. At around eleven o'clock that morning, Jo Ann headed for the Fox Hill apartments where Bill and their son Jeff had been living. As she drove, she received a phone call that no parent ever wants to receive.

A detective from the Austin Police Department told Jo Ann that he needed to speak with her and that he would meet her at her husband's apartment. Jo Ann pushed for the detective to reveal the reason for his call. Finally, he said, "It's Kelly." She nearly drove her car off the road before she stopped and broke down emotionally.

At the community center at the Fox Hill apartments, she found the detectives from members of the Austin Police Department waiting. Jo Ann met Bill and Jeff together with police detectives who shared the terrible details of the previous night's events.

Meanwhile, several patrol units and a helicopter from Austin Police Department began searching the woods in the Oak Hill area for Karr. Police captured him nearby on FM Road 1826 where it extends over Bear Creek. Still covered in Kelly's blood, Karr had slashed the inside upholstery of Darling's Jeep and had attempted to stab himself in the neck with the murder weapon.[3]

Judge Cliff Brown appointed criminal attorney Keith T. Lauermann to represent Karr on charges of first-degree murder and vehicle theft for fleeing the scene in Darling's Jeep.[4]

Kelly's friends at Southwest Airlines and throughout Austin held two memorials for her. The first one was held at a place off the Drag—Guadalupe Street across from the University of Texas—at a business that doubled not only as a restaurant but also as a theater. More than five hundred people attended the memorial, including Gary Kelly, the president of Southwest Airlines.

All of the Southwest Airlines' flight attendants who were unable to attend the memorial donated their "wings," or nametags. One of the flight attendants based in Houston gathered up all of the pins and put them together in a huge shadow box that measured thirty-six by thirty-six inches. A local graphics company in Houston mounted the nametags along with Kelly's Southwest ID badge, her scarf, and a watch that she always wore.

In addition, friends installed a memorial bench at Walsh Landing, just north of the Hula Hut restaurant off Town Lake Blvd. Austin Parks and Recreation Department also planted a tree in Kelly's memory. Weeks later, Jo Ann flew to Oakland to help Kelly's friends move her late daughter's personal things out of an apartment.

Before Karr's trial, Austin Police confiscated Kelly's computer, iPad, and iPhone as evidence. Jo Ann never contacted any of Kelly's friends unless they reached out to her first because she didn't have any means to contact them.

Chapter 24

Every day, Jo Ann drove to the Travis County Courthouse to listen to the pretrial and the trial proceedings when they began in 2016.

Before Kelly's death, Jo Ann had worked as a cashier at the H-E-B grocery located off Highway 71 and US 209 West in Oak Hill, but after Kelly died, Jo Ann could no longer find the strength to work. She also could not bear to hear her customers and fellow employees talking about Kelly's murder.

Darling and Hammond both testified at Karr's trial. Detectives produced the knife that Karr used to kill Kelly and forensic evidence that linked him to the scene. Karr pleaded not guilty, but a jury deliberated for less than an hour in 147th Travis County District Court to sentence the 53-year-old to life in prison, eligible for parole in thirty years.[5] He remains incarcerated at the William G. McConnell Unit in Beeville, Texas. In her thoughts, Jo Ann continued to have daily one-sided conversations with her daughter.

"I would say how sorry I was. 'It's been devastating being without you. I'm sorry you had to go through this. You were the sweetest, nicest, most well-mannered, most-loved child I've ever known. Everybody thought so much of you,'" she said.

25

The ROT Today

AT LEAST ONE of the original founding members of the Republic of Texas (ROT) group to this day has survived without being incarcerated since the 1997 standoff in the Davis Mountains. ROT president Ed Brannum,[1] a Southwestern Bell retiree, joined the ROT in 1995. Brannum said that over the last twenty-five years, the ROT has suffered from internal bickering and chaos within its ranks. Members have elected six different presidents and no longer associate themselves with Richard Lance McLaren.

"He was drawing just too much attention from everybody," Brannum said. "He declared war, but he was the paper writer pushing the paper for the Tenth Congress. Actually, what he [was,] was a paper pusher."

Brannum said that before he had ever heard about the ROT group, McLaren had already acquired hundreds of acres in the Davis Mountains and had filed liens against several local businesses. Brannum joined the ROT on December 9, 1995, in Victoria, Texas, after his friend Coolidge Gerdes invited him to attend a meeting there at a local restaurant.

"Coolidge Gerdes asked me, 'How would you like to go to West Texas and meet some people that are forming the Republic of Texas?' At that time, I didn't even know there was such a thing as the Republic of Texas," Brannum said.

He recalls that Gerdes introduced him to three other men at that meeting: Darrell Franks, Don Vernell Brooks, and Robert Taylor. Franks operated an ostrich farm in Shiner, and Brooks had retired from a twenty-eight-year career as an engineer working for Shell Oil Company. Brannum claims he never learned what Taylor did for a living.

The group immediately appointed Franks treasurer when he proposed a plan to set up a banking system called the Central Dominion Trust. Brannum also recalls that, at a follow-up meeting in San Antonio, someone volunteered his name to become the new secretary of state when a former nominee failed to attend.

Brannum shares McLaren's belief that a faulty treaty with the Republic of Texas and the United States Congress in 1844 had never been signed before Congress approved Texas' annexation by resolution in 1845.

He claims that the FBI has investigated members of the ROT continuously for more than twenty-five years. Demonstrations by the ROT continue to draw attention from the FBI and IRS.

"They've been investigating us since ninety-five. In early February 1996 we were bringing charges against the IRS and the Department of Justice, and we were in a Holiday Inn across the street from the IRS offices in Austin," he said.

"I was there when we marched down Congress Street in 1996, and we went to the IRS district office, and Archie Lowe carried those papers in. They wouldn't let seven hundred people in that office, so Archie Lowe delivered the papers," Brannum said.

He recalled that Richard McLaren led the march that day from the Congress Avenue Bridge to the state capital in Austin. McLaren told the delegation that he would file papers to ask the members of Congress to protect the ROT's capitol building. McLaren had insisted that everyone refer to him as Chief Ambassador and Counsel General of the Republic of Texas, a title that began to appear in all of the group's paperwork—both international and local.

The group began to self-destruct in July 1996 when Texas Attorney General Dan Morales issued a restraining order to stop McLaren from filing false liens against private and public property. "We were all with him [McLaren] for several years there before we started figuring out that he started turning against the people and trying to wheel and deal that property out in Fort Davis," Brannum said.

Brannum recalled that in January 1997, he and two other ROT members, Franks and Brooks, traveled to Fort Davis to try to remove McLaren from office. Brannum blames a professional agitator, Arthur Griesacker,[2] with "poisoning" McLaren with grandiose ideas.

"We could be in the embassy, and if Rick was in there and this other guy was in there at the same time—Rick would not be himself. He would be a completely different guy," Brannum said. "He [Griesacker] would leave, and it wouldn't be but a little while and Rick would be his old self again. I don't know what it was."

During March 1997, ROT president Archie Lowe formally impeached McLaren as its ambassador during a special hearing held in Arlington. After being served impeachment papers, McLaren attempted to move his impeachment hearing to Lubbock.

"He was going to have the court out there because he didn't think anyone would show. Well, there was about two hundred people who showed," Brannum said.

Afterward, McLaren split from the ROT to form his own group in the Davis Mountains, which he referred to as the Tenth Congress. McLaren later named Boyce Halbison president and assigned the office of auditor to Betty VanDyke and the title of secretary to Carolyn Carney.

A third ROT faction was led by president Jesse Enloe,[3] convicted and sent to prison for plotting to kill government officials, including former President Bill Clinton.[4]

"As it turned out, [ROT] president after president had their own agenda; they weren't really there for the people—they were there for themselves," Brannum said.

"Well, following the problem with Rick McLaren when they got in all that trouble and everything, the feds came in and confiscated all of the records."

Brannum said today's newly reformed ROT more closely resembles the original delegation of 1845 formed by the 1836 Constitution of the Republic of Texas. Other ROT groups took donations from the public, and accumulated millions in their coffers. The newly formed ROT came together in Buffalo, Texas, at a delegates' convention in June 2005 to elect officers. However, Brannum could not provide the number of registered members. He said the group holds elections every year on the first Monday in September.

He recalled when former Texas Attorney General Morales made a promise to eradicate every member of the ROT from the state. Brannum claims that, in return for Morales's threats, he and other members acted quickly to expose Morales's behind-the-scenes dealings with the tobacco industry.[5]

"Dan Morales went after twenty-six of us, and we got him in prison instead of him getting us in prison," Brannum said. "You know who was [sic] telling people about that."

While running a campaign for Texas governor, Morales hired five private attorneys on a contingency fee to sue the tobacco industry for some of the $17.5 billion in damages.[6] Afterward, Morales secretly awarded a multimillion-dollar contract to Houston attorney Marc Murr, who acted as a consultant in exchange for a kickback.[7]

"Morales, he sued us five guys for ten thousand dollars a day. We turned around and countersued him. We added three or four zeroes to that per day. Anyway, everything he came at us with, we gave back at him, and we don't use attorneys. If we had had an attorney, we'd be in prison," Brannum said. "We never went to his court. We did it all on paperwork."

Brannum claims that Morales worked with Judge Joseph H. Hart to have ROT member Jo Ann Turner arrested on contempt charges and that Hart might have arrested more members of the antigovernment group in Austin if Morales hadn't been indicted first.

"Hart dropped all the cases against us. I think he wanted to get away from it [the ROT case] because Morales was getting caught up in the cigarette deal," he said.

Brannum claims that Morales may also have been involved in an insurance fraud scheme and an unsolved and controversial murder that occurred in Austin more than thirty years ago. The burned bodies of Sarah Harbison, fifteen; her sister Jennifer Harbison, seventeen; Amy Ayers, thirteen; and Eliza Thomas, seventeen, were found inside the I Can't Believe It's Yogurt shop in the 2900 block of Anderson Lane in Austin on December 6, 1991.[8]

"He [Morales] was also mixed up in the Yogurt Shop Murders there in Austin. He was in on some insurance deals in that. He was in with insurance companies and taking under-the-table money," Brannum said.

Brannum does not stand alone in his suspicions about a local conspiracy. Corey Mitchell suggests in her book, *Murdered Innocents*,[9] that the murder of the four young women resulted from an insurance fraud involving several Texas political heavyweights. Beverly Lowry, in her book *Who Killed These Girls? Cold Case: The Yogurt Shop Murders*. points a finger at former interim Austin Police Chief Bruce Mills along with Morales.[10]

Brannum claims his phone still rings ten times daily these days as president of the newly reformed ROT. People come to him for advice about how to avoid paying their mortgages, federal income taxes, and county taxes.

"We don't go around telling people that they don't have to pay their mortgages. IRS is a different story. We've got over probably a thousand people we've saved their retirements and their social securities and all that. We've helped people all over the United States," he said.

"It's called helping people; it really doesn't have anything to do with the Republic of Texas; we help people any way we can. We done [*sic*] proved that the IRS doesn't really have any jurisdiction over people. You become a volunteer is what you do, and they've got you then."

He uses forms provided by the United States Tax Court to help people avoid paying federal income taxes and mortgages. He claims the federal court hears cases submitted by the ROT regularly.

The ROT meets in Kerrville once a month and survives on the sales of novelty coins in silver, gold, and copper. While the IRS has not formally investigated the ROT, several members of the group have been audited.

ROT members refuse to maintain official Texas driver licenses. "We don't respond to your ordinary licenses and fees and all that kind of stuff," Brannum said. "We're a country within a state."

Members of the ROT recognize the original independent nation of Texas created in 1837 that included parts of Kansas, Colorado, Oklahoma, and New Mexico. However, the newly reformed ROT group also supports a referendum of Texas voters suggested in Daniel Miller's book *Texit: Why and How Texas Will Leave the Union*.[11]

Today's ROT members do not have an embassy, but they meet the second Saturday of every month in Kerrville or Bryan. During the mornings, the ROT conducts business, such as passing bills or resolutions. In the afternoons, they often schedule guest speakers followed by a question-and-answer session. All meetings are live streamed on the ROT website: http://thetexasrepublic.com.

Brannum said the group plans to appeal to the Hague Academy of International Law[12] to have Texas returned to them as an independent country. In the meantime, he does not worry whether he or other members of the ROT will be arrested for sedition. He claims to have God on his side.

"Jesus has a place for me to go if it comes down to it. I don't have that many more years to go anyway. I'm seventy-seven," he said. "Yeah. After seventy years old, then you're on borrowed time. I've had seven years of borrowed time already."

Epilogue

Jo Ann Canady Tuner never considered herself a religious person, but in the remaining years of her life, she prayed daily to God to ask Him to free her from both her physical and her mental pain. Her faith had waned early in her married life. She had blamed God for all the bad things that happened to her—Bill's drinking, Bill's anger, Bill's abuse of their son Jeff, the foreclosure of their home, her arrest, and their daughter Kelly's death. Before her death on April 8, 2020, she and God reconciled; she received blessed assurance that she had been absolved.

"I don't blame Him anymore. We make our own beds; we cause our own problems. I realized that probably after I got out of jail. I talked to God about it to a certain extent. I said I regretted blaming Him, and I told Him that He was not the cause; He was not the enabler. I asked Him to help me to move forward to a better life in the future, and He did," she said.

Whenever she shared her story, people often asked her how she survived the past twenty-something years.

"God wanted me to survive because He had another purpose for me and another purpose for me to live. Hopefully, other people will benefit in some way. Don't do like Jo Ann did. Don't do what she did. Don't deliver documents for the ROT, and especially don't deliver documents to the IRS," she said.

Of all her regrets, Jo Ann regretted delivering liens that Richard McLaren wrote against the IRS, Stewart Title, and Travis County.

"That was playing with fire. I can't believe I did that. When I look back on that, I realize I probably would have been okay if I hadn't done that—that one thing. That took a heck of a lot of courage that I don't think anyone in their right mind would do. They'd have to be loaded on booze to do that," she said.

"I walked in there—into the offices of the IRS—as cool as a cucumber, very calm. I wasn't shaking. I walked into the main office there with all those security guards standing all around who said, 'Yes ma'am, how can we help you?' I said, 'I'm here to deliver this to the IRS.' Man, that box was heavy; it was a big box."

She often wished that she had questioned McLaren about his plans to reclaim Texas.

"He had me believing that he could help me recover my house from Stewart Title, but I didn't know, and frankly I didn't concern myself with all of the back taxes. I should have been very concerned," she said.

"He was charismatic. He had some kind of an emotional hold over me. He convinced me to help him with his secretarial work. He convinced me to deliver documents. I was not an official member of the ROT, but I did all of this willingly, with no compensation other than the promise that he would help me get my house back."

Jo Ann realized far too late that she might have solved her own problems better than McLaren ever could. In essence, Jo Ann had abandoned her husband, abandoned her family, abandoned all of her friends, abandoned God, and followed a false prophet.

People always asked her why. That is a question that she asked herself many times.

"The only thing I can say is that I felt that I needed to. I believed him. I felt that he could help me save my house," she said. "I must have been in shock."

At her lowest point, Jo Ann had once considered suicide.

"I'm surprised that I didn't find someone to shoot me, really. I was so distraught about everything. The fact is, I was in shock and not coherent enough to understand what kind of trouble I was really in and what more trouble I was going to be in," she said.

"I remember standing in one of the lanes on US 290 West in the middle of the night, hoping someone would run over me."

Richard and Evelyn McLaren never delivered on their promises. Though they kept promising that they would help, nothing they ever did truly improved Jo Ann's life. Had he lived in another time and place, McLaren might have been called a shaman. An ancient shaman might have sprinkled Jo Ann with herbs and potions and danced around her while casting incantations about her to remove evil spirits or to remove an evil eye. Instead, McLaren cast nothing but evil upon Jo Ann's life.

In 2016, when Jo Ann went to work full time as a cashier at the H-E-B grocery store in Oak Hill, Lonnie Burris came through her checkout line. The handsome and tall civil engineer had recently lost his wife. Jo Ann felt a sudden connection, and the two struck up a friendship that quickly turned to love.

In January 2018, Jeff moved out of the Fox Hill apartment that he shared with his parents and moved to Pensacola, Florida, to work as a scuba diving instructor. At ninety years old, Bill had become frail and suffered ill health. Jo Ann found that she could no longer take care of him alone.

She moved Bill into Elmcroft Senior Living, an assisted-living health center. Soon afterward, Jo Ann received a call from one of the nurses there. Bill had fallen out of bed and had likely spent some time alone on the floor of his room before the nurse found him just as her morning shift began. The nurse, whose name Jo Ann never wished to reveal, told her that she wanted to take care of Bill in her own home with her husband and two daughters. So, Jo Ann moved Bill into the nurse's home, where he remained until his death five months later on May 18, 2018.[1]

Bill's memorial was held June 13, 2018, at All Faiths Funeral Services. He had been a thirty-second-degree Mason of Masonic Lodge #456 and a long-standing member of Ben Hur Shrine Temple in Austin. Several members of his Masonic Lodge provided his eulogy at the memorial. All of Bill's surviving children attended the service, including Jeff, who had flown in from Pensacola for a few days.

Soon afterward, Jo Ann hired an attorney who helped her to finally clear her debt with the IRS. Her days of running from her past ended in more ways than one.

Jo Ann had suffered from back problems for nearly forty years since her 1980s car accident, but she finally decided to endure intensive back surgery on March 21, 2019, at St. David's Medical Center. Following her surgery, she was transferred to Deer Creek Rehabilitation Center in Wimberley, on April 2, 2019. When she was released on May 29, 2019, she returned to the house that she shared with Lonnie Burris in Canyon Lake. Soon the nerve pain migrated to her legs and she started using a rolling walker to get around.

Over the next few months, Lonnie cared for Jo Ann and took her to see several doctors for treatments to alleviate her physical suffering, but nothing seemed to help. She underwent acupuncture, massage therapy, a spinal block, and often relied on prescription pain medications. Soon she could no longer walk unassisted and began using a wheelchair.

On October 18, 2019, at the Comal County Tax Office in New Braunfels, Lonnie and Jo Ann Burris said their marriage vows and exchanged rings in front of Justice of the Peace Jennifer Saunders. The couple wore black, Jo Ann's favorite color, and the bride wore tiny white baby's breath flowers in her hair. Afterward, their friends celebrated with the newlyweds at Café Guadalajara in Canyon Lake. Jo Ann told everyone in attendance that day that she had never felt happier in her life, nor had she felt so beloved. Finally, she had begun to live the life that she always wanted. She and Lonnie hoped to begin traveling together soon. The newlyweds made plans to visit Europe.

However, on the morning of April 1, 2020, Lonnie awoke to find Jo Ann unresponsive while lying in their bed. She seemed dazed and could not speak. He immediately took his wife of six months to the nearest medical facility, Resolute Health Hospital in New Braunfels. In the emergency department, doctors learned that Jo Ann suffered from a heart infection and the beginning stages of liver failure from cirrhosis. Immediately, the medical staff began administering antibiotics and intravenous fluids.

Lonnie visited with Jo Ann only briefly at her bedside before the hospital's staff asked him to leave. As a result of the COVID-19 pandemic and the state's social distancing orders, the nurses isolated Jo Ann and sent Lonnie home to wait. He waited three days. Finally, on the third day, doctors phoned him to tell him they were moving Jo Ann to the PAM Specialty Hospital of New Braunfels for long-term acute medical care. Again Lonnie could not visit Jo Ann at the facility, but he called morning and night every day for the following four days to inquire about Jo Ann's condition. He called to ask if he could drop off her cell phone, but nurses told him that his wife's eyes fluttered open for only a few moments each day. For the most part, Jo Ann remained unconscious.

Early in the morning hours of April 8, 2020, a doctor telephoned Lonnie to tell him that Jo Ann had died. The news hit him hard and left him in shock. Lonnie's son Regan Burris took his father to stay with him and other extended family members in Round Rock. When Lonnie mustered the courage and composure, he called Jo Ann's son, Jeff, who at the time lived in South America. He also began calling Jo Ann's friends to share the sad news. Lonnie had Jo Ann's body cremated, and did not hold a memorial for her because of the ongoing pandemic.

Jo Ann would have loved to have witnessed this book's publishing. She had looked forward to one day attending a book signing to talk about her part in the ROT war. Despite her regrets, she felt proud to have survived all of the terrible things that had happened to her over the course of her lifetime. Jo Ann Canady Turner-Burris survived an impoverished childhood, an abusive first marriage, the murder of her only daughter, disabilities caused by a car accident, and a lifetime of physical and emotional suffering.

She had hoped that her part in this story might discourage others from following a similar path. Jo Ann mistakenly put her faith in Richard Lance McLaren and the Republic of Texas militia members who believed that Texas could become its own independent nation. For her part, she paid an extreme price. Though she never returned to jail or served prison time, she spent the remainder of her life regretting her involvement with the ROT and their 1997 fight for Texas' independence.

At the time of Jo Ann's death, Jeff Turner had moved to South America to escape unrelated charges of domestic violence in Florida. The whereabouts of Jeff's son and Jo Ann's only grandson, Chance Turner, remain unknown. April 27, 2022 marked the twenty-fifth anniversary of the standoff between a little more than a handful of Republic of Texas militia members and 300 law enforcement officers in the Davis Mountains.

Acknowledgments

First and foremost, I am grateful for the time given to me by Jo Ann Canady Turner-Burris, whom I met with regularly up until shortly before her death on April 8, 2020. She and I became very close friends. Her personal story provides a unique thread throughout this book.

Second, I am thankful for Molly McKnight, who first introduced me to Jo Ann. Molly sat in and listened to several of our interviews over lunches that I provided at my house. Since Jo Ann passed away, Molly and I have continued our friendship.

I am appreciative of the insight that former FBI consultant Gary Noesner provided to me during my research for this book and for writing my book's forward.

Several of the Texas Rangers, including Barry Caver, David Duncan, and Jess Malone, supplied me with details, names, and photographs from the seven-day standoff that I could not have obtained anywhere else. Caver also granted me two long phone interviews. In addition, Duncan and Malone met with me in person for breakfast and for lunch respectively on March 17, 2019. I am indebted to each of them.

Former Sheriff Steve Bailey, with his colorful language and sensory-filled descriptions about the standoff, allowed me to feel as if I had witnessed the action leading up to the event. I also learned a great deal about bass and striper fishing from our phone conversations.

One of the ROT hostages, Joe Rowe, invited my husband and me into his beautiful home in the DMR on St. Patrick's Day, March 17, 2019, to hear his story. After about an hour, we became fast friends and promised to visit him again whenever we pass through that stretch of road between Austin and El Paso.

Dessie Andrews, in person, divulged her insights about the members of the Republic of Texas militia during her time spent working with Richard Lance McLaren. I truly appreciate her story.

Thank you to Chuck Samson, who provided me with details about his cousin Richard Lance McLaren as a boy, as an adolescent, and as a young man; he also supplied me with several family photographs.

I enjoyed speaking with residents of the Davis Mountain Resort, former volunteers of the EMS and DMR fire departments, and others who continue to live in Fort Davis. They regaled me with stories about the standoff that cannot be matched.

I also would like to thank Robert Hurst, the public relations officer for the Texas Department of Criminal Justice. Hurst assisted in scheduling my interview with Richard Lance McLaren and, through regular emails and phone calls, confirmed the status of remaining ROT prisoners.

My interviews with all the attorneys, prosecutors, and judges about the ROT trials made this an exciting experience for me. I have not had so much fun researching crime since my days working as a police reporter for several Texas newspapers. Thank you all.

I especially wish to thank TAMU editor-in-chief Thom Lemmons for his continued support. Thanks to his early written endorsement of this project, I was able to conduct a one-on-one exclusive interview with Richard Lance McLaren on May 15, 2018, inside William P. Clements Unit prison in Amarillo. Thanks also goes to Pat Clabaugh, senior editor at TAMU, and to Carol Lallier, of Progressive Publishing Services, who copy edited this manuscript. I also appreciate Sue Gaines, who provided this book's index.

Last, but not least, I wish to thank my husband and son, and all of my extended family and friends for their loving support of my continued writing endeavors.

Notes

Introduction

1. Wood, "Movement to Make Texas Its Own Country."
2. Enclopedia.com, "Republic of Texas."
3. Blejwas, Griggs, and Potok, "Almost 60 Terrorist Plots Uncovered."
4. Ed Brannum, telephone interview by the author, April 5, 2018.
5. Gracy, "Austin, Moses."
6. Barker, "Mexican Colonization Laws."
7. Selin, "Stephen F. Austin."
8. History.com Editors, "Jan. 3, 1834."
9. Donald S. Frazier, PhD, telephone interview by the author, May 1, 2019.
10. History.com Editors. "Sam Houston."
11. History.com Editors, "Battle of San Jacinto."
12. Texas State Library and Archives Commission, "Treaties of Velasco."
13. U-S-history.com, "Adams-Onís Treaty."
14. Gambrell, "Lamar, Mirabeau Buonaparte."
15. Texas State Library and Archives Commission, "Republic of Texas."
16. Long, "Sabine River."
17. Davis, "History of the Short-Lived Florida Republic."
18. Bromley and Smith, "Historical Significance."
19. Bromley and Smith, "Historical Significance"; *Texas Almanac*, "Capitals of the Republic of Texas."
20. Texas Almanac, "Capitals of the Republic of Texas."
21. Texas State Library and Archives Commission, "Early Statehood."
22. Christian, "Mirabeau Buonaparte Lamar."
23. Moneymaker, "Wild Days of Texas."
24. Office of the Historian, "Annexation of Texas."
25. Joint Resolution, March 1, 1845.
26. Elliott, "Henderson, James Pinckney."
27. *Encyclopaedia Britannica*, "Treaty of Guadalupe Hidalgo."
28. GaVette, "Mexican-American War."
29. Wooster, "Civil War."

30. Glass, "Texas Is the 7th State to Secede."
31. Whitehurst, "Civil War and Reconstruction."
32. *Encyclopaedia Britannica*, "*Texas v. White*."
33. Kohout, "Jeff Davis County."
34. Strode, "Jefferson Davis."
35. Martin, "Why Did Texas Secede?"
36. Anti-Defamation League, "Militia Movement."

Chapter 1

1. All information and direct statements in this chapter attributed to Jo Ann Canady Turner are based on a series of exclusive interviews by the author, at a South Austin private residence, September 2017 to May 2019.
2. Holmes, "Texas Group Accused of 'Paper Terrorism.'"

Chapter 2

1. Marten, "Brackenridge Hospital."
2. Kemp, "Brackenridge, Robert J."
3. Barnes, Michael, "Austin Bids Farewell."
4. Brewer, "Fire Destroys AJH School"; *Old Austin High School* [photograph].
5. Roberts, "Junior High Led Austin Desegregation."
6. Austin History Center, "What Is the History of Barton Springs?"
7. Bueche, "A Splashy History of Deep Eddy."
8. Cinema Treasures, "Chief Drive-In."
9. CaptainChicken.org, "South Austin Drive-In Theater."
10. Hormel Historic Home History, "Woolworth's Store."
11. Great Indoorsman, "Austin Askew."
12. Hill, "Historic Dancehall."
13. Billboard Top 100, "1962."
14. Sports Reference LLC, "Ken McMinn."
15. Barnes, "Briscoe Center Offers a Staggering Look."
16. Austin History Center, "Desegregation in Austin."

Chapter 3

1. Pitzulo, "Insight."
2. All information and direct statements in this chapter attributed to Jo Ann Canady Turner are based on a series of exclusive interviews by the author, at a South Austin private residence, September 2017 to May 2019.
3. Bizjournals.com. "Pier today, gone tomorrow; Historic Austin establishment loses lease."

4. Corcoran, "A Closing Set."
5. Hodson, "The Continental Club."
6. Austin-Bergstrom International Airport, "History of the Airport."
7. Vanderstel, "Native Americans in Indiana."
8. Mayo Clinic, "Bipolar Disorder."
9. Miller, "Edinburg."
10. KRGV.com, "Station Information."
11. Leerhsen, "Who Was Ty Cobb?"
12. Interlandi, "How Safe Is Deet?"
13. Feigenbaum, "NSA Agrees to Offer Refunds."
14. D'Onofrio, "Herbalife 'Scam.'"
15. All information and direct statements in this chapter attributed to Jeff Turner are based on a telephone interview by the author, March 27, 2018.
16. Lee, "Texas' First African-American Judge."
17. King, "Peck Young Goes Away Mad."
18. Trejo, "Intersection Changes Proposed."
19. O'Keefe, *Texas Banking Crisis*.
20. Robinson, "Savings and Loan Crisis."
21. Moore, "Trucking Deregulation"; Friedman, "Rocky Road for Truckers."
22. Rich, "Drinking Through the Ages."
23. Financial Samurai, "How Much Can an Adjustable Rate Mortgage Go Up?"

Chapter 4

1. All information and direct statements in this chapter attributed to Jo Ann Canady Turner are based on a series of exclusive interviews by the author, at a South Austin private residence, September 2017 to May 2019.
2. All information and direct statements in this chapter attributed to Molly McKnight are based on an interview by the author, at a private residence, November 9, 2017.
4. Mississippi Sports Hall of Fame and Museum, "Dwight 'D.D.' Lewis."
3. United States v. Gold Unlimited Ltd.
4. Sheffield, "Is Network Marketing Just a Scam?"
5. Yeomans, "NSA's Recruitment Methods"; Guina, "Multi-Level Marketing."
6. *Slaying the Dragon of Debt*, "1990–92 Early 1990s Recession."
7. LendingTree, "Adjustable Rate Mortgage."

Chapter 5

1. All information and direct statements in this chapter attributed to Jo Ann Canady Turner are based on a series of exclusive interviews by the author, at a South Austin private residence, September 2017 to May 2019.

2. Winston & Strawn LLP, "What Is a Temporary Restraining Order (TRO)?"
3. All information and direct statements in this chapter attributed to Chuck Samson are based on a telephone interview by the author, August 20, 2019.
4. Atkins, *Encyclopedia of Right-Wing Extremism,* 249.
5. Richard Lance McLaren, in-person interview by the author, at William P. Clements Unit prison in Amarillo, May 16, 2018.
6. Associated Press, "Richard McLaren."
7. *Wilmington News-Journal,* "WHS to Graduate 263."
8. Pressley, "Cyber-Savvy 'Texians.'"
9. *Wilmington News-Journal,* "Miss Sandra Kay Denkenberger."
10. *The Eagle,* "Mary June McLaren.":
11. Texas A&M University, "Chuck H. Samson, Jr. PhD."
12. Hotel Limpia, "History."
13. Carl Covington, telephone interview by the author, December 3, 2019.
14. Jerry Rhea, telephone interview by the author, April 5, 2019.
15. All information and direct statements in this chapter attributed to Joe Rowe are based on an in-person interview by the author, at Davis Mountain Resort, March 17, 2019.
16. Verhovek, "Before His Armed Standoff."
17. Ibid.
18. All information and direct statements in this chapter attributed to Johnny Wofford are based on a telephone interview by the author, January 23, 2019.
19. Brock, "Republic of Texas Is No More."
20. Hill and Hill, "Lis Pendens."
21. Patoski, "Land That I Love."
22. All information and direct statements in this chapter attributed to Scott McIvor are based on a telephone interview by the author, April 17, 2019.
23. All information and direct statements in this chapter attributed to Mike Ward are based on a telephone interview by the author, April 5, 2019.
24. Farkas, "Who Can Claim Property?"
25. Bob Dillard, telephone interview by the author, April 4, 2019.

Chapter 6

1. Utterback, "Statewide Militia Muster."
2. Ibid.
3. All information and direct statements in this chapter attributed to Jo Ann Canady Turner are based on a series of exclusive interviews by the author, at a South Austin private residence, September 2017 to May 2019.
4. All information and direct statements in this chapter attributed to Dessie Andrews are based on an in-person interview by the author, at Jack Allen's restaurant in Oak Hill, Texas, October 25, 2017.
5. Clemons, *Branding Texas,* 2–9.

6. Atkins, *Encyclopedia of Right-Wing Extremism*, 249.
7. Ibid.
8. Richard Lance McLaren, in-person interview by the author, at William P. Clements Unit prison in Amarillo, May 16, 2018.
9. Vattel, *Law of Nations*, 10.
10. Brock, "Republic of Texas Is No More."
11. Watts, "Independent Spirits."
12. McCracken, "Feds Downplay New McLaren Arrest Warrant."
13. McCracken, "Republic of Texas Ambassador."
14. All information and direct statements in this chapter attributed to Michael T. Morgan are based on a telephone interview with the author, May 1, 2019.
15. McCracken, "Bunton Hears McLaren Contempt Charges."
16. Verhovek, "Pecos Journal."
17. McCracken, "Judge Wipes Smile Off McLaren's Face."
18. McCracken, "Bunton Hears McLaren Contempt Charges."
19. McCracken, "Attorney General Warned by McLaren."
20. Langford, "Fines Mount for Texas Separatist Group."
21. All information and direct statements in this chapter attributed to Ward Tisdale are based on a telephone interview by the author, June 2, 2020.
22. Erwin, *Declaration of Independence*, 205.
23. Nathan, "Christmas in the Republic of Texas."
24. Associated Press. "Standoff."
25. Verhovek, "Serious Face on Texas Independence."
26. Holmes, "Texas Group Accused of 'Paper Terrorism.'"
27. Korosec, "We Are the R.O.T."
28. Anti-Defamation League, "Vigilante Justice."
29. Cromeens Law Firm, "Fraudulent Liens in Texas."
30. Michael F. Hord Jr., telephone interview by the author, February 26, 2020.
31. All information and direct statements in this chapter attributed to Todd Jaggar are based on a telephone interview by the author, August 19, 2019.
32. Langford, "State Demands Militia Group's Email."
33. Harper, *And That's the Way It Will Be*, 164.
34. Pressley, "Cyber-Savy 'Texians.'"
35. Electronic Communications Privacy Act of 1986 (ECPA), U.S.C. §§ 2510–2523.
36. Craddock, "Texas ISP Targeted in Secessionist Case."
37. Brekke, "Wave of Support for Defiant Texas ISP."
38. Sears, "Elements of Cache Programing."
39. McKay, "Constitution of 1845."
40. Korosec, "Soul Food and Crackers."
41. Katz and Hart, "Two Hostages in Texas Standoff Released."
42. Batista, "Rick Perry's Ties to a Terrorist Militia."
43. Korosec, "Soul Food and Crackers."
44. Hollingsworth, "Up in Smoke."
45. Ramsey, "An Unreliable Narrator."

Chapter 7

1. All information and direct statements in this chapter attributed to Jo Ann Canady Turner are based on a series of exclusive interviews by the author, at a South Austin private residence, September 2017 to May 2019.
2. Texas Academy of Distinguished Neutrals, "Hon. Joseph H. Hart."
3. Scheibal, "Republic of Texas Member Arrested."
4. Ando and Chu, "Deposition Tips."
5. Scheibal, "Republic of Texas Member Arrested."
6. Caver and Nieman, "Captain Barry Caver on the Republic of Texas Standoff."
7. Vocabulary.com, "Operative."
8. CNN Interactive, "One Injured in Separatist Standoff."
9. Walsh, "Ex-Judge John Dietz Cancels His Courthouse Contract."
10. All information and direct statements in this chapter attributed to Nick Milam are based on a telephone interview by the author, March 1, 2019.
11. Katz, "Two Hostages in the Texas Standoff Released."
12. History.com Editors, "Confederate States of America."
13. Verhovek, "Hostages Taken in Standoff."

Chapter 8

1. All information and direct statements in this chapter attributed to Jo Ann Canady Turner are based on a series of exclusive interviews by the author, at a South Austin private residence, September 2017 to May 2019.
2. The Nature Conservancy, "Chihuahuan Desert."
3. All information and direct statements in this chapter attributed to Joe Rowe are based on an interview by the author, at Davis Mountain Resort, March 17, 2019.
4. Pressley, "Peaceful End Achieved in Texas Siege."
5. ATF, "National Firearms Act."
6. Verhovek, "Texas Swaps a Jailed Militant."
7. Military-Today.com, "SKS: Semi-Automatic Rifle."
8. Schuppe, Jon. "America's Rifle."
9. Ledin, "How to Understand Spotting Scope Features."
10. All information and direct statements in this chapter attributed to Jerry Rhea are based on a telephone interview by the author, April 5, 2019.

Chapter 9

1. All information and direct statements in this chapter attributed to Jo Ann Canady Turner are based on a series of exclusive interviews by the author, at a South Austin private residence, September 2017 to May 2019.
2. Blakinger, "Can We Build a Better Women's Prison?"

3. All information and direct statements in this chapter attributed to Steve Bailey are based on a telephone interview by the author, September 15, 2018. Juelene Jasper with the Sheriff's Association of Texas stated in an email to the author that Bailey served as sheriff from January 1, 1997, until December 31, 2004.

4. Bockhauser, "What Is an M16?"

5. Adam, "History of the SKS"; *Britannica*, "AK-47: Soviet Firearm."

6. Armalite, "AR-50."

7. All information and direct statements in this chapter attributed to David Duncan are based upon an interview by telephone by the author, November 27, 2018, and an in-person interview by the author, in Alpine, Texas, March 17, 2019.

8. *Britannica*, "Waco Siege."

9. All information and direct statements in this chapter attributed to Barry Caver are based on a telephone interview by the author, April 30, 2018.

10. Draper, "Twilight of the Texas Rangers."

11. Sheffield, "Joaquin Jackson"; Price, "Joaquin Jackson, Iconic Texas Lawman Dies."

12. Forstall, *Population of States and Counties of the United States*, 156.

13. Cox, *Stand-Off in Texas*, 118.

14. Patoski, "Out There."

15. Banta and Osborn, "Fort Davis-Area Residents Say Standoff Was Inevitable."

16. *Britannica*, "Janet Reno."

17. *US Customs*, "Marfa Station" and "CBP Through the Years."

Chapter 10

1. All information and direct statements in this chapter attributed to Jo Ann Canady Turner are based on a series of exclusive interviews by the author, at a South Austin private residence, September 2017 to May 2019.

2. Banta and Osborne, "Militant Separatists Take 2 Hostages."

3. All information and direct statements in this chapter attributed to Barry Caver are based on a telephone interview by the author, April 30, 2018.

4. All information and direct statements in this chapter attributed to Jess Malone are based on a telephone interview by the author, September 21, 2018, and in-person interview March 17, 2019, in Iraan.

5. All information and direct statements in this chapter attributed to David Duncan, are based upon an interview by telephone by the author, November 27, 2018, and an in-person interview by the author, in Alpine, Texas, March 17, 2019.

6. Mike Ward, telephone interview by the author, April 5, 2019.

7. George Grubb, telephone interview by the author, April 4, 2019.

8. All information and direct statements in this chapter attributed to Joe Rowe are based on an interview by the author, at Davis Mountain Resort, March 17, 2019.

9. Alison, "Stagecoach Service."

10. Brune, *Springs of Texas,* 261.

11. All information and direct statements in this chapter attributed to Carl Covington are based on a telephone interview by the author, December 3, 2019.

12. All information and direct statements in this chapter attributed to Steve Bailey are based on a telephone interview by the author, September 15, 2018.

13. Chan, "The Real Story Behind the Waco Siege."

14. History.com Editors, "Waco Siege."

15. *Britannica,* "Ruby Ridge."

16. Lewis, "Twenty Years Ago Today."

17. Noesner, Gary. *Stalling for Time: My Life as an FBI Negotiator,* chap. 10.

18. All information and direct statements in this chapter attributed to Gary Noesner are based on a telephone interview by the author, September 4, 2018.

19. DeNevi and Campbell, *Into the Minds of Madmen,* 74.

20. Campbell, "1997 Republic of Texas Standoff Intense."

21. *Ruidoso News.* "Robert Braxton 'Bobby' Holt."

22. All information and direct statements in this chapter attributed to Terence L. O'Rourke are based on a telephone interview by the author, January 16, 2019.

23. The Texas attorney general at the time was Dan Morales; see Rozen and Jeffreys, "Rise & Fall." For a perspective on the New World Order, see Hsu, "A Global Government Is Waiting in the Wings."

24. Draper, "The Great Defenders."

25. Killelea, "Flashback."

26. Rosenbloom, "Waco: More than Simple Blunders?"

Chapter 11

1. All information and direct statements in this chapter attributed to Jo Ann Canady Turner are based on a series of exclusive interviews by the author, at a South Austin private residence, September 2017 to May 2019.

2. Campbell, "Ranger Captain Reflects on Waco."

3. Federal Writers Project, *WPA Guide to Texas.*

4. All information and direct statements in this chapter attributed to Jess Malone are based on a telephone interview by the author, September 21, 2018.

5. Nash, "Medium Recovery Vehicle M88."

6. Lind, "Waco and Ruby Ridge."

7. Campbell, "1997 Republic of Texas Intense."

8. All information and direct statements in this chapter attributed to Gary Noesner are based on a telephone interview by the author, September 4, 2018.

9. All information and direct statements in this chapter attributed to Albert Valadez are based on a telephone interview by the author, April 20, 2018.

10. Farkas, "Who Can Claim Property?"

11. *Ruidoso News.* "Robert Braxton 'Bobby' Holt."

12. All information and direct statements in this chapter attributed to Terence L. O'Rourke are based on a telephone interview by the author, January 16, 2019.
13. National Governors Association, "Gov. George W. Bush."
14. Death Penalty Information Center. "Texas Pushes Nation's Executions to Record Numbers in 1997; but Opposition Grows."

Chapter 12

1. All information and direct statements in this chapter attributed to Jo Ann Canady Turner are based on a series of exclusive interviews by the author, at a South Austin private residence, September 2017 to May 2019.
2. All information and direct statements in this chapter attributed to Barry Caver are based on a telephone interview by the author, April 30, 2018.
3. All information and direct statements in this chapter attributed to Gary Noesner are based on a telephone interview by the author, September 4, 2018.
4. Settler, "David Koresh and the Waco Siege."
5. Noesner, *Stalling for Time*, 185.
6. Associated Press, "Mexican Standoff?"
7. Fulbright and Smith, "Seven Suspects Arrested."
8. Terence L. O'Rourke, telephone interview by the author, January 16, 2019.
9. All information and direct statements in this chapter attributed to Albert Valadez are based on a telephone interview by the author, April 20, 2018.
10. Farkas, "Who Can Claim Property Based on Adverse Possession in Texas?"
11. International Committee of the Red Cross, "Treaties, States Parties and Commentaries."
12. Honigsberg, "The Real Origin of the Term 'Enemy Combatant.'"
13. Military Factory, "Armored Personnel Carriers."

Chapter 13

1. All information and direct statements in this chapter attributed to Jo Ann Canady Turner are based on a series of exclusive interviews by the author, at a South Austin private residence, September 2017 to May 2019.
2. All information and direct statements in this chapter attributed to Barry Caver are based on a telephone interview by the author, April 30, 2018.
3. Cox, *Stand-Off in Texas*, 170.
4. All information and direct statements in this chapter attributed to Terence L. O'Rourke are based on a telephone interview by the author, January 16, 2019.
5. Kuempel, "Separatists End Standoff Peacefully."
6. A faxed copy of the letter handwritten by Julie Hopkins, daughter of Evelyn McLaren, was provided by Sarah Jackson, archivist for Harris County, with permission from attorney Terence O'Rourke for the author.

Chapter 14

1. All information and direct statements in this chapter attributed to Jo Ann Canady Turner are based on a series of exclusive interviews by the author, at a South Austin private residence, September 2017 to May 2019.
2. Rivas, "When Texas Was the National Leader."
3. McGaughy, "First to Ban Open Carry."
4. *Edmonton Journal,* "Surrender Ends Siege in Texas."
5. All information and direct statements in this chapter attributed to Terence L. O'Rourke are based on a telephone interview by the author, January 16, 2019.
6. All information and direct statements in this chapter attributed to Barry Caver are based on a telephone interview by the author, April 30, 2018.
7. Draper, "The Great Defenders."
8. TXMountaineer. "Davis Mountains." Summitpost.org.
9. Cox, *Stand-Off in Texas,* 166.
10. Johnny Wofford, telephone interview by the author, January 23, 2019.
11. Cox, *Stand-Off in Texas,* 182–83.
12. Cox, 178–79.

Chapter 15

1. All information and direct statements in this chapter attributed to Jo Ann Canady Turner are based on a series of exclusive interviews by the author, at a South Austin private residence, September 2017 to May 2019.
2. Dillman, "Eviction Process in Texas."
3. All information and direct statements in this chapter attributed to Barry Caver are based on a telephone interview by the author, April 30, 2018.
4. Utley, *Lone Star Lawmen,* 324.
5. Gambino, "Wife's Phone Call."
6. National Academies, "IED Attack."

Chapter 16

1. All information and direct statements in this chapter attributed to Jo Ann Canady Turner are based on a series of exclusive interviews by the author, at a South Austin private residence, September 2017 to May 2019.
2. Judges Hill, "William Caswell House."
3. ABC13, "A Look Back at Houston's Six Flags Astroworld."
4. Herman, "Robert Mueller Is Not That Robert Mueller."
5. Downs-Clark, "History of Shoal Creek."
6. Forever Resorts, "The History of Southfork Ranch."
7. Whittaker, "Still Working on It."
8. Mowreader, "What Are Cigarette Boats?"

9. *Britannica*, "Davis Mountains."
10. Campbell, "Republic of Texas Leader Unrepentant."
11. US Army, "Explosive Ordnance Disposal (EOD) Specialist."
12. All information and direct statements in this chapter attributed to Barry Caver are based upon a telephone interview by the author, January 23, 2019.
13. Cox, *Stand-Off in Texas*, 196.
14. Johnny Wofford, telephone interview by the author, January 23, 2019.
15. Chan, "Real Story Behind the Waco Siege."
16. All information and direct statements in this chapter attributed to Gary Noesner are based on a telephone interview by the author, September 9, 2018.
17. Federal Communications Commission, "Citizens Band Radio."
18. Ray, "Governor cites Fort Davis resolution as warning to other militia groups."

Chapter 17

1. All information and direct statements in this chapter attributed to Jo Ann Canady Turner are based on a series of exclusive interviews by the author, at a South Austin private residence, September 2017 to May 2019.
2. LeBlanc, "At Davis Mountains Preserve."
3. All information and direct statements in this chapter attributed to Jess Malone are based on a telephone interview by the author, September 21, 2018.
4. All information and direct statements in this chapter attributed to Eric Pechacek are based on telephone interviews by the author, March 29, 2019, and February 4, 2020.
5. National Shooting Sports Foundation, "Understanding America's Rifle."
6. Ruger, "Mini-14® Ranch."
7. Boddington, "The .270 Winchester Cartridge."
8. Cox, *Stand-Off in Texas*, 203–4.
9. Jorden, "Dead Separatist's Brother Says Man Was Betrayed by McLaren."
10. Associated Press, "Republic Member's Son Charged in Bomb Scare."

Chapter 18

1. All information and direct statements in this chapter attributed to Jo Ann Canady Turner are based on a series of exclusive interviews by the author, at a South Austin private residence, September 2017 to May 2019.
2. Allighieri, *Dante's Inferno*, 62–68.
3. Aron, "Authorities Scale Back Search."
4. All information and direct statements in this chapter attributed to Barry Caver are based on a telephone interview by the author, January 23, 2019.
5. Johnson, *Right Wing Resurgence*, 93–94.
6. *New York Times*, "Texas Takes Custody of 400 Children."
7. Texas Independence List, "Keyes Arrested."

8. Langford, "FBI Arrests Republic of Texas Fugitive Richard Keyes."
9. All information and direct statements in this chapter attributed to Chris Swecker are based on a telephone interview by the author, January 17, 2020.
10. Little, "Why the Hunt for the Real Atlanta Bomber Took Nearly 7 Years."
11. *Houston Chronicle,* "Texans Fear 'Republic' Fugitive Will Seek Revenge."
12. Moore, "FBI, Rangers taking Republic of Texas Fugitive Seriously."
13. Dyer, "Desperate Measures."
14. Dyer, "On the Run."
15. Ibid.
16. Dyer, *Harvest of Rage.*
17. *Los Angeles Times,* "Last Republic of Texas Separatist Sentenced."
18. Wilson, "Ruby Ridge 1992."
19. Barcella, "The Waco Siege."
20. Lewis, "Twenty Years Ago Today."
21. *FBI News,* "Oklahoma City Bombing."
22. *Austin American-Statesman,* "Morales Sues Separatist."
23. Associated Press, "Phony-Liens Bill."

Chapter 19

1. All information and direct statements in this chapter attributed to Jo Ann Canady Turner are based on a series of exclusive interviews by the author, at a South Austin private residence, September 2017 to May 2019.
2. Banta, "Fort Davis-area Residents Say Standoff Was Inevitable."
3. TexasEscapes.com, "Brewster County Courthouse."
4. Waymarking.com, "Brewster County Courthouse, Alpine, TX"; Kiddle, "Alpine Texas Facts for Kids."
5. All information and direct statements in this chapter attributed to Albert Valadez are based on a telephone interview by the author, April 20, 2018.
6. Kay, "Victim: Error led to siege."
7. Tribune News Services, "Texas Separatist Gets 99 Years."
8. Montes, "Texas Militants Sentenced."
9. Typewriter Database, "1997 Brother WP-5600 MDS."
10. Trottier, *Screenwriter's Bible.*

Chapter 20

1. All information and direct statements in this chapter attributed to Jo Ann Canady Turner are based on a series of exclusive interviews by the author, at a South Austin private residence, September 2017 to May 2019.
2. Simnacher, "Robert Hughes, 91, ex-Dallas Lawyer, Judge and State Representative."
3. Trip Advisor, "Explore Roatan."
4. United States District Court Northern District of Texas, "History."

5. Rosenwald, "Row vs. Wade's Forgotten Loser"; Faux, *Roe vs. Wade,* 86–89.
6. GSA, "Federal Building, Dallas, TX."
7. All information and direct statements in this chapter attributed to Mike Uhl are based on a telephone interview by the author, September 10, 2018.
8. Rozen, "The Man Who Knew Too Much."
9. All information and direct statements in this chapter attributed to U.S. Judge of the Northwestern District Joe Fish are based on a telephone interview by the author, September 7, 2018.
10. Kook Science Research Hatch, "Richard Kieninger."
11. Watkins, "Utopian Society."
12. All information and direct statements in this chapter attributed to Tom Mills are based on a telephone interview by the author, September 7, 2018.
13. Rozen, "The Man Who Knew Too Much."
14. *Orlando Sentinel,* "Man Linked to Separatists Charged with Bank Fraud."
15. History.com Editors, "Oklahoma City Bombing."
16. FindLaw, "Jury Nullification."
17. *Britannica,* "Texas v. White."
18. *Washington Post,* "Eight Republic of Texas' Separatists Convicted of Fraud."
19. Paul Coggins, telephone interview by the author, September 7, 2018.
20. Watts and Slover, "McLarens Face Federal Charges."
21. United States of America v Richard Lance McLaren, Linh Ngoc Vu, Evelyn Ann McLaren, Jasper Edward Baccus, Richard George Kieninger, Erwin Leo Brown, Joe Louis Reece, Stephen Craig Crear.
22. McLaren v. State.
23. McLaren, Richard Lance v. State of Texas
24. All information and direct statements in this chapter attributed to Richard Lance McLaren are based on an in-person interview by the author, at William P. Clements Unit prison, Amarillo, TX, May 16, 2018.
25. McLaren's reference to IMF refers to the International Monetary Fund.
26. History.com Editors, "War Powers Act."
27. US Legal, "Treasury Warrant Law and Definition."; Law Dictionary, "What Is Foreign Bill of Exchange?"
28. Authority, *Laws of the Eighth Legislature.*
29. Sharp. Republic of Texas officials contend that state should stand alone."
30. Definitions, "Provisional Government."
31. Pfeiff, "The Beach Life."
32. Baysider.com, "Sueno del Mar Diving Resort."

Chapter 21

1. All information and direct statements in this chapter attributed to Jo Ann Canady Turner are based on a series of exclusive interviews by the author, at a South Austin private residence, September 2017 to May 2019.

2. MilitaryBases.us, "Camp Mabry."
3. United States v. McLaren.

Chapter 22

1. All information and direct statements in this chapter attributed to Jo Ann Canady Turner are based on a series of exclusive interviews by the author, at a South Austin private residence, September 2017 to May 2019.

2. All information and direct statements in this chapter attributed to Gerald Carruth are based on a telephone interview by the author, February 22, 2019.

3. FJC, "Furgeson, William Royal, Jr."; FEDARB, "Judge W. Royal Furgeson Jr. (Retired)."

4. FJC, "Historic Federal Courthouses."

5. Vanderlaan, "Midland Federal Courthouse Renamed."

6. Flores, "New Weapons Charges."

7. UPI Archives "Republic of Texas Members Plead Guilty."

8. All information and direct statements in this chapter attributed to Robert Leahey are based on a telephone interview by the author, March 19, 2019.

9. UPI Archives, "Republic of Texas Members Plead Guilty."

10. United States of America v. Richard Lance McLaren, Defendant.

11. UPI Archives, "Republic of Texas Members Plead Guilty."

12. Robert Hurst, telephone interview by the author, June 7, 2021.

13. Bier, "Extreme Vetting of Immigrants."

14. *Daily Courier*, "Obituary: Robert Jonathan Scheidt."

Chapter 23

1. All information and direct statements in this chapter attributed to Richard Lance McLaren are based on an in-person interview by the author, at William P. Clements Unit prison in Amarillo, Texas, May 16, 2018.

2. Rogers, "Congress, the President, and the War Powers."

3. Aceris Law, "International Court of Arbitration."

4. History.com Editors "Texas Enters the Union."

5. Permanent Court of Arbitration. "About Us."

6. *Chicago Tribune*, "If It's War They Want."

7. *Wired*, "Texas ISPs Targeted."

8. Dubose, "So What's the Truth about Dan Morales and Tobacco?"

9. Dubose, "Dan Morales v. Harry Potter."

10. *Pecos Enterprise*, "Republic of Texas."

11. Chatham House, *The Law of Armed Conflict*.

12. Markon, "Hamdi Returned to Saudi Arabia."

13. Legal Information Institute, "Tenth Amendment."

14. Facing History, "The Reconstruction Acts of 1867."
15. ICRC, "Occupation and International Humanitarian Law"; Chinkin, "Laws of Occupation."
16. Verhovek, "Separatists End Texas Standoff."
17. Wood, "The Movement to Make Texas Its Own Country."
18. Fernandez, "White Rejects Petitions."
19. Dessie Andrews, in-person interview by the author, at Jack Allen's restaurant in Oak Hill, Texas, October 25, 2017.

Chapter 24

1. Pino, "Guide to Austin's Dirty Sixth Street."
2. Devash, "Five Things to Know Before Doing Day of the Dead Makeup."
3. Arias, "Emeryville Artist Joe Karr Charged."
4. Arias, "Accused Killer Joseph Karr Enters Plea."
5. Arias, "Accused Killer Joseph Karr Enters Plea."

Chapter 25

1. All information and direct statements in this chapter attributed to Ed Brannum are based on a telephone interview by the author, April 5, 2018.
2. Rozen, "The Man Who Knew Too Much."
3. Korosec, "We Are the R.O.T."
4. Enclopedia.com, "Republic of Texas."
5. Associated Press, "Texas Attorney General Is Charged with Fraud."
6. Ramsey, "Dan Morales Indicted."
7. Dubose, "So What's the Truth About Dan Morales and Tobacco?"
8. Plohetski, "Why Is the FBI Withholding DNA Evidence?"
9. Mitchell, *Murdered Innocents.*
10. Lowry, *Who Killed These Girls?*
11. Miller, *Texit.*
12. The Hague Academy of International Law (https://www.hagueacademy.nl) offers higher education in and serves as a global center for research about international law, both public and private.

Epilogue

1. Statesman.com, "William K. Turner."

Bibliography

ABC13. "A Look Back at Houston's Six Flags Astroworld." *ABC 13 Eyewitness News,* August 16, 2019. https://abc13.com/community-events/a-look-back-at-houstons-six-flags-astroworld/1051306.
Abilene Christian University. "About ACU." Accessed June 25, 2019. https://www.acu.edu/online.html.
Aceris Law. "International Court of Arbitration." October 12, 2018. https://www.acerislaw.com/international-court-of-arbitration.
Adam. "History of the SKS." War Gun Mods. Accessed January 5, 2020. https://www.wargunmods.com/history-of-the-sks.
Alcohol Policy Information System. "The 1984 National Minimum Drinking Age Act." Accessed June 24, 2019. https://alcoholpolicy.niaaa.nih.gov/the-1984-national-minimum-drinking-age-act.
Alison, Charlie. "Stagecoach Service from St. Louis to San Francisco." *Butterfield Overland Mail Route,* April 2, 2012. https://butterfieldoverlandstage.com.
Allighieri, Dante. *Dante's Inferno; The Indiana Critical Edition.* Translated and edited by Mark Musa. Bloomington: Indiana University Press, 1995.
AmpliVox Sound Systems. "Public Safety—For Crowd Control and Emergency Communications Systems." Accessed January 19, 2020. https://www.ampli.com/public-safety.
Ando, Russell H., and Harold Chu. "Deposition Tips: What Is a Deposition?" Caught.net and the Pro Se Way. Accessed June 25, 2019. http://caught.net/prose/depositiontips.htm.
Anthony's Key Resort. Accessed September 10, 2019. https://anthonyskey.com.
Anti-Defamation League. "The Militia Movement." Accessed February 4, 2020. Fraudulent Liens in Texas https://www.adl.org/education/resources/backgrounders/militia-movement.
———. "Vigilante Justice: Militias and 'Common Law Courts' Wage War Against the Government." 1997. https://www.adl.org/sites/default/files/documents/assets/pdf/combating-hate/adl-report-1997-vigilante-justice.pdf.
Arias, Rob. "Accused Killer Joseph Karr Enters Plea in Murder Girlfriend Kelly Turner. Trial Date Set for March." *Crime & Public Safety: News & Commentary,*

January 26, 2016. https://evilleeye.com/news-commentary/crime/accused-killer-joseph-karr-enters-plea-murder-girlfriend-kelly-turner-trial-date-set-march.

———. "Emeryville Artist Joe Karr Charged with Murdering Girlfriend on Halloween." *Crime & Public Safety: News & Commentary,* November 6, 2014. https://evilleeye.com/news-commentary/crime/emeryville-artist-joe-karr-charged-murdering-girlfriend-halloween.

Armalite. "AR-50: .50BGM Bolt-Action Rifle 501A1BGGG." Accessed January 5, 2020. https://www.armalite.com/product/50a1bggg-50-cal-bolt-action.

Army Technology. "M88A2 Hercules Armored Recovery Vehicle." https://www.army-technology.com/projects/herculesrecoveryvehi.

Aron, Jaime. "Authorities Scale Back Search for Republic of Texas Member." *Corpus Christi Caller-Times,* May 7, 1997, B4.

Associated Press. "Mexican Standoff? Republic of Texas Crisis Brews in Fort Davis." *Galveston Daily News,* May 1, 1997, A12. https://www.newspapers.com/newspage/13996910.

———. "Phony-Liens Bill Awaits Bush's Signature." *Corpus Christi Caller-Times,* May 9, 1997, B4.

———. "Republic Member's Son Charged in Bomb Scare." *Corpus Christi Caller-Times,* May 10, 1997, B5.

———. "Richard McLaren." *Austin American-Statesman,* May 4, 1997, A21.

———. "Standoff: McLaren Was Thrown Out, Group Says." *Odessa American,* April 28, 1997.

———. "Texas Attorney General Is Charged with Fraud." *New York Times,* March 7, 2003. https://www.nytimes.com/2003/03/07/us/texas-ex-attorney-general-is-charged-with-fraud.html.

ATF (Bureau of Alcohol, Tobacco, Firearms and Explosives). Accessed January 19, 2020. https://www.atf.gov.

———. "Houston Field Division." Accessed August 2, 2019. https://www.atf.gov/houston-field-division.

———. "National Firearms Act." February 14, 2019. https://www.atf.gov/rules-and-regulations/national-firearms-act.

Atkins, Steven E. *Encyclopedia of Right-Wing Extremism in Modern American History.* Santa Barbara, CA: ABC-CLIO, 2011.

Austin American-Statesman. "Morales sues Separatist, Citing $32,000 in Unpaid Taxes, Interest." Compiled from staff and wire reports. May 8, 1997, B10.

Austin History Center. "Desegregation in Austin." Austin library.com. Accessed June 25, 2019. http://www.austinlibrary.com/ahc/desegregation/index.cfm?action=decade&dc=1960s.

———. "What Is the History of Barton Springs?" Accessed June 25, 2019. http://www.austinlibrary.com/ahc/faq10.htm.

Austin-Bergstrom International Airport. "History of the Airport: John August Earl Bergstrom." Accessed June 25, 2019. https://www.austintexas.gov/department/history-airport.

Bibliography

Austintexas.gov. "History of Mayors." Accessed June 25, 2019. http://www.austintexas.gov/page/history-mayors.

———. Austin Police Department. Accessed August 2, 2019. http://www.austintexas.gov/department/police.

Authority. *Laws of the Eighth Legislature of the State of Texas. Extra Session.* Austin, TX: John Marshall & Company, 1861. Documenting the American South project, Rare Book Collection, University of North Carolina at Chapel Hill, 1999. https://docsouth.unc.edu/imls/texaslaw/texaslaw.html.

Banta, Bob, and Claire Osborn. "Fort Davis-area Residents Say Standoff Was Inevitable." *Austin American-Statesman,* April 28, 1997, A1.

———. "Militant Separatists Take 2 Hostages." *Austin American-Statesman,* April 28, 1997, A6.

Barcella, Laura. "The Waco Siege: Little Known Facts." *History,* April 13, 2018. https://www.history.com/news/waco-siege-what-happened-little-known-facts.

Barker, Eugene C. "Mexican Colonization Laws." *Handbook of Texas Online.* Updated July 30, 2020. https://tshaonline.org/handbook/online/articles/ugm01.

Barnes, Michael. "Austin Bids Farewell to Brackenridge Hospital After 133 Years." *Austin American-Statesman.* May 19, 2017. https://www.statesman.com/story/news/2017/05/19/austin-bids-farewell-to-brackenridge-hospital-after-133-years/10054882007.

———. "Briscoe Center Offers a Staggering Look at Civil Rights Movement." *Austin American-Statesman,* April 18, 2018. https://www.statesman.com/NEWS/20180418/Briscoe-Center-offers-a-staggering-look-at-civil-rights-movement.

———. "Revisiting the Continental Club in the 1960s." May 24, 2018. http://austinfound.blog.statesman.com/2018/04/15/the-continental-club-in-the-1960s.

Barnett, Erica C. "Grow and Prosper: Hyde Park Baptist Church Marches Forward Forever." *Austin Chronicle,* November 19, 1999. https://www.austinchronicle.com/news/1999-11-19/74732.

Batista, Juan. "Rick Perry's Ties to a Terrorist Militia." *Indybay,* November 6, 2011. https://www.indybay.org/newsitems/2011/11/06/18697914.php.

Baysider.com. "Sueno del Mar Diving Resort." Accessed January 27, 2022. https://www.baysider.com/Business/Sueno_Del_Mar_Diving_Resort.

Ben Hur Shriners. Home page. Accessed December 8, 2020. https://www.benhurshrine.org.

Bier, David J. "Extreme Vetting of Immigrants: Estimating Terrorism Vetting Failures." CATO Institute, April 17, 2018. https://www.cato.org/policy-analysis/extreme-vetting-immigrants-estimating-terrorism-vetting-failures#.

Big Bend Regional Medical Center. Accessed November 11, 2019. http://www.bigbendhealthcare.com/big-bend-regional-medical-center/home.aspx.

Billboard Top 100. "1962." Accessed June 25, 2019. http://billboardtop100of.com/1962-2.

Biography.com Editors. "Ann Richards (1933–2006)." Accessed June 24, 2019. https://www.biography.com/political-figure/ann-richards.

———. "Buddy Holly (1936–1959)." April 27, 2017. https://www.biography.com/musician/buddy-holly.

Bizjournals.com. "Pier today, gone tomorrow; Historic Austin establishment loses lease." July 29, 2005. http://www.bizjournals.com/austin/stories/2005/07/25/daily49.html.

Blakinger, Keri. "Can We Build a Better Women's Prison?" *Washington Post Magazine,* October 28, 2019. https://www.washingtonpost.com/magazine/2019/10/28/prisons-jails-are-designed-men-can-we-build-better-womens-prison/?arc404=true.

Blejwas, Andrew, Anthony Griggs, and Mark Potok. "Almost 60 Terrorist Plots Uncovered in the U.S. Since the Oklahoma City Bombing." *Intelligence Report* (April 27, 2005). https://www.splcenter.org/fighting-hate/intelligence-report/2005/almost-60-terrorist-plots-uncovered-us-oklahoma-city-bombing.

Bloomberg. "Gary C. Kelly: Chairman Southwest Airlines." Accessed January 19, 2020. https://www.bloomberg.com/research/stocks/people/person.asp?personId=187856&privcapId=31726.

Board of Governors of the Federal Reserve System. Accessed December 11, 2019. https://www.federalreserve.gov/aboutthefed/federal-reserve-system.htm.

Bockhauser, Arthur. "What Is an M16 and Why Is It Called So?" *Quora.* Accessed January 6, 2020. https://www.quora.com/What-is-an-M16-and-why-is-it-called-so.

Boddington, Craig. "The .270 Winchester Cartridge." *American Rifleman,* April 20, 2016. https://www.americanrifleman.org/articles/2016/4/20/the-270-winchester-cartridge.

Boulder Weekly. "Dyer Succeeds White as Boulder Weekly Editor." November 17, 2011. https://www.boulderweekly.com/news/dyer-succeeds-white-as-boulder-weekly-editor.

Brand, Donald Dilworth, and Robert H. Schmidt. "Rio Grande River: United States-Mexico." *Encyclopaedia Britannica.* Updated February 10, 2016. https://www.britannica.com/place/Rio-Grande-river-United-States-Mexico.

Brekke, Dan. "Wave of Support for Defiant Texas ISP." *Wired,* May 2, 1997. https://www.wired.com/1997/05/wave-of-support-for-defiant-texas-isp.

Brewer, Anita. "Fire Destroys AJH School." *Austin American-Statesman,* March 21, 1956. https://www.newspapers.com/clip/30972939/allan-junior-high-school-fire.

Britannica, Editors of Encyclopaedia. s.v. "AK-47: Soviet Firearm." Accessed January 5, 2020. https://www.britannica.com/technology/AK-47.

———. s.v. "Coahuila: State of Mexico." Updated November 21, 2012. https://www.britannica.com/place/Coahuila.

———. s.v. "Davis Mountains." Accessed June 23, 2020. https://www.britannica.com/place/Davis-Mountains.

———. s.v. "Janet Reno: United States Attorney General." Britannica.com. Accessed January 5, 2020. https://www.britannica.com/biography/Janet-Reno.

Bibliography

———. s.v. "Ruby Ridge." Accessed December 10, 2019. https://www.britannica.com/event/Ruby-Ridge.

———. s.v. "Texas v. White: Law Case." Updated June 11, 2015. https://www.britannica.com/event/Texas-v-White.

———. s.v. "Treaty of Guadalupe Hidalgo." Updated February 23, 2018. https://www.britannica.com/event/Treaty-of-Guadalupe-Hidalgo.

———. s.v. "Waco Siege: American History [1993]." Accessed January 5, 2020. https://www.britannica.com/event/Waco-siege.

Brock, Ralph H. "The Republic of Texas Is No More: An Answer to the Claim that Texas was Unconstitutionally Annexed to the United States." School of Law, Texas Tech University, 1997. https://ttu-ir.tdl.org/ttu-ir/bitstream/handle/10601/356/brock1.pdf?sequence=1.

Bromley, David G., and Joel Smith. "The Historical Significance of Annexation as a Social Process." *Land Economics* 25, no. 1 (1973): 294–309. https://doi.org/10.2307/3145602.

Brownwood News. "Retired Texas Ranger Captain Carl A. Weathers Obituary." August 30, 2018. https://www.brownwoodnews.com/retired-texas-ranger-captain-carl-a-weathers-obituary.

Brune, Gunnar M. *Springs of Texas*. Vol. 1. College Station: Texas A&M University Press, 2002.

Bueche, Shelley. "A Splashy History of Deep Eddy—The Oldest Swimming Pool in Texas." *Culture Map Austin*, July 20, 2017. http://austin.culturemap.com/news/city-life/07-20-17-deep-eddy-pool-austin-history/#slide=0.

Burrough, Bryan and Jason Stanford. "We've Been Telling the Alamo Story Wrong for Nearly 200 Years. Now It's Time to Correct the Record." *Time*. June 21, 2021. Accessed February 17, 2022. https://time.com/6072141/alamo-history-myths/

Campbell, Bob. "1997 Republic of Texas Standoff Intense, Damaging to Participants." *Midland Reporter-Telegram*, April 21, 2007. https://www.mrt.com/news/article/1997-Republic-of-Texas-standoff-intense-damaging-7597664.php.

———. "Ranger Reflects on Waco, Fort Davis." *Midland Reporter-Telegram*, June 1, 2008. https://www.mrt.com/news/article/Ranger-captain-reflects-on-Waco-Fort-Davis-7487690.php.

———. "Republic of Texas Leader Unrepentant about Man's Shooting." *Midland Reporter-Telegram*, April 21, 2007. https://www.mrt.com/news/article/Republic-of-Texas-standoff-leader-unrepentant-7615626.php.

CaptainChicken.org. "South Austin Drive-In Theater." July 5, 2007. https://www.captainchicken.org/austindrivein/south_austin/south_austin.html.

Carlson High Performance Boats. "Glastron Carlsons." June 24, 2019. http://www.classicglastron.com/gl-carlson-index-web.html.

Carr, Lisa. "MCSO Gary Painter Dies in His Home." *Amarillo Globe-News*. May 27, 2019. Statesman.com. https://www.statesman.com/news/20190527/mcso-sheriff-gary-painter-dies-in-his-home.

Castro, April. "Former Attorney General Dan Morales Indicted on Fraud Charges." *Midland Reporter-Telegram.* March 6, 2003. https://www.mrt.com/news/article/Former-Attorney-General-Dan-Morales-indicted-on-7886669.php.

Caver, Barry, and Nieman, Robert. "Captain Barry Caver on the Republic of Texas Standoff." *Texas Ranger Dispatch.* 2016. https://www.texasranger.org/wp-content/uploads/2017/07/History-Republic-of-Texas-Standoff.pdf.

Chan, Melissa. "The Real Story Behind the Waco Siege: Who Were David Koresh and the Branch Davidians?" *Time,* January 24, 2018. https://time.com/5115201/waco-siege-standoff-fbi-david-koresh.

Charlie's Angels. IMDB.com. Accessed June 24, 2019. https://www.imdb.com/title/tt0073972.

Chatham House. *The Law of Armed Conflict: Problems and Prospects* (conference summary) April 18–19, 2005. https://www.chathamhouse.org/sites/default/files/public/Research/International%20Law/ilparmedconflict.pdf.

Chicago Tribune. "If It's War They Want." April 30, 1997. https://www.chicagotribune.com/news/ct-xpm-1997-04-30-9704300008-story.html.

Chinkin, Christine. "Laws of Occupation." Accessed January 9, 2020. http://removethewall.org/wp-content/uploads/2014/05/Laws-of-Occupation-Christine-Chinkin-2009.pdf.

Christian, A. K. "Mirabeau Buonaparte Lamar." *Southwestern Historical Quarterly* 24, no. 2 (October 1920): 87–139.

Cinema Treasures. "Chief Drive-In." Accessed June 25, 2019. http://cinematreasures.org/theaters/36531.

City of Austin. "Austin Police Department: One Austin, Safer Together." Accessed August 2, 2019. http://www.austintexas.gov/department/police.

Clemons, Leigh. *Branding Texas: Performing Culture in the Lone Star State.* Austin: University of Texas Press, 2008.

CNN Interactive. "One Injured in Separatist Standoff: 'Republic of Texas' Holds Two Hostages." April 27, 1997. http://www.cnn.com/US/9704/27/texas.update/index.html.

Corcoran, Michael. "A Closing Set that Still Reverberates." *Austin American-Statesman,* September 1, 2021. https://www.austin360.com/story/entertainment/music/2012/09/24/a-closing-set-that-still-reverberates/10182384007/

———. "Ramblin' Ray Remembers: Austin Music in the 1950s." *Austin's East End Cultural Heritage,* April 1, 2012. http://www.eastendculturaldistrict.org/cms/culture-art-music/ramblin%E2%80%99-ray-remembers-austin-music-1950s.

Cox, Mike. *Stand-Off in Texas: "Just Call Me a Spokesman for the DPS."* Austin, TX: Eakin Press, 1998.

Craddock, Ashley. "Texas ISP Targeted in Secessionist Case." *Wired,* April 11, 1997. https://www.wired.com/1997/04/texas-isps-targeted-in-secessionist-case.

Cromeens Law Firm. "Fraudulent Liens in Texas." Accessed November 11, 2019. https://thecromeenslawfirm.com/fraudulent-liens-in-texas.

Bibliography

D'Onofrio, Kaitlyn. "Herbalife 'Scam' Weight Loss Product Associated with Liver Failure." *Docwirenews,* May 3, 2019. https://www.docwirenews.com/docwire-pick/home-page-picks/herbalife-scam-weight-loss.

Daily Courier. "Obituary: Robert Jonathan Scheidt." October 10, 2012. https://www.dcourier.com/news/2012/oct/10/obituary-robert-jonathan-scheidt/.

Dallas Morning News. "James D. Cummins." October 31, 2007. https://obits.dallasnews.com/obituaries/dallasmorningnews/obituary.aspx?n=james-d-cummins&pid=97093186.

———. "Jenna Hawkins Welch (1919–2019)." May 10, 2019. https://obits.dallasnews.com/obituaries/dallasmorningnews/obituary.aspx?n=jenna-hawkins-welch&pid=192865079&fhid=11452.

Davis, William C. "The History of the Short-Lived Florida Republic." *Smithsonian,* May 2013. https://www.smithsonianmag.com/history/the-history-of-the-short-lived-independent-republic-of-florida-28056078.

Death Penalty Information Center. "Texas Pushes Nation's Executions to Record Numbers in 1997, but Opposition Grows." December 1, 1997.

Definitions. s.v. "Provisional Government." Accessed June 23, 2020. https://www.definitions.net/definition/provisional+government.

DeNevi, Don, and John H. Campbell. *Into the Minds of Madmen: How the FBI's Behavioral Science Unit Revolutionized Crime Investigation.* New York: Prometheus Books, 2004.

Devash, Meirav. "Five Things to Know Before Doing Day of the Dead Makeup." *Allure,* October 12, 2016. https://www.allure.com/story/dia-de-los-muertos-makeup-tradition.

Dignity Memorial. "Arval Wendell Bohn." March 17, 2016. https://www.dignitymemorial.com/obituaries/austin-tx/arval-bohn-8209393.

———. "Coolidge D. Gerdes." Accessed February 20, 2019. https://www.dignitymemorial.com/obituaries/victoria-tx/coolidge-gerdes-8146596.

Dillman, Beth. "The Eviction Process in Texas: Rules for Landlords and Property Managers." Nolo. Accessed September 19, 2019. https://www.nolo.com/legal-encyclopedia/the-eviction-process-texas-rules-landlords-property-managers.html.

Douglass, Neal. *Durham's Business College,* photograph. November 16, 1955. University of North Texas Libraries, The Portal to Texas History. https://texashistory.unt.edu/ark:/67531/metapth33147.

Downs-Clark, Leila. "The History of Shoal Creek." *Bryker Woods,* May 1954. https://brykerwoods.org/our-history/the-history-of-shoal-creek.

Draper, Robert. "The Great Defenders." *Texas Monthly,* January 1994. https://www.texasmonthly.com/articles/the-great-defenders.

———. "The Twilight of the Texas Rangers." *Texas Monthly,* February 1994. https://www.texasmonthly.com/articles/the-twilight-of-the-texas-rangers.

Dubose, Lou. "Dan Morales v. Harry Potter." *Austin Chronicle,* March 8, 2002. https://www.austinchronicle.com/news/2002-03-08/84912.

———. "So What's the Truth About Dan Morales and Tobacco?" *Texas Monthly*, March 2002. https://www.texasmonthly.com/politics/so-whats-the-truth-about-dan-morales-and-tobacco.

Dungan, Ron. "A Moving Border, and the History of a Difficult Boundary." *USA Today*. Accessed February 5, 2020. https://www.usatoday.com/border-wall/story/us-mexico-border-history/510833001.

Dyer, Joe. "Desperate Measures." *Mother Jones*. June 25, 1997. https://www.motherjones.com/politics/1997/06/desperate-measures/

Dyer, Joe. "On the Run." *Mother Jones*, June 25, 1997. https://www.motherjones.com/politics/1997/06/richard-keyes-texas-fugitive.

———. *Harvest of Rage: Why Oklahoma City is Only the Beginning*. Boulder, CO: Westview Press, 1998.

The Eagle. "Mary June McLaren: June 18, 1920–Feb. 26, 2004." February 27, 2004. https://www.theeagle.com/archives/february/article_366ebdfd-3357-5d1c-8b22-b37c5799ca5d.html.

Eanes History Center. "Eanes Elementary Class of 1902." June 24, 2019. http://ehc.eanesisd.net.

Edmonton Journal. "Surrender Ends Siege in Texas." May 4, 1997, A6. The Associated Press.https://www.newspapers.com/image/474542209/?terms=Surrender&match=1

Ehrlick, Allison. "Willie Nelson's Starring Movie Debut Began in Corpus Christi with 'Honeysuckle Rose,'" *Corpus Christi Caller Times*, November 17, 2017. https://www.caller.com/story/news/special-reports/building-our-future/throwback/2017/11/15/tbt-willie-nelsons-starring-movie-debut-began-corpus-christi-honeysuckle-rose/867118001/#.

Electronic Communications Privacy Act of 1986 (ECPA). U.S.C. §§ 2510–2523. Accessed April 27, 2020. https://it.ojp.gov/PrivacyLiberty/authorities/statutes/1285.

Elliott, Claude. "Henderson, James Pinckney." *Handbook of Texas Online*. Accessed October 10, 2019. https://tshaonline.org/handbook/online/articles/fhe14.

Enclopedia.com. s.v. "Republic of Texas." Accessed February 28, 2021. https://www.encyclopedia.com/politics/legal-and-political-magazines/republic-texas.

Erwin, James L. *Declaration of Independence: Encyclopedia of American Autonomous and Secessionist Movements*. Westport, CT: Greenwood Press, 1974.

Facing History and Ourselves. "The Reconstruction Acts of 1867." Accessed January 9, 2020. https://www.facinghistory.org/reconstruction-era/reconstruction-acts-1867.

Farkas, Brian. "Who Can Claim Property Based on Adverse Possession in Texas?" Nolo. Accessed September 8, 2019. https://www.nolo.com/legal-encyclopedia/who-can-claim-property-based-adverse-possession-texas.html.

Faux, Marian. *Roe vs. Wade: The Untold Story of the Landmark Supreme Court Decision That Made Abortion Legal*. New York: McMillan, 1988.

FBI (Federal Bureau of Investigation). Accessed August 2, 2019. https://www.fbi.gov.

FBI News, "Oklahoma City Bombing: 20 Years Later." April 16, 2015. https://www.fbi.gov/news/stories/oklahoma-city-bombing-20-years-later.

Bibliography

FEDARB. "Judge W. Royal Furgeson Jr. (Retired)." Accessed December 11, 2019. https://www.fedarb.com/professionals/w-royal-furgeson.

Federal Communications Commission. "Citizens Band Radio Service (CBRS)." Accessed January 18, 2020. https://www.fcc.gov/wireless/bureau-divisions/mobility-division/citizens-band-radio-service-cbrs.

Federal Writers Project. *The WPA Guide to Texas: The Lone Star State.* San Antonio, TX: Trinity University Press, 2013.

Feigenbaum, Nancy. "NSA Agrees to Offer Refunds." *Orlando Sentinel,* April 19, 1993.

Fernandez, Manny. "White Rejects Petitions to Secede, but Texans Fight On." *New York Times,* January 22, 2013. https://www.nytimes.com/2013/01/16/us/politics/texas-secession-movement-unbowed-by-white-house-rejection.html?_r=0.

Financial Samurai. "How Much Can an Adjustable Rate Mortgage Go Up after the Fixed Period Is Over?" Updated March 9, 2020. https://www.financialsamurai.com/how-much-can-an-adjustable-rate-mortgage-arm-go-up-after-the-fixed-period-is-over.

Find a Grave. "Mary June Samson." Accessed December 11, 2019. https://www.findagrave.com/memorial/74041949/mary-june-mclaren.

———. "Charles H. Samson." https://www.findagrave.com/memorial/114979741/charles-h_-samson. Accessed Dec. 11, 2019.

———. "Marie Gertrude Morris Samson." https://www.findagrave.com/memorial/114979876/marie-gertrude-samson. Accessed Dec. 11, 2019.

FindLaw. "Jury Nullification." Accessed December 11, 2019. https://criminal.findlaw.com/criminal-procedure/jury-nullification.html.

FJC (Federal Judicial Center). "Furgeson, William Royal, Jr." Accessed January 21, 2020. https://www.fjc.gov/node/1380981.

———. "Historic Federal Courthouses." Accessed January 21, 2020. https://www.fjc.gov/history/courthouse/midland-texas-1974.

Flores, Rosie. "New Weapons Charges Filed Against McLaren, Followers." *Pecos Enterprise,* December 5, 2000. http://www.pecos.net/news/arch2000a/120500p.htm.

Flueckiger, Barbara. "Kodachrome." *Timeline of Historical Film Colors.* Accessed November 6, 2020. https://filmcolors.org/timeline-entry/1277.

Forever Resorts. "The History of Southfork Ranch." Accessed June 24, 2019. https://www.southforkranch.com/southfork-ranch-history.

Forstall, Richard L. *Population of States and Counties of the United States: 1790 to 1990.* Washington, DC: US Department of Commerce, Bureau of the Census, 1996.

French Smith (Freda French Smith). Accessed September 19, 2019. https://www.frenchsmithart.com/mbr_bio.php.

Friedman, Thomas L. "The Rocky Road for Truckers." *New York Times,* January 24, 1982. https://www.nytimes.com/1982/01/24/business/the-rocky-road-for-truckers.html.

Fulbright, Jon, and Rick Smith. "Seven Suspects Arrested on Way to Standoff." *Pecos Enterprise,* April 30, 1997. http://www.pecos.net/news/arch97/043097p.htm.

Gambino, Denise. "Wife's Phone Call Brought Peaceful End to Tense Siege." *Austin American-Statesman,* May 5, 1997, A7.

Gambrell, Herbert. "Lamar, Mirabeau Buonaparte." *Handbook of Texas Online.* Updated March 15, 2016. https://tshaonline.org/handbook/online/articles/fla15.

Gaston & Sheehan Company. "About Us." Accessed September 19, 2019. https://www.txauction.com.

GaVette, Justin. "The Mexican-American War and Its Effects." *Student Theses, Papers and Projects (History),* 2005. https://digitalcommons.wou.edu/his/128.

Glass, Andrew. "Texas Is the 7th State to Secede from the Union, February 1, 1861." *Politico* (February 1, 2011). https://www.politico.com/story/2011/02/texas-is-the-7th-state-to-secede-from-the-union-feb-1-1861-048507.

Gracy, David B. II. "Austin, Moses." *Handbook of Texas Online.* Updated November 20, 2019. https://tshaonline.org/handbook/online/articles/fau12.

Great Indoorsman. "Austin Askew: Chapter XXI—Scarborough's Department Store, 1893–1982." February 23, 2006. https://thegreatindoorsman.wordpress.com/2012/04/29/are-you-being-served-scarboroughs-department-store-1893-1982-3-2.

GSA (US General Services Administration). "Federal Building, Dallas, TX." Accessed January 21, 2020. https://www.gsa.gov/historic-buildings/federal-building-dallas-tx#architecturaldesc.

Guina, Ryan. "Multi-Level Marketing—Business Opportunity or a Scam?" *Cash Money Life,* May 6, 2019. https://cashmoneylife.com/multi-level-marketing-business-opportunity-or-a-scam.

H&MUA Team. "Women's 1960s Hairstyles: An Overview." *Hair and Makeup Artist Handbook.* March 12, 2012. Hair-and-makeup-artist.com http://hair-and-makeup-artist.com/womens-1960s-hairstyles.

Hague Academy of International Law. Accessed January 19, 2020. https://www.hagueacademy.nl.

Hardin-Simmons University. "History of Hardin-Simmons." Accessed June 25, 2019. https://www.hsutx.edu/about-hsu/the-hsu-difference/history.

Harper, Christopher. *And That's the Way It Will Be.* New York: New York University Press, 1998.

Harrigan, Stephen. *Big Wonderful Thing: A History of Texas.* Austin: University of Texas Press, 2019.

Heard, Alex. "If At First You Don't Secede: The Eyes of the Nation Are on the New Republicans of Texas." *Slate,* May 11, 1997. https://slate.com/news-and-politics/1997/05/if-at-first-you-don-t-secede.html.

Herman, Ken. "Robert Mueller is Not That Robert Mueller." *Austin American-Statesman,* December 7, 2018. https://www.statesman.com/news/20181207/herman-austins-robert-mueller-is-not-that-robert-mueller.

Bibliography

Hicks, Josh. "Congress passes bill to rename U.S. courthouse after Bush presidents." *Washington Post.* December 18, 2012. https://www.washingtonpost.com/news/federaleye/wp/2012/12/18/congress-passes-bill-to-rename-u-s-courthouse-after-bush-presidents/.

Hill, Gerald, and Kathleen Hill. "Lis Pendens." *The People's Law Dictionary.* Accessed September 8, 2019. https://dictionary.law.com/Default.aspx?selected=1172.

Hill, Shay. "Historic Dancehall 'Grande Ole Oplin' Re-Opens." *KEAN.1051-FM.* July 18, 2017. http://keanradio.com/historic-dancehall-grand-ole-oplin-re-opens.

Historic Landmark Commission [City of Austin, TX]. "Demolition and Relocation Permits." Accessed June 25, 2019. http://www.austintexas.gov/edims/document.cfm?id=304440.

History.com Editors. "Andrew Jackson." October 29, 2009. https://www.history.com/topics/us-presidents/andrew-jackson.

———. "Battle of the Alamo." Updated February 28, 2020.

———. "Battle of San Jacinto." November 9, 2009. https://www.history.com/topics/mexico/battle-of-san-jacinto.

———. "Confederate States of America." Updated August 21, 2018. https://www.history.com/topics/american-civil-war/confederate-states-of-america.

———. "Jan. 3, 1834: Stephen Austin Imprisoned by Mexicans." November 16, 2009. https://www.history.com/this-day-in-history/stephen-austin-imprisoned-by-mexicans.

———. "Oklahoma City Bombing." *History.* Updated August 21, 2018. https://www.history.com/topics/1990s/oklahoma-city-bombing.

———. "Sam Houston." November 9, 2009. https://www.history.com/topics/mexico/sam-houston.

———. "Texas Enters the Union." Accessed January 9, 2020. https://www.history.com/this-day-in-history/texas-enters-the-union.

———. "Waco Siege." Updated August 21, 2018. https://www.history.com/topics/1990s/waco-siege.

———. "War Powers Act." Updated June 10, 2019. https://www.history.com/topics/war-powers-act.

Hodapp Funeral Homes. "Robert 'Mac' McLaren." December 17, 2017. https://www.hodappfuneralhome.com/obituary/robert-mac-mclaren.

Hodson, Christy Lynn. "The Continental Club." *Handbook of Texas.* July 8, 2014. https://tshaonline.org/handbook/online/articles/xdc07.

Hollingsworth, Skip. "Up in Smoke: How Dan Morales Beat Big Tobacco but Lost His Reputation." *Texas Monthly,* August 1999. https://www.texasmonthly.com/politics/up-in-smoke.

Holmes, Michael. "Texas Group Accused of 'Paper Terrorism.'" *Los Angeles Times,* February 2, 1997. https://www.latimes.com/archives/la-xpm-1997-02-02-mn-24625-story.html.

Honigsberg, Peter Jan. "The Real Origin of the Term 'Enemy Combatant.'" *Huffington Post,* March 11, 2014. https://www.huffpost.com/entry/the-real-origin-of-the-te_b_4562216.

Hormel Historic Home History (blog). "Woolworth's Store A Landmark in Downtown." October 22, 2012. https://hormelhistorichome.blogspot.com/2012/10/woolworths-store-landmark-in-downtown.html.

Hotel Limpia. "History of Hotel Limpia in Fort Davis, Texas." Accessed September 9, 2019. https://www.hotellimpia.com/history-of-hotel-limpia-in-fort-davis.

Houston Chronicle. "Plea bargain reached in Republic of Texas trial." August 8, 2001. https://www.chron.com/news/houston-texas/article/Plea-bargain-reached-in-Republic-of-Texas-trial-2019437.php

Houston Chronicle. "Texans Fear 'Republic' Fugitive Will Seek Revenge." August 31, 1997.

Houston's Original Social Network. "Join Houston Mod in Celebrating Our Modern Legacy." April 8, 2010. https://www.houstonarchitecture.com/haif/topic/23172-april-is-modern-month-in-houston.

Hsu, Hua. "A Global Government Is Waiting in the Wings." *New York Magazine,* November 15, 2013. https://nymag.com/news/features/conspiracy-theories/new-world-order.

Huang, Charlene, Johnny Hsueh, Emily Goll-Broylles, and Srijith Kambala. "Founding Fathers of Texas." Accessed February 5, 2020. https://texasfoundingfathers.weebly.com/founding-fathers.html.

Hulse, Carl. "Janet Reno: First Woman to Serve as US Attorney General, Dies at 78." *New York Times.* November 7, 2016. https://www.nytimes.com/2016/11/08/us/janet-reno-dead.html.

Hume, Martha. "Abortion in Texas." *Texas Monthly* 2, no. 3 (March 1974): 57.

ICRC (International Committee of the Red Cross). "Occupation and International Humanitarian Law: Questions and Answers." April 8, 2004. https://www.icrc.org/en/doc/resources/documents/misc/634kfc.htm.

Images of Austin. "Mary Doerr: Meet an Austin Original." Accessed September 19, 2019. https://imagesofaustin.com/?page_id=344.

Interlandi, Jeneen. "How Safe Is Deet?" *Consumer Reports.* April 24, 2019. https://www.consumerreports.org/insect-repellent/how-safe-is-deet-insect-repellent-safety.

International Committee of the Red Cross. "Treaties, States Parties and Commentaries: Resolutions of the Diplomatic Conference. Geneva, 12 August 1949." Accessed February 20, 2020. https://ihl-databases.icrc.org/ihl/INTRO/385?OpenDocument.

International Monetary Fund. Accessed December 11, 2019. https://www.imf.org/en/About.

Jackson Pollack: Biography, Painting, Quotes. "Jackson Pollack and His Paintings." Accessed August 5, 2019. https://www.jackson-pollock.org.

Jackson, Charles Christopher. "San Felipe de Austin, TX." *Handbook of Texas Online.* Updated May 3, 2016. https://tshaonline.org/handbook/online/articles/hls10.

JackWhiteArtist.com. "Jack White: Artist-Author." Accessed February 17, 2022. http://jackwhiteartist.com/

https://bojanb.jeunesseglobal.com/en-US.

Jimmie Rodgers Foundation. "Biography." Accessed June 25, 2019. https://www.jimmierodgers.com/biography.

John F. Kennedy Presidential Library and Museum. "Life of Jacqueline B. Kennedy." Accessed January 19, 2020. https://www.jfklibrary.org/learn/about-jfk/life-of-jacqueline-b-kennedy.

Johnson, Daryl. *Right Wing Resurgence: How a Domestic Terrorist Threat Is Being Ignored.* Lanham, MD: Rowan & Littlefield, 2012.

Joint Resolution of the Congress of the United States, March 1, 1845. In *Treaties and Other International Acts of the United States of America* (Vol. 4. Documents 80–121, 1836–1846), ed. Hunter Miller. Washington: Government Printing Office, 1934. https://avalon.law.yale.edu/19th_century/texan01.asp.

Jorden, Jay. "Dead Separatist's Brother Says Man Was Betrayed by McLaren." *Corpus Christi Caller-Times,* May 10, 1997, B5.

Judge Paul Davis. "About Judge Davis." Accessed September 19, 2019. https://www.judgepauldavis.com/about.

Judge Pete Lowry. "Judge Pete Lowry: Two High Courts Determine Texas Appeals." January 5, 2016. https://medium.com/@JudgePeteLowry/judge-pete-lowry-two-high-courts-determine-texas-appeals-ec99f6e742e9.

Judges Hill. "William Caswell House—1904." Accessed December 11, 2019. https://judgeshill.org/homes/west/caswell.html.

Jung, Helin. "What No One Has Ever Told You About the O.G. Lazy Girl Hairstyle: The Iconic Beehive Has an Amazing Origin Story." *Cosmopolitan,* June 15, 2016. https://www.cosmopolitan.com/style-beauty/a59958/beehive-hairstyle-creator-margaret-vinci-heldt.

Kaku, Michio. "Albert Einstein: German-American Physicist." *Britannica.* July 19, 2019. https://www.britannica.com/biography/Albert-Einstein.

Katz, Jesse, and Lianne Hart. "Two Hostages in Texas Standoff Released." *Los Angeles Times.* April 29, 1997. http://articles.latimes.com/1997-04-29/news/mn-53617_1_hostages-in-texas-texas-standoff-released.

Kay, Michelle. "Victim: Error led to siege." *Austin American Statesman.* B1, B5. October 29, 1997. Accessed February 17, 2022. https://www.newspapers.com/image/356891436/?terms=%22joe%20Rowe%22&match=1

Kemp, Elizabeth A. "Brackenridge, Robert J. (1839–1918)." *Handbook of Texas Online.* June 12, 2010. https://www.tshaonline.org/handbook/entries/brackenridge-robert-j.

Kiddle. "Alpine Texas Facts for Kids." Accessed June 18, 2020. https://kids.kiddle.co/Alpine,_Texas.

Killelea, Eric. "Flashback: Waco Cult Showdown Ends in Disaster." *Rolling Stone*, January 4, 2018. https://www.rollingstone.com/culture/culture-news/flashback-waco-cult-showdown-ends-in-disaster-124074.

King, Michael. "Peck Young Goes Away Mad." *Austin Chronicle*, February 8, 2013. https://www.austinchronicle.com/daily/news/2013-02-08/peck-young-goes-away-mad/.

Kohout, Martin Donell. "Jeff Davis County." *Handbook of Texas Online*. Accessed October 10, 2019. https://tshaonline.org/handbook/online/articles/hcj04.

Kook Science Research Hatch. s.v. "Richard Kieninger." Accessed December 11, 2019. https://hatch.kookscience.com/wiki/Richard_Kieninger.

Korosec, Thomas. "Soul Food and Crackers." *Dallas Observer*, September 18, 1997. https://www.dallasobserver.com/news/soul-food-and-crackers-6429104.

———. "We Are the R.O.T." *Dallas Observer*, May 8, 1997. https://www.dallasobserver.com/news/we-are-the-rot-6402797.

KRGV.com. "Station Information." Accessed June 19, 2019. https://www.krgv.com/station-information.

Kuempel, George. "Separatists End Standoff Peacefully." *Cult Education Institute*, May 4, 1997. https://culteducation.com/group/1119-republic-of-texas-militia/17934-separatists-end-standoff-peacefully.html.

Kyprianou, Mario (dir.). *The Republic of Rick*. ROR Productions, 2014.

Kuhlmann, Steve. "Books in the Basin: Former Texas Ranger doesn't consider himself an author." *Midland-Reporter Telegram*. September 29, 2014. Accessed February 17, 2022. https://www.mrt.com/news/article/Books-in-the-Basin-Former-Texas-Ranger-doesn-t-7416224.php.

Langford, Mark. "Fines Mount for Texas Separatist Group." UPI Archives, November 27, 1996. https://www.upi.com/Archives/1996/11/27/Fines-mount-for-Texas-separatist-group/7294849070800.

Langford, Terri. "FBI Arrests Republic of Texas Fugitive Richard Keyes." *AP News*, September 20, 1997. https://apnews.com/407225bf861f18679092a5362c8ac64e.

———. "State Demands Militia Group's Email: Attorney General Subpoenas Internet Providers of Republic of Texas for Documents." *Austin American-Statesman*, April 11, 1997, B11.

Law Dictionary. "What Is Foreign Bill of Exchange?" Accessed December 11, 2019. https://thelawdictionary.org/foreign-bill-of-exchange.

LeBlanc, Pam. "At Davis Mountains Preserve, Explore 'A Sky Island.'" *Austin American-Statesman*, February 27, 2018. https://www.statesman.com/lifestyle/20170227/at-davis-mountains-preserve-explore-a-sky-island.

Ledin, Steve. "How to Understand Spotting Scope Features." OpticsPlanet.com. August 19, 2013. https://www.opticsplanet.com/howto/how-to-understand-spotting-scope-features.html.

Lee, Michael. "Texas' First African-American Judge Remembers Her Life and Career." KUT 90.5. January 31, 2018. http://www.kut.org/post/texas-first-african-american-female-judge-remembers-her-life-and-career.

Leerhsen, Charles. "Who Was Ty Cobb? The History We Know That's Wrong." *Imprimis* 45, no. 3 (March 2016). https://imprimis.hillsdale.edu/who-was-ty-cobb-the-history-we-know-thats-wrong.

Legal Information Institute. "Tenth Amendment." Accessed January 9, 2020. https://www.law.cornell.edu/constitution/tenth_amendment.

LendingTree. "Adjustable Rate Mortgage (ARM)." Accessed September 19, 2019. https://www.lendingtree.com/glossary/adjustable-rate-mortgage.

Lewis, Danny. "Twenty Years Ago Today, the Montana Freemen Started Its 81-Day Standoff." *Smithsonian,* March 25, 2016. https://www.smithsonianmag.com/smart-news/twenty-years-ago-today-the-montana-freeman-started-its-81-day-standoff-180958568.

Lewis, Emily. "A Brief History of the History of TSD." Reprinted from October 1, 1909, issue of *The Lone Star,* Texas School for the Deaf. Accessed June 25, 2019. https://www.tsd.state.tx.us/apps/pages/index.jsp?uREC_ID=173757&type=d&pREC_ID=359032.

Lieck, Ken. "On a Carousel: Jay Clark's Legacy." *Austin Chronicle,* July 31, 1998. https://www.austinchronicle.com/music/1998-07-31/523686.

Lind, Dara. "Waco and Ruby Ridge: The 1990s Standoffs Haunting the Oregon Takeover, Explained." *Vox,* January 5, 2016. https://www.vox.com/2016/1/5/10714746/waco-ruby-ridge-oregon.

Lindsay. "West Texas Films: 11 Films Set or Filmed in West Texas." *Road Trip Soul.* January 31, 2018. https://roadtripsoul.com/11-films-set-or-filmed-in-west-texas.

Lit2Go, "The Rime of the Ancient Mariner" by Samuel Taylor Coleridge [synopsis]. Accessed February 5, 2020. https://etc.usf.edu/lit2go/181/the-rime-of-the-ancient-mariner.

Little, Betty. "Why the Hunt for the Real Atlanta Bomber Took Nearly 7 Years." History.com, December 13, 2019. https://www.history.com/news/atlanta-bombing-richard-jewell-domestic-terror-investigation.

Long, Christopher. "Sabine River." *Handbook of Texas Online.* Updated October 3, 2017. https://tshaonline.org/handbook/online/articles/rns03.

Los Angeles Times. "Last Republic of Texas Separatist Sentenced to 90 Years in Prison." June 20, 1998. https://www.latimes.com/archives/la-xpm-1998-jun-20-mn-61862-story.html#:~:text=Last%20Republic%20of%20Texas%20Separatist%20Sentenced%20to%2090%20Years%20in%20Prison,-L.A.%20Times%20Archives&text=The%20last%20of%20five%20Texas,Pecos%20County%20Dist.

Lowry, Beverly. *Who Killed These Girls?* New York: Knopf, 2016.

Markon, Jerry. "Hamdi Returned to Saudi Arabia." *Washington Post,* October 12, 2004. http://www.washingtonpost.com/wp-dyn/articles/A23958-2004Oct11.html?noredirect=on.

Marten, James. "Brackenridge Hospital." *Handbook of Texas Online.* November 1, 1994. https://www.tshaonline.org/handbook/entries/brackenridge-hospital.

Martin, Paul C. "Why Did Texas Secede from the Union & Join the Confederate States of America?" *Classroom,* September 29, 2017. https://classroom.synonym

.com/why-did-texas-secede-from-the-union-join-the-confederate-states-of-america-12084236.html.

Maslin, Janet. "Honeysuckle Rose." *New York Times,* July 18, 1980, C14. https://www.nytimes.com/1980/07/18/archives/honeysuckle-rose.html.

Mattel. "The Barbie Story." Accessed June 24, 2019. https://barbie.mattel.com/en-us/about/our-history.html.

Mayo Clinic. "Bipolar Disorder." Accessed June 25, 2019. https://www.mayoclinic.org/diseases-conditions/bipolar-disorder/symptoms-causes/syc-20355955.

McCracken, Peggy. "Attorney General Warned by McLaren." *Pecos Enterprise,* July 19, 1996. http://www.pecos.net/news/archives/0796fed.htm

———. "Bunton Hears McLaren Contempt Charges." *Pecos Enterprise,* May 2, 1996. http://www.pecos.net/news/archives/mclaren.htm.

———. "Feds Downplay New McLaren Arrest Warrant." *Pecos Enterprise,* December 20, 1996. http://www.pecos.net/news/archives/122096p.htm.

———. "Judge Wipes Smile Off McLaren's Face." *Pecos Enterprise,* May 17, 1996. http://www.pecos.net/news/archives/0596fed.htm.

———. "Republic of Texas Ambassador Summoned to Court." *Pecos Enterprise,* April 25, 1996. http://www.pecos.net/news/archives/0496fed.htm.

McGaughy, Lauren. "First to Ban Open Carry, Texas Could Be One of the Last to OK It." *Houston Chronicle,* December 22, 2014. https://www.houstonchronicle.com/news/politics/texas/article/First-to-ban-open-carry-Texas-could-be-one-of-5974401.php.

McKay, S. S. "Constitution of 1845." *Handbook of Texas Online.* Updated December 10, 1994. https://tshaonline.org/handbook/online/articles/mhc03.

McLaren v. State. No. 08-97-00651-CR (Texas Ct. App. Aug. 26, 1999). https://caselaw.findlaw.com/tx-court-of-appeals/1079500.html.

McLaren, Richard Lance v. State of Texas—Appeal from 394th District Court of Brewster County. No. 08-97-00651-CR (TC# 3346 Apr. 10, 2003). https://law.justia.com/cases/texas/eighth-court-of-appeals/2003/62226.html.

McMurry University. "About McMurry." Accessed June 25, 2019. https://about.mcm.edu.

Memorial Hermann Southwest Hospital. Accessed September 3, 2019. http://www.memorialhermann.org/locations/southwest.

Military Factory. "Armored Personnel Carriers (APC)." Accessed February 20, 2020. https://www.militaryfactory.com/armor/armored-personnel-carriers.asp.

MilitaryBases.us. "Camp Mabry." Accessed February 20, 2019. http://www.militarybases.us/camp-mabry.

Military-Today.com. "SKS: Semi-Automatic Rifle." Accessed November 11, 2019. http://www.military-today.com/firearms/sks.htm.

Miller, Daniel. *Texit: Why and How Texas Will Leave the Union.* Conroe, TX: Defiance Press, 2018.

Miller, Hubert J. "Edinburg, a Story of a Town." *Handbook of Texas Online.* Updated January 1, 1995. https://tshaonline.org/handbook/online/articles/hee02.

Bibliography

Mississippi Sports Hall of Fame and Museum. "Dwight 'D.D.' Lewis." Accessed September 19, 2019. https://msfame.com/inductees/dwight-lewis.

Mitch LaPointe's Classic Boat and Motor. "1960 19' Chris-Craft Capri." Accessed June 25, 2019. http://www.classicboat.com/chris-craft-19-capri-runabout-103n.htm.

Mitchell, Corey. *Murdered Innocents*. New York: Kensington, 2005.

Modisett, Bill, and Nancy Rankin McKinley, ed. *Historic Midland; An Illustrated History of Midland County*. Historical Publishing Network. San Antonio, Texas. January 1, 1998.

Moneymaker, Will. "The Wild Days of Texas: When Texas was a Country." AncestralFindings.com. Accessed September 19, 2019. https://ancestralfindings.com/wild-days-texas-texas-country.

The Monitor. "Alfonzo Al Ramirez." April 26, 2009. https://www.legacy.com/obituaries/themonitor/obituary.aspx?page=notice&pid=126582415.

Montes, Eduardo. "Texas Militants Sentenced." *Standard Times,* November 5, 1997. https://www.southcoasttoday.com/article/19971105/news/311059967.

Moore, Evan. "FBI, Rangers taking Republic of Texas Fugitive Seriously." *Houston Chronicle*. Reprint. Aug. 31, 1997. *Greenville News*. 25A.

Moore, Thomas Gale. "Trucking Deregulation." *The Concise Encyclopedia of Economics*. Accessed June 24, 2019. https://www.econlib.org/library/Enc1/TruckingDeregulation.html.

Mountain Project. "Point of Rocks Climbing." Accessed January 5, 2020. https://www.mountainproject.com/area/106389388/point-of-rocks.

MountainZone.com. "Sleeping Lion Mountain." Accessed November 11, 2019. https://www.mountainzone.com/mountains/texas/jeff-davis-tx/summits/sleeping-lion-mountain.

Mowreader, Jim. "What Are Cigarette Boats? How Did They Get Their Name? *Quora*. Accessed June 24, 2019. https://www.quora.com/What-are-cigarette-boats-How-did-they-get-their-name.

Nash, Mark. "Medium Recovery Vehicle M88." *Online Tank Museum,* March 5, 2019. https://tanks-encyclopedia.com/coldwar-us-medium-recovery-vehicle-m88/

Nathan, Debbie. "Christmas in the Republic of Texas." *Texas Observer,* January 17, 1997, 8.

National Academies and Department of Homeland Security. "IED Attack: Improvised Explosive Devices." *News & Terrorism*. Accessed February 28, 2021. https://www.dhs.gov/xlibrary/assets/prep_ied_fact_sheet.pdf.

National Governors Association. "Gov. George W. Bush." Accessed January 17, 2020. https://www.nga.org/governor/george-w-bush.

National Park Service. "Big Bend: How Big Is It?" December 14, 2018. https://www.nps.gov/bibe/learn/management/park_sizes.htm.

National Shooting Sports Foundation. "Understanding America's Rifle." Accessed January 19, 2020. https://www.nssf.org/msr.

Nature Conservancy. "Chihuahuan Desert." Accessed March 10, 2020. https://www.nature.org/en-us/get-involved/how-to-help/places-we-protect/chihuahuan-desert.

New York Times. "Texas Takes Custody of 400 Children after Raid on Polygamist Compound." April 8, 2008. https://www.nytimes.com/2008/04/08/world/americas/08iht-texas.1.11761542.html.

Ninesling, Rosie. "Haunted Austin: Metz Elementary." *Austin Monthly.* October 2019. Accessed Feb. 2, 2022. https://www.austinmonthly.com/haunted-austin-metz-elementary/

Noesner, Gary. *Gary Noesner: Former FBI Negotiator and Author.* http://garynoesner.com.

———. *Stalling for Time: My Life as a Hostage Negotiator.* New York: Random House, 2010.

O'Keefe, John. *The Texas Banking Crisis Causes and Consequences, 1980–1989.* Federal Reserve Bank of St. Louis, 1990. https://fraser.stlouisfed.org/files/docs/publications/texasbankcrisis_1980_1989.pdf.

Office of the Historian, "Annexation of Texas, the Mexican-American War, and the Treaty of Guadalupe Hildalgo, 1945–1848." Accessed October 10, 2019. https://history.state.gov/milestones/1830-1860/texas-annexation.

Old Austin High School/John T. Allan Junior High School, photograph. [1900–20?]. University of North Texas Libraries, Portal to Texas History. Accessed June 25, 2019. https://texashistory.unt.edu/ark:/67531/metapth124256.

Online Highways. "Adams-Onís Treaty." U-S-history.com. Accessed October 10, 2019. https://www.u-s-history.com/pages/h3985.html.

Orlando Sentinel. "Man Linked to Separatists Charged with Bank Fraud." March 22, 1998. https://www.orlandosentinel.com/news/os-xpm-1998-03-22-9803220173-story.html.

Patoski, Joe Nick. "Land That I Love." *TexasMonthly,* March 2000. https://www.texasmonthly.com/articles/land-that-i-love-2.

———. "Out There: What I Saw at the Republic of Texas Standoff." *TexasMonthly,* June 1997. https://www.texasmonthly.com/articles/out-there.

Pecos Enterprise. "Republic of Texas: Action Taken Against Three Republic Members." May 8, 1997. http://www.pecos.net/news/arch97/050897r.htm.

Permanent Court of Arbitration. "About Us." Accessed June 7, 2021. https://pca-cpa.org/en/about.

Pfeiff, Margo. "The Beach Life Is the Best Life on Roatan Island in Honduras." *Los Angeles Times,* February 20, 2016. https://www.latimes.com/travel/la-tr-d-honduras-main-20160221-story.html.

Pino, Jessica. "Guide to Austin's Dirty Sixth Street." *The Austinot,* February 4, 2016. https://austinot.com/guide-dirty-6th-street-austin-texas.

Pitzulo, Carrie. "Insight: Playboy Let Me View Its Archives. Here's What I Learned." *Austin American-Statesman.* October 4, 2017. https://www.statesman.com/news/20171004/insight-playboy-let-me-view-its-archives-heres-what-i-learned.

Plohetski, Tony. "Why is the FBI Withholding DNA Evidence in Austin's 1991 Yogurt Shop Murders?" KVUE.com, February 8, 2020. https://www.kvue.com/article/news/investigations/defenders/1991-austin-yogurt-shop-murders-killer-dna-fbi/269-d28e6099-7c69-4e10-bb45-3054fde938aa.

Preferred Hotels and Resorts. "A Hillside Paradise Spread Across 40 Acres Overlooking Acapulco Bay." Accessed June 24, 2019. https://preferredhotels.com/hotels/mexico/las-brisas-acapulco.

Pressley, Sue Anne. "Cyber-Savvy 'Texians' Are Papered into a Corner of the Southwest." *Washington Post,* March 12, 1997, A03. https://www.washingtonpost.com/wp-srv/national/daily/march/12/republic.htm?noredirect=on.

———. "Peaceful End Achieved in Texas Siege." *Washington Post,* May 4, 1997. https://www.washingtonpost.com/archive/politics/1997/05/04/peaceful-end-achieved-in-texas-siege/4f968b33-922c-4ba9-a7d4-051946f99e50.

Price, Asher. "Joaquin Jackson, Iconic Texas Lawman Dies." *Austin American-Statesman,* September 3, 2016. https://www.statesman.com/story/news/2016/09/03/joaquin-jackson-iconic-texas-lawman-dies/10127536007/.

Raivio, Ville. "A History of Saddle Shoes." Keikari.com. May 23, 2014. https://www.keikari.com/english/a-history-of-saddle-shoes.

Ramis, Harold (dir.). *Groundhog Day.* Culver City, CA: Columbia Pictures, 1993.

Ramsey, Ross. "An Unreliable Narrator with a Story to Tell." *Texas Tribune,* September 30, 2013. https://www.texastribune.org/2013/09/30/unreliable-narrator-story-tell.

———. "Dan Morales Indicted." *Texas Tribune,* March 10, 2003. https://www.texastribune.org/2003/03/10/dan-morales-indicted.

Ray, Steve. "Governor Cites Fort Davis Resolution as Warning to Other Militia Groups." *Corpus Christi Caller-Times.* May 4, 1997. A13.

Rescorla, Bob, and Molly Hults. *Public Schools Resources Guide.* 2013. http://www.austinlibrary.com/ahc/downloads/Public_Schools_Guide.pdf.

Rich, Gerald. "Drinking Through the Ages." *Daily Texan,* July 21, 2011. https://thedailytexan.com/2011/07/21/drinking-through-the-ages.

Rivas, Brennan Gardner. "When Texas Was the National Leader in Gun Control." *Washington Post,* September 12, 2019. https://www.washingtonpost.com/outlook/2019/09/12/when-texas-was-national-leader-gun-control.

Roberts, Stan. "Junior High Led Austin Desegregation." *Austin American-Statesman.* September 27, 2018. https://www.statesman.com/story/news/2012/09/01/junior-high-led-austin-desegregation/9778744007.

Robinson, Kenneth J. "Savings and Loan Crisis 1980–1989." Federal Reserve History. November 22, 2013. https://www.federalreservehistory.org/essays/savings_and_loan_crisis.

Rogers, William P. "Congress, the President, and the War Powers." *California Law Review* 59, no. 5 (1971): 1194–1214

Rosenbloom, Joe III. "Waco: More than Simple Blunders?" *Wall Street Journal,* October 17, 1995. https://www.pbs.org/wgbh/pages/frontline/waco/blunders.html.

Rosenwald, Michael S. "Row vs. Wade's Forgotten Loser: The Remarkable Story of Dallas Prosecutor Henry Wade." *Washington Post,* September 5, 2018. https://www.washingtonpost.com/news/retropolis/wp/2018/08/21/roe-v-wades-forgotten-loser-the-story-of-dallas-prosecutor-henry-wade.

Roufa, Timothy. "The History and Purpose of SWAT Teams." *The Balance Careers,* November 6, 2019. https://www.thebalancecareers.com/the-history-and-purpose-of-swat-teams-974567.

Rozen, Miriam. "The Man Who Knew Too Much." *Dallas Observer,* April 2, 1998. https://www.dallasobserver.com/news/the-man-who-knew-too-much-6401996.

Rozen, Miriam, and Brenda Sapino Jeffreys. "Rise & Fall: Why Did Dan Morales Exchange Good Judgment for the Good Life?" *Texas Lawyer,* October 27, 2003. https://www.law.com/almID/1066944923864/?slreturn=20190022100327.

Ruger. "Mini-14® Ranch." Accessed January 19, 2020. https://ruger.com/products/mini14RanchRifle/models.html.

Ruidoso News. "Robert Braxton 'Bobby' Holt." February 25, 2012. https://www.legacy.com/obituaries/ruidosonews/obituary.aspx?n=robert-braxton-holt-bobby&pid=156162132.

Scheibal, Steve. "Republic of Texas Member Arrested." *Austin American-Statesman,* April 23, 1997, B3.

Schuppe, Jon. "America's Rifle: Why So Many People Love the AR-15." *NBC News,* December 27, 2017. https://www.nbcnews.com/news/us-news/america-s-rifle-why-so-many-people-love-ar-15-n831171.

Sears, Chris B. "The Elements of Cache Programming Style." In *Proceedings of the Fourth Annual Linux Showcase & Conference,* 283–296. Atlanta, GA, October 10–14, 2000. https://www.usenix.org/legacy/publications/library/proceedings/als00/2000papers/papers/full_papers/sears/sears_html/index.html.

Second Amended and Restated Declaration of Covenants, Conditions and Restrictions (Vol. 75, p. 903). Davis Mountains Property Owners Association Inc. State of Texas, County of Jeff Davis. November 14, 2002.

Selin, Shannon. "Stephen F. Austin, Founder of Anglo-American Texas." Imagining the Bounds of History. Accessed October 10, 2019. https://shannonselin.com/2016/06/stephen-f-austin-founder-texas.

Settler, Sara. "David Koresh and the Waco Siege." *Biography.* Updated June 17, 2019. https://www.biography.com/news/david-koresh-waco-ae-documentary.

Shapiro & Dunn. "About Us: External Legal Counsel with Relevant In-House Experience and Real World Business Acumen." Accessed September 19, 2019. http://shapirodunn.com/about-us.

Sharp, Stan. "Republic of Texas officials contend that state should stand alone." Kilgore News-Herald. February 23, 1997. Accessed February 17, 2022. https://www.newspapers.com/image/612128386/?terms=%22War%20Powers%20Act%22&match=1.

Sheffield, Dick. "Joaquin Jackson." *Texas Monthly,* July 2002. https://www.texasmonthly.com/the-culture/joaquin-jackson.

Bibliography 271

Sheffield, Michael L. "Is Network Marketing Just a Scam?" *Entrepreneur*, December 25, 2000. https://www.entrepreneur.com/article/35744.

Simnacher, Joe. "Robert Hughes, 91, ex-Dallas Lawyer, Judge and State Representative." *Dallas Morning News*, February 13, 2017. https://www.dallasnews.com/news/obituaries/2017/02/13/robert-hughes-91-ex-dallas-lawyer-judge-and-state-representative.

Slaying the Dragon of Debt. "1990–92 Early 1990s Recession." Accessed September 19, 2019. https://bancroft.berkeley.edu/ROHO/projects/debt/1990srecession.html.

Spacek, Sissy. *My Extraordinary Ordinary Life*. New York: Hyperion, 2012.

Sports Reference LLC. "Ken McMinn." Accessed June 25, 2019. https://www.sports-reference.com/cfb/players/ken-mcminn-1.html.

Standard-Times. "Donald Davenport McIvor." Accessed September 8, 2019. https://www.legacy.com/obituaries/name/donald-mcivor-obituary?pid=135089476.

Statesman.com. "Camilo Joe Villegas. October 28, 2007. https://www.legacy.com/obituaries/statesman/obituary.aspx?n=camilo-joe-villegas&pid=97036657.

———. "Gisela Sterling." January 9, 2011. https://www.legacy.com/obituaries/name/gisela-sterling-obituary?pid=147667086.

———. "Jody Lynn Hagemann 1955–2017." August 13, 2017. https://www.legacy.com/obituaries/statesman/obituary.aspx?n=jody-lynn-hagemann&pid=186299680.

———. "Lightsey, Jerry Stephen." October 25, 2017. https://www.legacy.com/obituaries/statesman/obituary.aspx?n=jerry-lightsey&pid=187085655&fhid=19499.

———. "Robert Higgins Hughes: 1925–2017." *Austin American-Statesman*, January 22, 2017. https://www.legacy.com/obituaries/statesman/obituary.aspx?n=robert-higgins-hughes&pid=183679719.

———. "William K. Turner." Accessed January 19, 2020. https://www.legacy.com/obituaries/statesman/obituary.aspx?n=william-k-turner&pid=189253934&fhid=15362.

Strode, Hudson. "Jefferson Davis: President of Confederate States of America." *Encyclopaedia Britannica*. October 14, 2019. https://www.britannica.com/biography/Jefferson-Davis.

"Tack Room; Posada Hotel." Accessed February 17, 2022. https://www.laposada.com/the-tack-room#:~:text=The%20Tack%20Room%20provides%20an,race-track%20in%20Nuevo%20Laredo%2C%20Mexico.

Texas A&M University. "Chuck H. Samson, Jr. PhD: Acting President, July 10, 1980–August 31, 1981." Accessed December 10, 2019. https://president.tamu.edu/administration/past-presidents/index.html.

Texas Academy of Distinguished Neutrals. "Hon. Joseph H. Hart." Accessed June 25, 2019. https://www.texasneutrals.org/joseph-hart.

Texas Almanac. "Capitals of the Republic of Texas." Accessed February 5, 2020. https://texasalmanac.com/topics/history/capitals-texas.

Texas Archival Resources Online. "Hart Graphics, Inc. Records." Accessed June 25, 2019. http://www.lib.utexas.edu/taro/aushc/00169/ahc-00169.html.

Texas Department of Criminal Justice. "Lynaugh (LH)." Accessed July 19, 2019. https://www.tdcj.texas.gov/unit_directory/lh.html.

Texas Independence List. "Keyes Arrested." Tx.politics.republic forum, September 20, 1997. https://groups.google.com/forum/#!topic/tx.politics.republic/GMKH77cA9j4.

Texas Ranger Hall of Fame and Museum. "Jesse Carl 'Jess' Malone." Accessed December 10, 2019. http://texasrangerregister.org/malone-jesse-carl-iii.

Texas State Historical Association. "Davis Mountains." *Handbook of Texas Online*. Modified June 28, 2019. https://tshaonline.org/handbook/online/articles/rjd03.

Texas State Library and Archives Commission. "Early Statehood: The 1850 Boundary Act." December 5, 2017. https://www.tsl.texas.gov/treasures/earlystate/boundary.html.

———. "The Republic of Texas." December 5, 2017. https://www.tsl.texas.gov/treasures/republic/index.html.

———. "The Republic of Texas—The Texas Revolution: The Treaties of Velasco." Modified December 5, 2017. https://www.tsl.texas.gov/treasures/republic/velasco-01.html.

Texas Tribune. "Dobie Middle School." June 24, 2019. https://schools.texastribune.org/districts/austin-isd/dobie-middle-school.

TexasEscapes.com. "Brewster County Courthouse." Accessed June 18, 2020. http://www.texasescapes.com/WestTexasTowns/AlpineTexas/AlpineBrewsterCountyCourthouse.htm.

Timothy Bible College. Facebook page. Accessed September 8, 2019. https://www.facebook.com/timothybiblecolllege.

Travis County Sheriff's Office. Accessed August 2, 2019. www.tcsheriff.org.

Trejo, Rebecca. "Intersection Changes Proposed for 360 and RM 2222." KVUE.com. March 7, 2019. https://www.kvue.com/article/news/intersection-changes-proposed-for-360-and-rm-2222/269-bfcad157-de11-4310-94eb-173c8c30a213.

Tribune News Services. "Texas Separatist Gets 99 Years." *Chicago Tribune*, November 5, 1997. https://www.chicagotribune.com/news/ct-xpm-1997-11-05-9711050042-story.html.

Trip Advisor. "Explore Roatan." Accessed September 9, 2019. https://www.tripadvisor.com/Tourism-g292019-Roatan_Bay_Islands-Vacations.html?fid=9f8ce95e-5ee9-4c9a-80da-711edaa9b62b.

Trottier, David. *The Screenwriter's Bible: Complete Guide to Writing, Formatting, and Selling Your Script*. 3rd ed. Los Angeles: Silman-James Press, 1998. https://www.keepwriting.com/tsc/swbible.htm.

The Twilight Zone. IMDB.com. Accessed May 11, 2020. https://www.imdb.com/title/tt0052520.

The Typewriter Database. "1997 Brother WP-5600 MDS." October 25, 2014. https://typewriterdatabase.com/1997-brother-wp5600-mds.3510.typewriter.

TXMountaineer. "Davis Mountains." Summitpost.org. July 27, 2009. https://www.summitpost.org/davis-mountains/335829.

Bibliography

United States District Court Northern District of Texas. "History." Accessed January 21, 2020. http://www.txnd.uscourts.gov/history.

United States of America v Richard Lance McLaren, Linh Ngoc Vu, Evelyn Ann McLaren, Jasper Edward Baccus, Richard George Kieninger, Erwin Leo Brown, Joe Louis Reece, Stephen Craig Crear. No. 98-10762 (5th Cir. 2000). http://www.ca5.uscourts.gov/opinions%5Cunpub%5C98/98-10762.0.wpd.pdf.

United States of America v. Richard Lance McLaren, Defendant. No. P-00-CR-400-F (01). Judgment in a criminal case (for offenses committed on or after November 1, 1987), pp. 1–5.

United States Tax Court. Accessed February 25, 2021. https://www.ustaxcourt.gov.

United States v. McLaren. No. 98-10762 (5th Cir. 2000). https://www.courtlistener.com/opinion/21818/united-states-v-mclaren.

United States v. Gold Unlimited Ltd. No. 96-6713 (6th Cir. 1999). https://caselaw.findlaw.com/us-6th-circuit/1390933.html.

UPI Archives. "Republic of Texas Members Plead Guilty." August 9, 2001. https://www.upi.com/Archives/2001/08/09/Republic-of-Texas-members-plead-guilty/1621997329600.

Urban Dictionary. s.v. "Banana Clip." April 23, 2004. https://www.urbandictionary.com/define.php?term=banana%20clip.

US Army. "Explosive Ordnance Disposal (EOD) Specialist." Accessed January 23, 2019. https://www.goarmy.com/careers-and-jobs/browse-career-and-job-categories/intelligence-and-combat-support/explosive-ordnance-disposal-specialist.html.

US Customs and Border Protection. "CBP Through the Years." Modified May 5, 2021. https://www.cbp.gov/about/history.

———. "Marfa Station." Modified March 10, 2014. https://www.cbp.gov/border-security/along-us-borders/border-patrol-sectors/big-bend-sector-texas/marfa-station-mrs.

US Immigration and Customs Enforcement. "Office of Intelligence." Accessed January 5, 2020. https://www.ice.gov/intelligence.

USLegal. "Treasury Warrant Law and Definition." Accessed December 11, 2019. https://definitions.uslegal.com/t/treasury-warrant.

Utley, Robert M. *Lone Star Lawmen: The Second Century of the Texas Rangers*. New York: Oxford University Press, 2007.

Utterback, Bill. "Statewide Militia Muster and Patriot Rally at the Alamo on November 12, 1994." *Texas Constitutional Militia: Southern Region*, September 28, 1994. https://constitution.org/1-Activism/mil/pr_4928.txt.

Vanderstel, David G. "Native Americans in Indiana." *Conner Prairie Interpreter Resource Manual*. 1985. https://www.connerprairie.org/historyonline/indnam.html.

Vattel, Emmerich. *The Law of Nations; Principles of the Law of Nature*. London: Merriam, 10.

Verhovek, Sam Howe. "Before His Armed Standoff, Texan Waged War on Neighbors in Court." *New York Times*, May 2, 1997. https://www.nytimes.com/1997/05/02/us/before-his-armed-standoff-texan-waged-war-on-neighbors-in-court.html.

---. "Hostages Taken in Standoff with Militant Texas Group." *New York Times,* April 28, 1997. https://www.nytimes.com/1997/04/28/us/hostages-taken-in-standoff-with-militant-texas-group.html.

---. "Pecos Journal; New Courthouse Is Raising Texas-Size Questions." *New York Times,* November 30, 1995. ttps://www.nytimes.com/1995/11/30/us/pecos-journal-new-courthouse-is-raising-texas-size-questions.html.

---. "Separatists End Texas Standoff as 5 Surrender." *New York Times,* May 4, 1997. https://www.nytimes.com/1997/05/04/us/separatists-end-texas-standoff-as-5-surrender.html.

---. "Serious Face on Texas Independence." *New York Times,* January 24, 1997. https://www.nytimes.com/1997/01/24/us/serious-face-on-a-texas-independence-group.html.

---. "Texas Swaps a Jailed Militant for Hostages in Tense Siege." *New York Times,* April 29, 1997. https://www.nytimes.com/1997/04/29/us/texas-swaps-a-jailed-militant-for-hostages-in-tense-siege.html.

Vintage Dancer. "1950s Petticoat History." November 11, 2013. https://vintagedancer.com/1950s/1950s-petticoat-history.

---. "1950s Socks—Women's Bobby Socks." Accessed June 25, 2019. https://vintagedancer.com/1950s/1950s-socks-bobby-socks.

Vintage Traveler. "Vintage Shoes—The Loafer." June 13, 2011. https://thevintagetraveler.wordpress.com/2011/06/13/vintage-shoes-the-loafer.

Vocabulary.com. s.v. "Operative." Accessed June 25, 2019. https://www.vocabulary.com/dictionary/operative.

Vox Nutrition. "Private Label Nutrition Supplements." Accessed September 19, 2019. https://www.voxnutrition.com/products.

Walsh, Sean Collins. "Ex-Judge John Dietz Cancels His Courthouse Contract." *Austin American-Statesman,* September 4, 2016. https://www.statesman.com/story/news/2016/09/04/ex-judge-john-dietz-cancels-his-courthouse-contract/9981955007/.

Washington on the Brazos Historical Foundation. "Where Texas Became Texas." Accessed October 10, 2019. http://wheretexasbecametexas.org.

Washington Post. "Eight Republic of Texas' Separatists Convicted of Fraud." April 15, 1998. https://www.washingtonpost.com/archive/politics/1998/04/15/eight-republic-of-texas-separatists-convicted-of-fraud/7403f84f-f3d7-4171-a3ec-9468673e24bf.

Watkins, Chelsea. "Utopian Society Built in Texas Town in 1984 to Survive the End of the World." *Dallas Morning News,* August 16, 2018. https://www.dallasnews.com/news/2018/08/16/utopian-society-built-in-texas-town-in-1984-to-survive-the-end-of-the-world.

Watts, Thomas G. "Independent Spirits Declare Texas Free." *Dallas Morning News,* January 17, 1996, 17A.

Watts, Thomas G., and Pete Slover. "McLarens Face Federal Charges." *Dallas Morning News.* May 6, 1997. https://culteducation.com/group/1119-republic-of-texas-militia/17936-mclarens-face-federal-charges.html.

Waymarking.com. "Brewster County Courthouse, Alpine, TX." Accessed June 18, 2020. https://www.waymarking.com/waymarks/WMH52T_Brewster_County_Courthouse_Alpine_TX.

WebstaurantStore. "Everything You Need to Know About Melamine Dinnerware." July 7, 2018. https://www.webstaurantstore.com/article/61/top-eight-benefits-of-melamine-dinnerware.html.

Weddle, Robert S. "Nueces River." *Texas Handbook Online.* Updated March 23, 2019. https://tshaonline.org/handbook/online/articles/rnn15.

Whitehurst, Katie. "Civil War and Reconstruction, 1861–1870." Texas PBS. Accessed October 10, 2019. https://texasourtexas.texaspbs.org/the-eras-of-texas/civil-war-reconstruction.

Whittaker, Richard. "Still Working on It: Actor Brian O'Halloran on the Enduring Appeal of 'Clerks.'" *Austin Chronicle,* July 29, 2011. https://www.austinchronicle.com/screens/2011-07-29/still-working-it.

Wilmington News-Journal. "Miss Sandra Kay Denkenberger and Mr. Richard Lance McLaren Exchanged Wedding Vows." April 24, 1975, 6. https://www.newspapers.com/newspage/62377760.

———. "WHS to Graduate 263." May 10, 1972, 22. https://www.newspapers.com/image/65819465/?terms=Richard%20Lance%20McLaren&match=1.

Wilson, Jason. "Ruby Ridge 1992: The Day the American Militia Movement Was Born." *The Guardian,* August 26, 2017. https://www.theguardian.com/us-news/2017/aug/26/ruby-ridge-1992-modern-american-militia-charlottesville.

Winston & Strawn LLP. "What Is a Temporary Restraining Order (TRO)?" Accessed September 19, 2019. https://www.winston.com/en/legal-glossary/temporary-restraining-order.html.

Wired. "Texas ISPs Targeted in Secession Case." March 11, 1997. https://www.wired.com/1997/04/texas-isps-targeted-in-secessionist-case.

Wood, Graeme. "The Movement to Make Texas Its Own Country." *The Atlantic,* December 2019, ruaryhttps://www.theatlantic.com/magazine/archive/2019/12/the-secessionist/600739.

Wooster, Ralph A. "Civil War." *Handbook of Texas Online.* Accessed October 10, 2019. https://tshaonline.org/handbook/online/articles/qdc02.

World Class Travel Network. "Welcome to World Class Travel Network: An Affiliation Program for Travel Professionals." Accessed September 19, 2019. http://www.worldclassnetwork.net.

Yeomans, Adam. "NSA's Recruitment Methods Come Under Attack." *Orlando Sentinel,* October 19, 1992. https://www.orlandosentinel.com/news/os-xpm-1992-10-19-9210170166-story.html.

Index

NOTE: Family relationships shown in parentheses refer to Jo Ann Canady Turner unless otherwise specified.

Abbott, Greg, 212, 214
ABC media, 111, 118
Adams, Harvey. *See in photo gallery*
Adams, Matt, 117, 118
Adams-Onís Treaty, 5
Adelphi spiritual group, 187
adjustable-rate mortgage (ARM), 38, 42, 45
adverse possession principle, 61, 130–31, 213
air traffic restrictions over siege area, 110–11, 122
Alamo Mission, 63
Alamo Title Company, 46, 47, 88
Alar Moving Company, 48, 52–53, 80, 150, 181
alcohol and drinking, 1, 32, 33, 41
Alexander, Dan, 95
Allen, Johnny, 111–12, 116. *See also in photo gallery*
"ambassador" title adopted by McLaren, 4, 65, 67, 188, 193, 213, 222
American Terrorist (Michael and Herbeck), 3
Andrews, Dessie, 64, 67, 68, 68–69, 73, 75, 75–76, 215

annexation of Texas: historical background, 5–7; ROT arguments against legality of, 2, 14, 65–66, 178, 188–89, 210–11, 222. *See also* sovereignty of Texas, McLaren's claims regarding
antigovernment militia groups, 3, 8, 135. *See also* separatist movements (other than ROT); tax evasion/protest
Anzaldua, Johnny. *See in photo gallery*
armored vehicles, 129, 137, 147. *See also in photo gallery*
Army (US), 6, 157
arrests: Evelyn McLaren, 148, 150–51; of incoming ROT members, 136; Jo Ann, 11–15, 13, 82; Keyes, 169–70; McLaren, 66, 149–50; Otto, 149–50, 151; Paulsons, 151, 166; Scheidt, 96–97, 107–8
ATF (Bureau of Alcohol, Tobacco, Firearms and Explosives). *See* Bureau of Alcohol, Tobacco, Firearms and Explosives (ATF)
attachment liens, McLaren's use of, 212, 214
AT&T communication lines, 112–13
Austin, Moses, 4
Austin, Stephen F., 4–5
Austin American-Statesman, 49, 80, 115, 176

Austin Police Department: and Jo Ann's arrest, 12; and Kelly's murder, 218–19; and Yogurt Shop Murders (1991), 224–25

Baccus, Jasper Edward, 193–94
Bailey, Steve: and arrival of federal agencies, 119; burglary charges against McLaren, 69; earlier troubles with ROT, 111, 120–21; first contact with Texas Rangers, 72; guard for home and family, 121; and Rowe kidnapping incident, 95–97, 106–9, 110; siege daily routine, 122. *See also in photo gallery*
Baker, David, 110–11
Baldy Peak (Mount Livermore), 4, 156
bank and mail fraud, 14, 75–76, 77, 186–87, 189–94, 191–94, 193, 200. *See also in photo gallery*
Barry B. Telford Unit, Texarkana (state prison), 171
Battle of San Jacinto, 5
Beames, Ron, 141
Becker, Curtis. *See in photo gallery*
Bell, Jack and Elaine, 118
Ben Hur Shriners, 154
Big Bend Regional Medical Center, Alpine, 117
Big Bend Sentinel, 121
Big Wonderful Thing (Harrigan), 4
Billings, John. *See in photo gallery*
Blakely, Sue, 57–58
Blue Mountain Bar and Grill, Fort Davis, 57
"bogus lien bill." *See under* liens, fraudulent/bogus
Bohn, Walter and Frieda, 35
bomb squad/explosive ordnance disposal (EOD), 121, 157. *See also in photo gallery*
booby traps, 96, 152, 157. *See also* explosives and IEDs

Border Patrol, 58–59, 113, 122, 157
Boulder Weekly, 170–71
Brackenridge Hospital, Austin, 17
Branch Davidians, 109, 119. *See also* Waco siege of 1993
Brannon, John, 146
Brannum, Ed, 3, 214, 221–26
Brantley, Al, 120
Brewster County Courthouse, Alpine, 177–78
Brooks, Don Vernell, 221–22, 223
Brown, Cliff, 219
Brown, Erwin Leo, 194
Brown, Randall, 108
Brown, Tom, 117, 118
Bunton, Lucius Desha, 66–67
Bureau of Alcohol, Tobacco, Firearms and Explosives (ATF), 12, 109, 119, 124, 157
Burris, Lonnie, 229–31
Burris, Regis, 230–31
Bush, George H. W., 204
Bush, George W., 14, 65, 113, 122, 132, 159, 169, 204
Byrne, Jerry. *See in photo gallery*

California Rangers (militia group), 8
Campbell, Mike, 107, 109
Camp Mabry Army Base, Austin, 129, 198
Canady, Becky (sister), 19, 23, 177
Canady, Jimmie (brother), 18, 19, 21, 33
Canady, Lillian (aunt). *See* Nelson, Lillian (née Canady, aunt)
Canady, Lillian (sister). *See* Lehman, Lillian Mae (née Canady) (sister)
Canady, Margaret (mother) "Maggie," 17, 18, 21–22, 85
Canady, Sydney Carroll (father), 18, 19, 21, 25
Canady, Sydney Jr. (brother), 19, 33
Carney, Carolyn, 147, 172, 211, 223

Carruth, Gerald, 204–6
Casteel, Bruce, 130, 151
Castillo, Tony, 22
Caver, Barry: background and career, 109, 119, 169; and George W. Bush, 169; and incoming ROT members, 134, 136, 140; on McLaren's character and psyche, 146, 148; and O'Rourke's negotiations, 123, 124, 140, 141, 144, 145; Rowe kidnapping and hostage exchange, 101, 104, 111–12, 116; on Scheidt's surrender, 147; Sheriff Bailey's call for assistance, 72; staging and strategic planning, 110–11, 128, 128–30; on surrenders and escapes, 151–52. *See also in photo gallery*
CBS media, 118
cease-fire agreement, 123, 151, 214
Central Dominion Trust (banking system), 222
Chamberlain, Melissa, 177, 182
check writing schemes, 77, 189–90
Chihuahuan Desert, 3–4, 95
Childress, George C., 5
Christian Front, 8
Christopher, Warren, 66–67
civil contempt fines (accumulated), 68
civil rights movement, 24–25
Civil War, 7–8, 88, 118, 213. *See also* "indestructible union" concept
Clinton, Bill, 2, 223
CNN, 82, 111, 117, 118
Cobb, Molton "Ty," 34
Coggins, Paul, 189, 191
Collins, Buster. *See in photo gallery*
communications. *See* power and communication lines; radio communications
Concerned Property Owners Association (CPOA) (of DMR), 57
Conejo, Carlos, 121
Confederacy, Texas in, 7, 88

Contract Microfilm Co./Protek Archival Labs, 211
convictions and sentencing: federal firearms trial, 206–7; federal fraud trial, 186, 193–94; Keyes, 171; state trial, 179; state trial reversal and reinstatement, 191, 200
Cornyn, John, 77
Counsel General of the Republic of Texas (title adopted by McLaren), 222
counterfeit money/documents, 188, 190–91
COVID-19, impact of, 230
Covington, Carl (Covington Enterprises), 57, 118–19
Cox, Calvin. *See in photo gallery*
Cox, Mike, 3, 111, 134, 135–36, 140, 158
Crear, Steven Craig, 194
credit card fraud, 189–90. *See also in photo gallery*
Cummings, James, D., 72
currency created by ROT, 75, 190

Darling, Jancy, 217–20
Davis, Jefferson, 7
Davis, Paul, 52–53
Davis, Tommy, 140
Davis Mountain Resort (DMR), 57–60, 59, 60, 141, 168. *See also in photo gallery*
Davis Mountains, 3–4, 94, 118, 156, 163
Davis Mountains Land Commission (DMLC), 57–58
Davis Mountains State Park, 4, 156
de-escalation strategies, 130, 134, 135–36, 145–46
DeGuerin, Dick, 124, 145
DeHart, Kenneth, 178, 179
DeMoss, Harold R. Jr, 200
Denkenberger, Sandra Kay, 55

Denkenberger, Sandra Kay (first wife of McLaren), 55
Department of Public Safety (DPS). *See* Texas Department of Public Safety (DPS)
De Pena, Alex, 64
Depew family, 154
Dietz, John, 86–89, 89
Dillard, Bob, 61
diplomatic pouches, use of, 137, 141
DMR (Davis Mountain Resort). *See* Davis Mountain Resort (DMR)
Dodge, Larry, 63
dogs: Joe Rowe's dog, 98–99, 103; Turner family dog, 161–62; used in tracking escapees, 159, 161, 162–64, 165 (*See also in photo gallery*)
domestic terrorism, 128, 168–69, 171–72
Dominguez, Danny, 108–9
Dowd, David D., 200
Downs, Roger, 189
Driscoll, Mike, 123
Duffy, Jim, 137
Duncan, David, 97, 101, 108–9, 111–12, 116, 119. *See also in photo gallery*
Durham's Business College, 25
Dyer, Joe, 170–71
Dyer, William, 37

Earle Cabell Federal Building and Courthouse, Dallas, 186
Eckhart, Steve, 48
Edmonton Journal, 144
Eighth Legislature of Texas, 193, 213
Eldorado, Tex. siege, 169
Electronic Communications Privacy Act of 1986, 71
emails, subpoenas for, 70, 71
"embassy" of ROT, 57, 120, 129. *See also in photo gallery*
employment, Jo Ann's: architecture firm, 34; Dell Children's Hospital, 203; Gulf Oil Company, 35; H-E-B grocery store, 203, 220, 229; house staging, 201–3; KRGV television, 34; networking/marketing pursuits, 38, 43–45, 82–83; real estate business, 34, 37; Shoal Creek Hospital, 37; teen years, 20–21, 23, 25; temporary work, 34, 176, 203; truck driving, 197–99
Empress Verdiacee "Tiari" Washitaw Turner Goston El Bey, 68
Enloe, Jesse, 2, 69, 223
escape of Matson and Keyes, 151, 156, 156–57, 161, 169–70
evacuation of DMR residents, 118
Evans, Paula, 111
Evans, Tracee, 112
eviction of Turners from home, 12, 46–49
Executioner's Song, The (Mailer), 3
executions, penal, 132
explosives and IEDs, 121, 136, 152, 157, 205, 206. *See also* Bureau of Alcohol, Tobacco, Firearms and Explosives (ATF); *in photo gallery*

false lien bill of Texas Legislature, 13–14, 69, 69–70, 172
Fandango (film), 4
Faucett, Michelle, 47
FBI (Federal Bureau of Investigation). *See* Federal Bureau of Investigation (FBI)
Federal Aviation Administration (FAA), 122
Federal Bureau of Investigation (FBI), 12, 109, 119, 120, 130, 157, 222. *See also* Noesner, Gary
Federal Deposit Insurance Corporation (FDIC), 48
Federal Reserve Bank, 192
Federal Savings & Loan Insurance Corporation (FSLIC), 41

Federal Trade Commission (FTC), 44
Fields, Earl, 180
Fifth Circuit Court of Appeals, 192, 200
firearms violations (federal), 96, 98, 136, 180, 191, 200, 204–7. *See also in photo gallery*
fire station command post, siege team, 128, 130, 134. *See also in photo gallery*
Fish, Joe, 186
Flying J truck stop, Pecos, 136
foreclosures on Turners, 41, 47–49
Fort Bliss, El Paso, 121, 169
Fort Davis, Tex., 4, 7, 57, 132
Fort Worth, McLaren apartment in, 55, 73–74
Foster, Terry. *See in photo gallery*
Franks, Darrell, 75, 221–22, 223
Friedman, Paul L., 191
Friend, J. W. "Skinny," 58
Furgeson, William Royal Jr., 204–6

Gaston & Sheehan Auctioneers, 49, 53
Geneva Convention demands from ROT, 67, 137, 213
George H. W. Bush and George W. Bush United States Courthouse and George Mahon Federal Building, Midland, Tex., 204
Gerdes, Coolidge, 221–22
Giant (film), 4
Gilbreath, Larry, 136
Global Land Corporation, 57
Gold Unlimited Network, 44
Gonzales, Gonzalo and Maria, 20–21
Graham, Gary, 63
Grand Prairie, Tex. ROT location, 74
"Great Lien," 65, 67, 68–69
Grebe, Jack Abbot Jr., 2
Griesacker, Arthur, 187–88, 223
Grubb, George, 117, 118
Gruggs, Bobby. *See in photo gallery*

gun modifications, illegal. *See* firearms violations (federal)

Hagar, Ralph, 163. *See also in photo gallery*
Hagemann, Jody L., 48, 53
Hague Academy of International Law, 226
Halbison, Boyce Eugene, 147–48, 223
Hamilton, John, 63
Hammond, Michael, 217–18, 220
Hannes, Kenneth and Mickey, 154–55
Harbison, Sarah and Jennifer, 224
Hardin-Simmons University, 23
Harper, Cathy, 24
Harrigan, Stephen, 4
Harris County Jail, 123, 170
Harrison, Dorothy, 40
Harrison, George (Bill's drummer), 27, 37
Harrison, Joyanna, 40
Hart, Joseph H., 68, 80, 89, 172, 214, 224
Hart Graphic company, 25
Hartnett, Will, 69
Heaman/Sweat Historic County Courthouse, 80
Hedrick, Judith, 23
helicopters: Jo Ann's concerns about, 15, 128, 139; reconnaissance operations, 122; and search for Kelly's killer, 219; and search for ROT escapees, 163, 164–65, 219
Henderson, Gary, 136
Henderson, J. Pinckney, 6
Herbalife Nutrition, 38
Herbeck, Dan, 3
Hightower, Allen, 172
Holder, Nellie (aunt), 27
Holloman Air Force Base, N. Mex., 169
Holt, Robert Braxton "Bobby," 122, 132

homes. *See* residences of Turners
Honduras, 181–83, 185, 194–96
Hopkins, Julie, 141, 144–46
Hord, Michael F. Jr., 70
Hotel Limpia, Fort Davis, 57, 132
Houston, Sam, 5
Houston, Tex., 6, 34–36
Hughes, Robert "Bob" Higgins and Kay, 181–82, 185, 194
Hunt, Joe. *See in photo gallery*
Hurst, Robert, 206–7

immigration violation (Karen Paulson), 205, 207
impeachment of McLaren by ROT, 193, 223
improvised explosive devices (IEDs), 152. *See also* explosives and IEDs
"indestructible union" concept, 7, 189
Indybay (newswire website), 76
insurance fraud accusations, 224–25
Internal Revenue Service (IRS). *See* tax evasion/protest
international courts, ROT appeals to, 188, 210–11, 226
Internet use by ROT, 70–73, 226
Isaacs, Joyce, 52
Ivor, Donald Davenport, 59–60

Jackson, Andrew, 5
Jackson, Joaquin, 110
Jaggar, Todd, 70–71, 72
jailbreak rumors, 127–28
James Lynaugh Unit, Fort Stockton (state prison), 159. *See see also in photo gallery*
James V. Allred Unit, North Iowa Park (state prison), 207
Jeff Davis County, founding of, 7
Jeff Davis County Commissioners, 58
Jeff Davis County County Courthouse, 58, 61, 97, 120

Jeff Davis County Dispatch, 61
Jeff Davis County Sheriff's Department, 95, 111, 157
Jeffs, Warren, 169
Jenkins, Hoff, Oberg, and Saxe architects, 34
Jeunesse Global, 43
Johnson, Daryl, 168–69
Johnson, David, 2, 69
Jolly, E. Grady, 200
Jordan, Mont. *See* Montana Freemen incident of 1996
jury nullification concept, 188
Just Call Me a Spokesman for DPS (Cox), 3
Justice Department. *See* US Department of Justice

Karr, Joseph Frederick, 217–20
Kea, Gene. *See in photo gallery*
Keesey Canyon, 4
Kelly, Bob and Margaret, 153–54
Kelly, Gary, 219
Kelly Services, 176
Kerrville, Tex., 2, 225
Key, Gene, 164
Keyes, Richard Frank III: arrest of in September 1997, 169–70; convictions and sentences, 171, 207; end of search for, 168; escape of and search for, 151, 152, 156–57, 163–66, 164, 165, 168, 170–71; federal firearms violations trial, 204–7; and Rowe kidnapping incident, 98–101, 99, 100, 101, 104, 116–17; state trial, 180. *See also in photo gallery*
kidnapping incident: conviction of McLaren and Otto, 179–80; home invasion and shooting of Rowe, 82, 97–104; Keyes's account of, 171; prisoner/hostage exchange, 104, 111–12, 116–17; radio confusion and miscommunications, 96–97,

107–8; reversal and reaffirmation of conviction, 191
Kieninger, Richard George (pseud. Ekial Kueshana), 187
Kilpatrick, Arvin, 121. *See also in photo gallery*
Kinkaid, Terry. *See in photo gallery*
Koresh, David, 119, 124, 158. *See also* Waco siege of 1993
Kriewald, Melvin Louis, 147–48
KTRH radio, 111
Kueshana, Ekial. *See* Kieninger, Richard George
KVET-AM radio, 52
KVLF/KALP radio, 140

Ladies' Oriental Shrine of North America, 154
Lamar, Mirabeau B., 5
land grants in Texas, 4
Larsen, Susan, 206
Lauermann, Keith T., 219
Law of Adverse Possession. *See* adverse possession principle
Law of Nations concept, 65
Laws of Occupation in international law, 213
Leahey, Robert, 205
Leal Trucking Company, 11, 41, 49, 176, 203
Lehman, Lillian Mae (née Canady) (sister), 18–19, 33, 177
Lewis, Dwight Douglas "D. D." and Margaret, 44
liens, fraudulent/bogus: Alar Moving and Storage Company, 80; attachment liens, 212, 214; DMR properties, 58–60; false lien bill of Texas Legislature, 13–14, 69, 69–70, 172; Jo Ann's regrets, 227–28; McLaren's acquired properties in DMR, 120; Morales's restraining order, 69, 222; Pope John Paul II,

69; Stewart Title Company, 66, 88
Limpia, Hotel. *See* Hotel Limpia, Fort Davis
Lincoln, Abraham, 7, 213
Lowe, Archie Huel, 65, 69, 222, 223
Lowry, Beverly, 225
Lowry, Pete, 53
Lozano, Lupe (and family), 19
Luecke, James D., 117
Lujan, Jimmy, 108
Lynaugh Unit. *See* James Lynaugh Unit, Fort Stockton (state prison)

M88 armored recovery vehicle, 129
Mailer, Norman, 3
mail fraud. *See* bank and mail fraud
Malone, Jess, 116, 116–17, 121–22, 128, 131, 140. *See also in photo gallery*
marijuana, 136
Martínez, Antonio, 4
Masonic Lodge in Austin, 229
Matson, Mike, 147, 151, 156–57, 162–65. *See also in photo gallery*
Matson, Ralph, 165–66
McCollough, W. Scott, 71
McCorvey, Norma, 186
McDonald Observatory, 4, 60
McIvor, Donald Davenport (and family), 59–60
McKnight, Molly, 44
McLaren, Evelyn Ann (née Horak): federal trials, 179–80, 186; Jo Ann's observations on, 46, 73–74; O'Rourke's strategic use of pleas from daughters, 137, 141, 144–46; prison sentence, 193; surrender and arrest of, 148, 150–51. *See also in photo gallery*
McLaren, Mary June (née Samson) (McLaren's mother), 54, 55, 56, 61. *See also in photo gallery*
McLaren, Richard "Rick" Lance: appearance, 46, 209; arrests of,

66, 149–50; book written by, 215; family background and early years, 54–56; federal trials, 179–80, 204–7; impeachment of by ROT, 193, 223; interviews with in prison, 191–93, 209–15; personality and character, 46, 54, 58, 60, 146, 148–49, 158; property at DMR, 56–57, 61–62; state trial and conviction, 177–80. *See also in photo gallery*; sovereignty of Texas, McLaren's claims regarding; war/circumstances of war, McLaren's defense strategies and demands

McLaren, Robert "Mac" (McLaren's father), 55. *See also in photo gallery*

McMinn, Ken, 24

media: coverage of siege, 82, 111, 117, 144; O'Rourke's informal contact with, 132; requests for interviews with Jo Ann, 93; staging area at Point of Rocks, 111, 112, 118–19; strategic use of press releases, 134–36. *See also* radio stations

Messick, Gene and Peggy (née Turner) (Bill's sister and husband), 31–32

Mexican-American War, 7

Michael, Lou, 3

Midland, federal trial in, 204

Milam, Nick, 87–88, 181

military maneuvers and munitions practice by ROT, 72, 95, 111, 121

militia movements. *See* antigovernment militia groups

Miller, Daniel, 2, 69, 214, 225

Mills, Bruce, 225

Mills, Buster, 108

Mills, Tom, 187

Minutemen (militia group), 8

Mitchell, Corey, 225

money and economic issues: Bill's selfishness, 33; medical debt, 40; recession of 1990, 45; savings and loan crisis of 1980s, 40–41; Turners' failure to pay mortgage, 38, 42, 45; Turners' failure to pay taxes, 41, 80, 203, 229

Montana Freemen incident of 1996, 8, 119, 172

Morales, Dan (Texas Attorney General): controversies and misdeeds, 77, 224–25; McLaren's accusations of corruption, 211; and McLaren's false lien filings, 49, 69–70; media attack against ROT and call for arrests, 76, 87, 89; subpoena for Internet data, 70–72; suits against ROT members and actions, 172, 211, 224

Morgan, Michael T., 66–67

Mother Jones, 171

Motor Carrier Act of 1980, 41

Mount Livermore (Baldy Peak), 4, 156

munitions and bomb experts, 121

Murdered Innocents (Mitchell), 225

Murphy, Harriet Mitchell, 40

Murr, Marc D., 77, 224

Natasha (fellow inmate), 83, 86, 115

Nathan, Debbie, 68

National Firearms Act, violations of, 96, 98, 191, 200, 204, 205–6

National Guard. *See* Texas National Guard

National Minimum Drinking Age Act of 1984, 41

National Public Radio, 111

Native Americans, 6, 7, 8, 32, 68, 77, 118, 131

NBC media, 111, 118

NBC Nightly News, 72

negotiations and strategies: Caver's efforts, 104, 109, 111–12, 128–30; Noesner's efforts, 119, 120–21, 130,

134, 135, 135–36, 158–59. *See also* Malone, Jess; O'Rourke, Terrence "Terry" L.
Nelson, Lillian (née Canady, aunt), 18–19
Nelson, Patricia (cousin), 19
Nelson, Willie, 40
No Country for Old Men (film), 4
Noesner, Gary, 119, 120–21, 130, 134, 135, 135–36, 158–59. *See also in photo gallery*
NSA Water Filters, 38, 43, 44
Nygard, Janelle, 32

O'Halloran, Brian, 155
Oklahoma City bombing, 172, 187, 188
One Ranger. A Memoir (Jackson), 110
organized crime charges/conviction, 206
O'Rourke, Terrence "Terry" L.: background and early career, 123; as McLaren lawyer and liaison with siege team, 122–25; McLaren's dismissal of, 148; observations on siege operations, 132, 140–41; request for McLaren's surrender, 135; strategic use of Evelyn McLaren's daughters, 137, 141, 144–46
Ortega, Cosme, 136
Oswald, Lee Harvey, 186
Otto, Robert "White Eagle": demand for self-representation at trial, 178; federal firearms violations trial, 204–6; interactions with negotiators, 129–30; parole of, 206–7; state trial and conviction, 177–80, 181; surrender and arrest of, 149–50, 151. *See also in photo gallery*
Overland Network, 70–73

Pagnozzi family, 154
"paper war/terrorism" label, 13–14, 66, 69, 87
Paradise Ranch Bed and Breakfast, 58
parallel *v.* linear negotiation strategies, 130
Paris, Texas (film), 4
Parrack, Roy. *See in photo gallery*
Parrott, Jean, 122
Paulson, Gregg and Karen, 96, 98, 99, 147, 151, 180, 204–7
Paulson, John, 166
Pechacek, Eric, 163–64
Permanent Court of Arbitration, 213
Place Called Waco, A (Thibodeau), 3
Playboy Lounge, 27
Point of Rocks (landmark), 72, 111, 112, 118–19
Polk, James K., 6
Pope John Paul II, 69
power and communication lines: AT&T drop lines for law enforcement, 112–13; DMR phone lines cut, 141; Internet use by ROT, 70–73; McLaren shuts down communication with siege team, 134, 140; power for media at Point of Rocks, 118–19; ROT phone lines cut by siege team, 135, 137, 141
Pratt, Larry, 63
Presidio County Jail, Marfa, 97, 108
Pressley, Sue, 71
Print & Sign Designs, 189
prison experience, Jo Ann's: racism and violence, 85–86; solitary confinement cell, 127–28, 133–34, 139, 149; stress and mental coping mechanism, 106, 202–3; strip searches, 13, 81; suicidal thoughts, 228; Travis County Correctional Complex (solitary), 127–28, 133–34, 139, 149; Travis County

Correctional Complex (women's cellblock), 80–86, 105, 115, 149; Travis County Jail, 79–80; weight loss in prison, 83. *See also in photo gallery*
privacy rights of ROT, 70–72
Puerto Rico, McLean's dealings in, 76–77, 192

racism: historical profiles (segregation), 20, 24–25; and violence in prison, 85–86
radio communications: confusion and miscommunications, 96–97, 107–8; ROT use of, 96, 112, 135, 147, 158
radio stations: coverage of Jo Ann's story, 52, 82; strategic broadcasts by Texas Rangers, 134–36, 140; use of by McLaren, 14, 74–75, 112, 115, 135, 158. *See also* media
Ralph, Douglas, 67
Ramírez, Alfonso "Al," 33
Rayne, Wilma, 32
Raytheon Company, 146
Reconstruction Acts, 212–13
Reece, Joe Lewis, 194
Reeves, Lori (née Martin), 197, 217
religion, 22, 84–85, 227
Reno, Janet, 113, 130, 157
Republic of Texas (and historical separation from Mexico), 4–5
Republic of Texas (ROT) group: current profile and future outlook, 2–3, 221–26; federal trials of, 179–80, 186, 204–7; Noesner's profiling of ROT members, 120–21, 135, 158–59. *See also in photo gallery*
residences of Turners: Austin lake property purchase, 35; Canyon Lake with Lonnie Burris, 229; Fields duplex, 180–81; first home in Austin, 31; Fox Hill apartment, 203, 218–19, 229; Houston, Tex., 34–36; Liberty Hill home of Bill's daughter, 197–200; McAllen, Tex., 33; Quail Creek house (Austin), 37; Rivercrest Drive lake home (Austin), 12, 38–39, 47–49; Roatan, Honduras, 185, 194–96; Shepherd Mountain apartment, 49; Spicewood Springs (Austin), 36–37
Reyna, Pat, 101
Rhea, Jerry and Karen, 57, 101–3
Right Wing Resurgence (Johnson, Daryl), 168
Rio Grande (river), 5, 6, 7
Rio Grande Savings and Loan, 57
Roatan, Honduras, 195. *See also* Honduras
Robertson, Peggy, 122
Roe v. Wade, 186
ROT (Republic of Texas). *See* Republic of Texas (ROT) group
Rowe, Joe and Margaret Ann "M. A.": background and early issues with McLaren/ROT, 57–58, 59, 95–96; Bob Dillard on, 61; home/property in DMR, 94–95, 109–10; ROT attack and kidnapping, 82, 97–104, 107; as witness at state trial, 179. *See also in photo gallery*
Rowe, Mikel, 94
Ruby, Jack, 186
Ruby Ridge (Walter), 3
Ruby Ridge, Idaho incident of 1992, 8, 119, 172
Rudolph, Eric, 170
Ruiz, Bernice and family, 20–21, 22
Rutledge, Lisa, 141, 144–46

Sam Houston National Forest, 169
Samson, Charles "Chuck" III (and family), 54–57. *See also in photo gallery*

Sanders, Joe. *See in photo gallery*
San Felipe de Austin (early colony), 4–5
Santa Anna, Antonio López de, 5
Santa Fe Federal Building, Dallas, 186
"Satellite City," 118
savings and loan crisis of 1980s, 40–41, 42
Scheibal, Steve, 80
Scheidt, Robert Jonathan: arrest on highway, 96–97, 107–8; death of, 207; diplomatic pouch pickup, 141; federal firearms violations trial, 204–7; prisoner/hostage exchange, 104, 111–12, 116–17; "prison of war," McLaren's declaration as, 8, 82, 112; surrender of, 147. *See also in photo gallery*
Schneider Trucking Company, 197–99
Screenwriter's Bible, The (Trottier), 182
Searchers, The (film), 4
sentencing. *See* convictions and sentencing
separatist movements (other than ROT), 63–64, 68, 214–15. *See also* antigovernment militia groups
Shannon, Barbara (and family), 197
Shapiro & Dunn PLLC, 49, 88
Sharpley, Christian, 217
Shepherd Mountain apartment, 49
Shoal Creek Hospital, 37, 154
Shriners (Ben Hur Shrine, Austin), 154
Silver Shirt Legion, 8
Sims, Larry and Linda, 92
Skyline Drive Trail (Davis Mountains State Park), 4
slavery in Texas history, 4, 7
Smathers, John and Lillie (grandparents), 22
Smith, Coy, 112, 164
Smith, J. B., 137
Smith, Kelly, 189
Sonleitner, Karen Marie, 47

Southwest Airlines, 177, 183, 219
sovereignty of Texas, McLaren's claims regarding, 88, 141, 158, 178, 212, 225. *See also* annexation of Texas
Spain, Tinker, 63–64
squatting and land possession. *See* adverse possession principle
Stalling for Time (Noesner), 3, 119
Stand-Off in Texas (Cox), 111
Sterling, Gisela, 48
Stewart Title Company, 66, 88
"Sugar" (tracking dog), 162–64, 165
survivalist mindset, 60, 156, 170
Swecker, Chris, 169–70
Sweeney, Richard, 140

tax evasion/protest: actions against IRS, 13, 88, 227–28; and antigovernment extremists, 3, 8, 191; ROT disputes and claims, 69, 120, 158, 222, 225; sales tax suit against ROT, 172, 211; Turners' failure to pay, 41, 80, 203, 229
Taylor, Robert, 221–22
Tenth Amendment, 212–13
Tenth Congress (name for McLaren's faction of ROT), 221, 223
Terrell, Tex., 187
Texas, historical overview of, 4–8
Texas A&M University, 55, 56
Texas Constitution, 5
Texas Constitutional Militia (TCM) rally, 63–64
Texas Department of Corrections, 159
Texas Department of Motor Vehicles (TXDMV), 28, 30, 33, 34, 35, 38
Texas Department of Public Safety (DPS), 111, 132, 157, 168–69. *See also* Cox, Mike; *in photo gallery*; Texas Rangers
Texas DMV, Bill's job with, 28, 30, 33, 34, 35, 38

288　Index

Texas Highway Patrol, 121–22, 128–29
Texas Highways, 55
Texas National Guard, 112, 129, 140
Texas Nationalist Movement, 2, 214
Texas Observer, 68, 187
Texas Rangers, 72, 134–36, 140, 158. *See also* Caver, Barry; Duncan, David; Malone, Jess
Texas Revolution and independence from Mexico, 4–5
Texas State Guard, 112
Texas Tribune, 77
Texas v. White, 7, 189
"Texian" identity, 65, 66, 131, 193
Texit (Miller), 2, 225
There Will be Blood (film), 4
Thibodeau, David, 3
Thomas, Dudley, 140
Time, 72
Timothy Bible College, Bastrop, 64
Tisdale, Ward, 68, 77
Townsend, Nancy, 154
Travis, William Barret, 65
Travis County Correctional Complex: solitary confinement cell, 127–28, 133–34, 139, 149; women's cellblock, 80–86, 105, 115, 149
Travis County Courthouse, 31, 87, 88, 220
Travis County Jail, 13, 37, 79–80
Travis County Sheriff, 12
Treasury, State of Texas, 188, 190, 192
Treaties of Velasco, 5
Treaty of Guadalupe Hidalgo, 7
TRO (Temporary Restraining Order), 52–53
Trottier, David, 182
trucking industry/jobs: Leal Trucking Company, 11, 41, 49, 176, 203; team driving for Schneider Trucking Company, 197–99; Turner Trucking company, 38, 40–41

Turner, Bill: alcohol and drinking, 1, 32, 33; appearance, 27–28, 94; background, 30; boats and boating, 29–30, 35, 155, 180; courtship with Jo Ann, 27–31; death of, 229; home staging career, 201–3; Leal Trucking Company job, 11, 41, 49, 176, 203; music career, 27, 39–40; Texas Department of Motor Vehicles (TXDMV) job, 28, 30, 33, 34, 35, 38; Turner Trucking company, 38, 40–41. *See also in photo gallery*; residences of Turners
Turner, Chance (grandson), 177, 182, 231
Turner, Cleofas and Anna (née Ross) (Bill's parents), 31–32, 36
Turner, Jeff (son): Bill's aggression toward, 33, 36, 37, 39; birth of, 33; childhood friends, 154; contractor work in Austin, 197; escape to South America, 231; and family dog, 161–62; high school years, 37, 39; in Lake Tahoe area, 177, 182, 200; move to Dallas, 39; move to Honduras with parents, 182, 194–95; risky-taking behavior, 36; son Chance, 177, 182, 231. *See also in photo gallery*
Turner, Jo Ann (née Canady): accident, back surgery, and chronic pain, 40, 203–4, 229, 229–30; arrest of, 11–15; auto accident 1984, 40; birth of daughter, 36; birth of son, 33; book/screenplay, 182, 195, 196; courtship with Bill, 27–31; death of, 230–31; early childhood, 17–20; education, 20, 23–24; marriage 2019, 230; photographs (family), return of, 54, 150; "prisoner of war," McLaren's declaration as, 8, 82, 89, 112, 115; regrets for trusting McLarens, 2, 139–40, 153, 227–28; release of

and aftermath, 175–77; social life prior to ROT involvement, 153–56; typing work for ROT, 74. *See also* employment, Jo Ann's; prison experience, Jo Ann's; residences of Turners

Turner, Kelly (daughter): avoidance of parents, 85, 155, 197, 203; Bill's affection for, 36, 155; birth and childhood, 36, 37; character profile, 155–56; murder of, 217–20; refusal to move to Honduras, 183; school and activities, 38, 39, 155–56; Southwest Airlines career, 177, 200, 217. *See also in photo gallery*

Turner Trucking, 38, 40–41

Turpin, Bill, 38

Tyler, John, 6

Uhl, Mike, 186, 189, 190–91

Ultimate Frontier, The (Kieninger, pseud. Ekial Kueshana), 187

Union reclamation of Texas, 7, 88, 189

United Nations, ROT communications to, 66

US Border Patrol, 58–59, 113, 122, 157

US Customs and Border Protection, 113

US Department of Immigration and Naturalization Service (INS), 113

US Department of Justice, 113, 212, 222

US Department of State, 212

US Immigration and Customs Enforcement (ICE), 113

US Postal Service. *See* bank and mail fraud

Utterback, Bill, 64

U Up U Down Ranch, 59–60

vacations/trips (Turners), 36, 106

Valadez, Albert, 130–31, 151, 178–79

VanDyke, Betty, 223

Van Kirk, J.C., 45, 63, 64–65, 69

Varnell, Donald J., 67, 172, 211

Vickers, George, 164

Villalobos, Gerry. *See in photo gallery*

Villegas, Camilo Joe "C. J." and Gudelia, 40

Vocational Office Educational (VOE), 22–23

voting process claims by McLaren, 193

Vox Nutrition, 43

Vu, Lihn Ngoc, 193

Waco siege of 1993, 8, 109, 119, 158, 172

Wade, Henry, 186

Walter, Jess, 3

war/circumstances of war, McLaren's defense strategies and demands: declaration of war against United States, 8; laws of war and prior acts claims, 193, 213–14; "prisoners of war" label for ROT members, 8, 82, 89, 112, 115; War Powers acts, 192, 193, 210, 212; warrant bills of war procedures, 190, 192–93; war reparations demands, 69

Ward, Mike and Cathy, 60, 117

Ward County Jail, 66, 67

warrants (securities), ROT use of, 190, 192–93

Washington on the Brazos, Tex., 5, 6

Washington Post, 71

Washita/Washitaw de Dugdahmoundyah tribe/Nation, 68, 77

WBAP radio, 111

Weathers, Carl, 136, 164, 165

Wendlant, Buddy, 34–35

West Texas Utility (WTU) powerlines, 118–19

Whitehead, L. D., 214

Who Killed These Girls? (Lowry, B.), 225
William G. McConnell Unit, Beeville (state prison), 220
William P. Clements Unit, Amarillo (state prison), 2, 191–92. *See also in photo gallery*
Williamson, James Leslie, 136
Wilson, Lisa Ann, 197
Wind River Office Park office, Jo Ann's office in, 37, 180
Wireless Internet Service Providers Association (WISPA), 71
Wise, Johnnie, 2
WOAI radio, 111, 112
Wofford, Jake, 112, 113
Wofford, Johnny and Mary Lynn "Rusty," 58–59, 101, 111, 112–13, 122, 146, 157
World Class Travel Network, 44
World Court, ROT communications to, 66
Wright, Troy, 43

Yogurt Shop Murders, 224–25
Young, William "Peck," 40